i Refuse
–TO–
DIE!

"It's My Time To Live!"

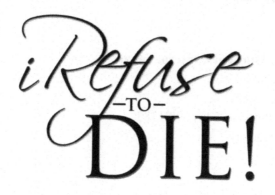

i Refuse –TO– DIE!

"It's My Time To Live!"

DR. MATTIE NOTTAGE

I Refuse To Die!
"It's My Time To Live!"

Published By:
Mattie Nottage Ministries, International
P.O. Box SB–52524
Nassau, N. P. Bahamas
Tel: (888) 825-7568 or (242) 698-1383
www.mattienottage.org

Unless otherwise indicated, all Scripture quotations are taken from the King James Version, biblegateway.com and The Amplified Bible ©1987 by the Zondervan Corporation and the Lockman Foundation, Grand Rapids, Michigan.

Cover design by: Beyond All Barriers Publications & Media Group
Edited by: Beyond All Barriers Publications & Media Group
Format and Interior design by: BEYOND ALL BARRIERS PUBLICATIONS & MEDIA GROUP

Printed in the United States of America
First Printing: October 2013
ISBN-13: 978-0-9896003-2-3

DEDICATION

To my best friend, spiritual covering, husband and Senior Pastor, Apostle Edison Nottage; thank you for always being the wind beneath my wings, propelling me to greater dimensions in God. *I love you!*

To all my children: thank you for your motivation, your love and continued support. I love you all!

And finally, this book is dedicated to people from all walks of life who are willing to *"take their grave clothes off"* and *"refuse to die"* in their present condition. Also, to the thousands who have made a resolute decision that they were not going to die unfulfilled but, rather, choose to believe and pursue their dreams, even after experiencing adverse challenges in life.

ACKNOWLEDGEMENTS

"....He which hath begun a good work in you will perform it until the day of Jesus Christ:" (Philippians 1:6)

I count it an honor and a privilege to be a vessel used by God in these last days. Therefore, without question or reservation God will always be first in my life. It is to Him that I give all the glory, honor and praise. I acknowledge the Holy Spirit, who is my compass and orders my every step.

To my spiritual sons and daughters of Believers Faith Outreach Ministries, International, Nassau, Bahamas, especially my "A" Team: I appreciate you more than I can say. To my faithful sons and daughters of Believers Faith Breakthrough Ministries, South Florida, the partners and friends of Mattie Nottage Ministries International: thank you. Your prayers and support have been a source of encouragement and strength to me.

My greatest appreciation is to my mother, Minister Daiseymae McKenzie, who has taught me the true art of survival from my childhood. She is worthy of double honor.

God bless you all!

APOSTOLIC ENDORSEMENT

It gives me great pleasure to give a word of endorsement for this life-changing book written by my darling wife, *Prophetess Dr. Mattie Nottage.* I have seen God use her in various ways over the years to help birth phenomenal change in the lives of scores of people. Her powerful, prophetic insight and keen sense of discernment have helped to deliver many people and set the captives free.

This book, so well written, has somewhat encapsulated the dramatic accounts of how she overcame some of the most challenging experiences of her life. There were times when she could have given up and died but, instead, she chose to persevere, trust God and live. I know personally the many obstacles she has faced, some of which occurred just prior to her writing this book. I watched as God began to mold and shape her into the woman of God that she has become today.

I can attest to the fact that every word, prophetic insight, kingdom revelation and power nugget in this book has been cultivated as a result of much sacrifice and divine inspiration by God. I pray that you are blessed as you read this dynamic book written by one of the greatest warriors I know in the Body of Christ, my wife, Prophetess Mattie Nottage.

Apostle Edison Nottage, Senior Pastor
Believers Faith Outreach Ministries, International ◊ Nassau Bahamas

OTHER ENDORSEMENTS

Dr. Myles Munroe, CEO/President/Founder
Myles Munroe International ◊ Nassau, Bahamas

Dr. Mattie is a true example of a Kingdom Ambassador who understands her assignment. I believe everyone will be touched and tremendously blessed by her ministry. In this book, she clearly and cleverly exposes various myths or misconceptions about "life and death". She has penned a brilliant work in which she shares personal experiences, candidly exposing the spirit of death and its tactics as it seeks to destroy the believer's relationship with God. She further unveils that fulfilling the purpose and mandate of God for your life is the truest definition of what it means to live.

Bishop Mark J. Chironna, MA, PhD
Mark Chironna Ministries ◊ Orlando, Florida

"Dr. Mattie Nottage has invited us to take a fresh look at the dogged-determination of those who walk by faith and not by sight and refuse to lay down and die, because they choose to live and tell the works of the Lord. Someone once said, "The future belongs to the dreamers". If you refuse to die, this book will provide you with the tools and resources to dream again, and not just live, but live BIG!"

Dr. Medina Pullings, Senior Pastor
United Nations Church Int'l ◊ Richmond VA

"Mattie Nottage has done it again! She has penned a script that speaks volumes to the reader right from the beginning! In her latest work, "I Refuse to Die!", Dr. Mattie speaks to the very core of your purpose, exposes its enemies and gives practical tools for you to live the highest expression of God's original intent for your life. I highly recommend this book!"

Dr. Jerry Grillo
Fogzone Ministries ◊ Hickory, NC. 28602

"I have read Dr. Nottage's books and talked extensively with her....anything she says will promote you to your future! Enemies come to steal your territory ...adversaries come to steal your anointing! In this book, "I Refuse to Die - It's My Time to Live," you will discover necessary keys to overcome every enemy and adversary assigned to rob you of your destiny!"

Evangelist Nichelle Early, Founder/CEO/Executive Editor
PreachingWoman.com ◊ Haymarket, VA 20169

"Dr. Mattie Nottage has penned a priceless, compelling work laced with profound truths that will set you on the path to overcoming life's greatest challenges!"

TABLE OF CONTENTS

TABLE OF CONTENTS CONT'D ...

TABLE OF CONTENTS CONT'D ...

TABLE OF CONTENTS CONT'D ...

I REFUSE TO DIE! – THE TRILOGY

First, I must say that I am both humbled and honored that God would entrust me to share His kingdom perspective on the typically "taboo" subject of "death and dying". I can truly admit that at first I was somewhat hesitant in writing this book because I believe that many people do not want to talk about death or the pain of losing something or someone that is near and dear to them. I further wrestled because I believe, in contrast to the concept of "death"; the essence of who God is represents hope, encouragement and empowerment.

My sincerest question to God was, "How do I share the *light* of the glorious gospel of the kingdom on the somewhat *dark* topic of death and dying?"

In my finite understanding, I never imagined that the Holy Spirit would have led me on such a profound journey of kingdom insight and revelation as to how He perceives "death" and its purpose. *(Ecclesiastes 3:1–2)* This extensive life-changing experience could not be captured within the confines of a single writing but, rather, has birthed the epic **"I REFUSE TO DIE" TRILOGY.** Through this multi-faceted compilation, the Holy Spirit seeks to guide every believer to a greater understanding of the very nature and characteristics of the spirit of death and how to overcome its diabolical schemes to live victoriously.

I REFUSE TO DIE! – "It's My Time To Live!" is the prophetic forerunner in this powerful series in which I share intimate details from my life while I was afflicted by the enemy. During that season, I truly felt as though the gates of death, hell and the grave had launched an all-out war against my health, my ministry and even my life.

It was by the grace of God that I overcame and am now able to share all that I have learned about the spirit of death and how I defeated this demonic nemesis.

I REFUSE TO DIE! – THE TRILOGY

The sophomore work in the TRILOGY, **"IT'S MY TIME TO LIVE!"** – **"Defeating The Spirit of Death!"** exposes how the spirit of death relentlessly goes after the life of *every* believer. It also reveals how this demonic spirit attacks entire families, communities, nations and regions. It further unveils kingdom strategies which every believer can employ in order to defeat the destructive spirit of death, regardless of how it manifests.

And, saving the best for last, the Holy Spirit unveils through the final book in this TRILOGY, **"THE POWER OF PROPHETIC REVERSAL!"** how the believer has been given power from God to "voice activate" change in his or her life. The *power of prophetic reversal* is an essential kingdom revelation which speaks to empowering believers with spiritual authority to prophetically declare the victory and turn every situation around for the good. *(Proverbs 18:21)*

As you read, I pray that the wisdom of the Holy Spirit will be your spiritual compass to help you navigate through the corridors of faith and understand how the Spirit of God sees every adversity, trial or challenge with which you are faced.

If you make a resolute decision to persevere to the end, you will see the power of God demonstrated like never before. Subsequently, all of your dreams, visions and ideas will come to pass as you see the goodness of the Lord manifesting in your life. *(Psalm 27:13)*

I believe that "I Refuse to Die!" is a ***prophetic brand*** that identifies every believer in this and future generations who has courageously faced life's greatest challenges and adversities but has made a resolute decision to refuse to die or give up and chose to live!

CHAPTER ONE

LEGENDS, LEGACY AND DEATH

WHY "I REFUSE TO DIE!"

Of all the things in the world, one might ask, why would anyone want to write a book about death? After all, no one likes to think about death and even fewer people wish to discuss it. It represents such finality to our human existence and leads us in our curiosity to wonder what happens afterwards.

By definition, *"death"* is said to be the cessation of life. However, in a spiritual context, to the one who dies in the Lord, death can be considered a higher promotion in life.

Statistics indicate that 130 million babies are born every year, and more than 6,800 people in the United States of America and 150,000 people around the world die every day. This averages to approximately 56 million people who die worldwide on an annual basis.

Based on these facts, it is my opinion that "death and life" is a much-needed discussion. I further believe that if we had a better understanding of the nature and "spirit" of death, we would have fewer unnecessary casualties in our homes, churches, and communities at large. Subsequently, we will also have a better understanding of "the spirit of life" and how Jesus has truly set us free from the law of sin and death. This liberty gives us the right to truly live our lives to the fullest.

In the natural or carnal way of thinking, *death* only has one meaning and that means *the end of life.* However, in the realm of God *death signifies the beginning of eternal life* and is a *spiritual promotion.*

This book seeks to expose **the nature of physical death, spiritual death** and the subtle workings of **the spirit of death.** Further, it seeks to reveal how, in the life of the believer, the process of "dying to the flesh" can also lead to a more meaningful life in God. It is also designed to reveal God's divine plan for your life and how you can live to overcome the diabolical workings of the enemy who seeks your ultimate demise.

"I Refuse To Die!" champions every survivor who has faced great challenges in life but made firm decisions not to give up – they refused to die and made a *deliberate* choice to persevere and live!

When I first started writing this book, I had absolutely no idea of the warfare I would encounter, not to mention how difficult it would be to get this book in publication. I completed the first draft, tore it up and rewrote the new book at least twelve times before moving forward.

When I finally thought I had completed it, I then had second thoughts and became uncertain as to whether or not I wanted to share some of the *intimate* details of my experiences or leave them hidden under the covers. Nevertheless, after several years of tearing up this manuscript, throwing it in the garbage and even setting it on fire, I decided to put pen to paper for one last time and finish it.

Subsequently, shortly thereafter my spiritual father and mentor, Dr. Myles Munroe, died unexpectedly. I knew then that I had one additional chapter to write because now this work would fulfill a much greater purpose.

LEGENDS, LEGACY & DEATH

A *legend* is someone whose life or life's work has made a significant or indelible impact on someone else, the community or the world at large. Legendary people have a positive impact that stimulates or evokes change. Unfortunately, we have a tendency to only acknowledge legends *upon or after their death.*

For the most part, when somebody dies the biggest question is "Why?" Similarly, if the death was tragic, we are more inclined to ask an even bigger "Why?" We may not always have *"explanations"* for all tragedies. However, we must consider the life and legacy that person has left; in this, I believe we will discover some *degree of resolution.*

I believe that great legends do not just simply die, but rather their death should be viewed as a promotion. In other words, in the life of someone who is considered to be great, death serves as a catalyst to a higher reward. To those who are left to mourn, the death of their loved one may be grievous. However, for the one who has departed having fulfilled his earthly mandate, death is glorious; a moment of celebration and pageantry.

"LEGENDS DON'T SIMPLY DIE...THEY GET PROMOTED!!"

The tragic death of a legend *through a beheading* like John the Baptist; *a stoning before an angry crowd* like Stephen, one of Jesus' disciples; *an assassination* like Dr. Martin Luther King, Jr.; *in a tragic plane crash* or even *being boiled in oil* like John the Divine Revelator; does not imply that the person sinned or was out of alignment with the will of God.

The best soldiers in the army receive commendations, stripes and badges of honor. These soldiers are the ones promoted to other ranks and higher positions of authority such as General or Commanding Officer, as they have proven to be faithful beyond their call of duty and trustworthy in acts of courage. They are the ones who are given *mantles* to pass on to those who may follow and ultimately succeed them.

In like manner, once a person fulfills his God-ordained mandate and purpose in the earth, God calls him from this realm and re-deploys him on greater assignments.

"Precious in the sight of the Lord is the death of His saints." (Psalm 116:15)

MANTLING A SUCCESSOR

A mantle is a specific mandate or responsibility given from one person to another and can be classified as follows:

- a spiritual impartation, anointing or ability given by God to complete a specific assignment and mission. It is the activation or release of the power of God in your life
- a spiritual endowment or directive transferred to a successor in order to carry on the work and legacy of his predecessor
- a transference of power to an heir; which can be bestowed by the conveyance of a crown, rod, sceptre, ring or inheritance
- a symbolic tangible token or point of contact such as a prayer cloth or cloak given by a Leader to fortify your spiritual relationship and signify that you have been call of God

4

- a symbolic tangible token or point of contact such as a handkerchief or anointing oil through which you may receive a miracle, healing, breakthrough or deliverance

Spiritual Mantles

A spiritual mantle is generally caught in the realm of the spirit first before it is received in the natural. These *power* mantles are activated by revelation and impartation. In other words, although you may not understand everything regarding the mandate you know within yourself that this supernatural ability and inner empowerment is God's will concerning you.

As spiritual mantles are activated and you begin to operate in a new level of power, you will begin to see the glory of God unveiled in ways unimagined. You will also begin to realize that your new prophetic empowerment was released based on the grace of God more so than your own personal accomplishments.

Although mantles are spiritual by nature there are physical items which can be used as conduits of the anointing to represent them. Generally, a physical representation of a mantle is a symbolic point of contact that a prophet, pastor, or leader has prayed over, consecrated and anointed before passing it on to its intended receiver.

Some examples of physical conduits of spiritual mantles include, but are not limited to: clothing, scarves, shoes, jewelry, prayer cloths, handkerchiefs, a cruse of oil or water. Whereas, mantles and blessings may be symbolic of eternal promises, they are not given as a personal trophy to be held onto forever. *They are meant to be passed on to a "worthy" successor. This process is called "mantling".*

Mantling is done in order to accomplish or carry out a specific assignment and can be likened to receiving tools, equipment and the instructions necessary to construct an ever evolving monument.

"Mantling" requires a covenantal agreement between two or more people and can be viewed as the process of spiritual enablement.

Upon researching my family's history I discovered that both my grand and great grandfathers on my mother's side of the family were Baptist preachers while their wives were prayer band leaders.

As a young child I greatly admired my grandfather and his love for God. Although my name was Mattie, he would affectionately call me *"Mattius", which means "gift from God."* Most times I was the only one in the car going with him and my grandmother to the weekly prayer meetings. He would always remind me that one day God would use me to preach the gospel.

I can distinctly remember one day when he took me by my hand, blessed me and told me again that God was going to use me to preach the gospel. However, on this day, along with his blessing, he gave me a small white handkerchief. This meant the world to me and in my eyes, was worth more than a million dollars. I received this mantle and from that day to the present, I have taken this mandate seriously. I thank God for His grace and mercy upon my life. I believe my faith in God and willingness to serve others have blessed me, for which I am grateful.

MANTLING THE NEXT GENERATION

Mantling this generation of young people became an integral part of my mandate from God and overall kingdom assignment. I understood most of their struggles and constant cries for help. As a spiritual leader and one called to this generation, I realized that I was equipped with an ability from God to bring transformation and change to their lives. Even as a pastor I am never too busy to pray for or counsel a young person. After all, Jesus also took time to do so.

As leaders, whether pastors, evangelists or prophets, we must take time to minister to this rising generation of youth and children. In so doing, we will have a greater global kingdom impact on future economies, communities and the nations at large.

A *"mantle"* in this regard represents a "spiritual grace" given by God to fulfill or accomplish a specific purpose which is designed for global impact. Generally, a spiritual mantle is accompanied with training, skills and instructions which are taught to a successor by the predecessor or carrier of the mantle. Although the mentee goes through this process of preparation there are some areas of expertise which can only be developed by the help and impartation of the Holy Spirit.

Every generation should seek to accomplish more by exceeding the achievements of the previous generation.

This generation of upcoming warriors must earnestly seek the face of God in prayer and fasting if they are going to receive mantles from the previous generation and, especially from God. However, there must also be a sense of urgency and desperation on the part of both generations to earnestly desire the manifestation of the kingdom of God. Therefore, it is imperative that the outgoing generation take the initiative to release the mantles of God while the upcoming generation seeks diligently to receive them.

This new generation of world changers will be mantled to dominate in every arena of government, medicine, science, education, creative wisdom, technology, media, the arts, entertainment and more. However, this global mantle will not only come from man; I believe that there will be a supernatural empowerment that comes from God, Himself. As believers, we must begin to posture ourselves to seek God for the mantle or spiritual responsibility that we are meant to carry within our generation.

Mantles Are Falling

If a mantle is not released before a legend dies then his mantle will continue to remain suspended in the atmosphere of the spirit for a period of time or until it is eventually "caught". If it is not caught then it will die with the legend. Successive mantles should be given by a leader, father or spiritual father to his spiritual sons and daughters.

If a leader passes on but does not transfer the mantle to someone else, when he is "taken up" the mantle falls in the spirit realm and has to be sought after by those who are willing to pay the price to pursue it and walk in his stead.

Joshua was well able and equipped to not only operate in Moses' stead but to also fulfill the assignment of carrying the children of Israel into the promised land. Joshua had served faithfully, humbly obeying every instruction while Moses was alive. Therefore, after Moses' death, he was prepared to carry on the mission.

There are three (3) basic ways that a mantle may be passed on:

1) **Through a transference anointing** - by the laying on of hands *(2 Timothy 1:6)*
2) **Through a prayer anointing** - where it may be "thrown" and "caught" through prayer *(1 Kings 19)*
3) **Through a prophetic anointing** – where it is given or bestowed through prophetic utterance *(1 Timothy 4:14 AMP)*

Spiritual Armour vs Spiritual Mantles

It is important to note that "spiritual armour" and a "spiritual mantle" are different. Your armour is birthed out of prayer and learning how to fight to overcome every trial or battle you face. Through your seasons of

Every warrior wears his armour with pride because he paid the price for it.

learning how to overcome, you will begin to develop a spiritual armour that is tailor-made to "suit" you or designed to your exact fit.

Although the mantle is given, the skilled warrior must train himself in order to effectively bear his armour. His level of proficiency is based on the weapons he chooses to employ. For example, when Saul tried to put his armor on David it did not fit. David had not proven the armour that Saul gave him, but he had without a doubt, proven his slingshot.

Mantles can be transferred; however, the armour worn for protection in spiritual warfare must "fit" and can only be given by the Spirit of God *(Ephesians 6:11)*.

"SOLDIERS FIGHT TO LIVE, WARRIORS LIVE TO FIGHT! IN OTHER WORDS, A SOLDIER MAY RETIRE FROM THE BATTLE, BUT A TRUE WARRIOR LIVES A 'LIFESTYLE' PERPETUALLY PREPARED FOR WAR!"

You must remain in spiritual alignment with the mantle carrier in order to truly catch a mantle. Elijah cast his mantle on Elisha and kept walking. Elisha caught the mantle from Elijah because he was in the right spiritual alignment with him. Regardless of how others may have felt about him, he stayed long enough to see his leader taken up in a chariot of fire.

Any person who seeks to compete with his leader is either a fool or is spiritually immature and has not yet embraced the significance and value of having a mentor.

Although Elisha was powerful, he elected to remain in Elijah's shadow, doing what was necessary to promote Elijah's ministry and serve him; he emerged from that shadow only upon Elijah's death. Elisha served with meekness, he never contended with Elijah. There was absolutely no competition! *(See more in book by author, IT'S MY TIME TO LIVE!)*

"LEAVING A LEGACY!"

Far too often we have a tendency to equate how a person dies with the life they lived, especially if they were someone of renown or prominence. If their death is viewed as a tragedy we may, unfortunately, ignore or devalue the significance of their life's contributions or legacy.

A *legacy* is an indelible impression that a trailblazing pioneer has left behind. Legacies are definitive in nature. Through the annals of time, history highlights many prominent individuals who have died. Though some died tragically, their life's work still lives on today.

"Verily, verily, I say unto you, Except a corn of wheat fall into the ground and die, it abideth alone: but if it die, it bringeth forth much fruit."
(John 12:24)

For example, Dr. Martin Luther King, Jr. was known for the mantra "I Have A Dream!", the beloved Mother Theresa will forever be immortalized as the "Queen of Calcutta" and her service to humanity as she cared for the *poorest of the poor* in India. Similarly, through the teachings of the legendary Dr. Myles Munroe, the world has gained a greater appreciation and understanding on the importance of fulfilling your God-given purpose.

"...Blessed are the dead who die in the Lord from henceforth. Yea, saith the Spirit, that they may rest from their labors, and their works do follow them." (Revelation 14:13)

The Power of A Righteous Seed

In and of itself, a seed is only a seed. However, if it dies it now has the potential to reproduce after its kind. When someone dies, is buried and goes into the ground, it is symbolic of a seed being planted which should yield crops, fields, vineyards, orchards, plantations and harvests; some thirty, some sixty, some one hundred fold.

In other words, at the time of your death there should be some discernable contribution you have made that will continue to nurture, inspire or impact generations to come. Jesus started His earthly ministry at the age of thirty and died by the age of thirty-three.

In every seed, there is a fruit, a tree and a bountiful

Although His death by Crucifixion was viewed by many as horrific, Jesus did more in His three (3) years of ministry than most people have done in their entire lifetime.

It is believed that more people were saved as a result of Jesus' death than were saved while He was alive, and His legacy continues to live on through believers today. Therefore, what we should consider at a person's death is their overall contribution to life rather than the manner in which they died.

I can clearly remember when the spirit of death came after my life to destroy me. I had to firmly resolve that I was not going to die, primarily because it was not my time to die. Further, I did not feel as if I had completed my God-given purpose or assignment. I chose not to die because I was not finished living! Based on how much of your life's divine goals you have accomplished, when death comes, you can choose whether or not to embrace it.

On the other hand, every individual in this world will come to the crossroads of what I call "choosing life or death!" In this context I am not only speaking of a physical death; I am speaking of any crisis or dilemma which may confront you. Although "death" has purpose, it is incumbent upon every individual faced with a dilemma to determine whether to give in or to rise above it.

If you are experiencing a crisis in your life you can either choose to succumb to or "come under" what you are facing, or you can choose to overcome it. Further, you can decide to settle for the circumstance that is confronting you or you can choose to fight against it. If you are going to survive or live beyond any challenging circumstance with which you are faced, you must be prepared to take your faith into a higher dimension and choose to live. The choice of whether you live or die is, ultimately, yours.

For example, if you are involved in an abusive relationship it is inevitable that if you stay under this type of oppression someone will die; if it is not physical, death will be mental, emotional and maybe, in some cases, spiritual.

If you believe that you have not fulfilled or accomplished your God-given assignment in the earth then, by all means, you should refuse to give up, refuse to throw in the towel, refuse to walk away and, most important of all, you should refuse to die!

"YOU CAN CHOOSE TO DIE ILL-ACCOMPLISHED OR CHOOSE TO LIVE 'TIL ACCOMPLISHED!"

PROPHETIC SUCCESSION
"How To Build A Legacy!"

Everyone, especially leaders should understand that we all have an unavoidable appointment with death. However, for the purpose of longevity, preparation should be made for the continuation of our visions and dreams.

During Jesus' time here on earth He was very clear about His mission, purpose and mandate. Early in His ministry He communicated His mandate and demonstrated the power of His kingdom to His disciples and the people who were following Him. This is a leadership strategy I call *"prophetic succession planning"*.

Prophetic Succession Planning is a strategy in which a leader makes plans for succession while he is still alive. This principle can be applied in corporate, civic, athletic, spiritual, or any other arena. Further, you must discover and rediscover your God-given vision, mission and purpose while planning for succession.

Leaders should have a development strategy outlining their lifelong plans which includes indentifying their successors. These are loyal people who can be trusted completely to carry on their mission while they are alive and even after they have died. True successors are like trustees, mandated to act on behalf of the leader while he is alive and even after his death.

Further, every leader should remain in a posture where he embraces "spiritual evolution", capturing everything that God is saying to and through him. These prophetic mandates should also be passed on to those who position themselves as faithful successors called to continue the vision of their leader.

Everything that Jesus did for the thirty-three years He was on earth, was centered around His purpose, because He knew that He was born to die! Therefore, in His final words, "It is finished!" Jesus made a prophetic declaration that His dying would put an end to the power of death in the life of every believer.

Jesus' legacy now lives on and, two thousand years later, people are still writing about Him and His ministry. I believe this occurred partly due to the fact that He practiced *Prophetic Succession* Planning. He clearly outlined his vision and mission, giving specific details as to how he started his ministry and how it should be continued. Jesus employed a three(3)-twelve(12)-seventy(70)-one hundred twenty(120) progressive approach in which he started with the three, added the nine, established the twelve, empowered the seventy, endowed the one hundred twenty and expanded to three thousand as outlined below:

As a leader, there are many strategies of prophetic succession planning you can learn from the example that Jesus demonstrated:

- Disseminate, inject, impart the dream, vision and idea that God has given you into the "3", even as He did with Peter, James and John. These "3" are the ones who capture the vision. Do not start with the masses *(Matthew 17:1).*

- Anticipate that these "3", once "activated" or "impregnated", will begin to disseminate to and infect another "9" with what has been deposited into them, even as Peter, James and John did with the other "9" disciples.

- The number "9" represents birthing. These "9" will begin to birth or give hands and legs to the vision.

- "3" plus "9" equals "12". Prophetically, "12" is the number of government. With the "12" enlisted, governmental structure and order are possible. *(Luke 9:12; Isaiah 9:6)*

- Once activated, the "12" will assist with establishing the structure and order within your organization that will, in turn, attract and impact the "70". *(Luke 10:1)*

- Prophetically, "70" is the number of totality which denotes something that is an all-encompassing entity and represents a level of spiritual evolution or spiritual maturity. The Bible reveals that the disciples had grown from the three to the twelve and then to the "70". They had also matured to the point where they were "doing what Jesus did" by demonstrating the power of

God. This demonstration of power and excitement caused the Church to grow to the 120 which had gathered in the Upper Room Acts 2.

- Prophetically "120 " represents overflow (Gk –*"nabi"*– is a prophetic term which represents a bubbling up in the spirit). This was demonstrated by the disciples' prophesying in various tongues and languages while they were in the "Upper Room". They could not stop speaking. It was like a well springing up on the inside of them.

- On the day of Pentecost the disciples had matured to a spiritual place where they had emptied themselves of their own personal issues and the cares of this life. They were now ready to be filled and endowed with the power of the Holy Spirit.

- As the "120" got on one accord and came together in unity, the Holy Spirit descended upon them like cloven tongues of fire and they all began speaking in other languages. This outpouring of the spirit represented the global impact the church would have as each man heard the gospel preached in his own language. This was evident as Peter stood up, now being endued with power from the Holy Spirit, and preached a sermon that added over three thousand souls to the church from various tribes, and nations *(Acts 2:14 – 41).*

The "Beauty" & "Tragedy" Of Death

It is undeniable that the death of our Lord and Savior, Jesus Christ, has left an indelible mark on the hearts and minds of every race, nationality, creed and culture from the day of His Crucifixion to this present time. His powerful message of self-sacrifice, even unto death, to fulfill God's will on His life to bring salvation to mankind, left a blueprint for the entire world to follow. It is, therefore, irrefutable that He, as the Savior of the whole world, is unsurpassed as we esteem Him to be the "Ultimate Legend!"

There are several truths about God's plans concerning your life that you should never forget:

- God adds the element of time to the coordinates of your life to predetermine your destiny and set your life in motion.

- God's times and seasons belong to Him. Your time and season to be born were always etched in the plan of God.

- You are not an accident or an afterthought in the mind of God. He sat down and architecturally designed you exactly how He wanted you to be and no one can change that.

- God knew exactly what the earth needed when He formed you.

DIVINE COORDINATES

In the natural sense coordinates are considered to be the location of various points, distances and angles marked by an ordered group of numbers.

In the spiritual sense, your *"Divine Coordinates"* refer to the map that God has designed for your life. Within this blueprint lies the discovery and the rediscovery of His original intent concerning you and the path that leads to His divine destiny.

As every seamstress knows, you should never cut a *pattern* to suit a *dress,* you cut the *dress* according to the *pattern.* In the "fabric" of your life, your divine coordinates represent the pattern or plan that God wants you to follow. His intention is that you come into divine

Seek out the will of God for your life, find your "co-ordinates" and set your compass towards your destiny.

alignment with His plan and begin to seek out and discover the pre-determined "co-ordinates" by which your life has been mapped.

In other words, because we live in a three-dimensional world that is physically defined by length, breadth and height, it is of paramount importance that you understand the following dynamics of your:

- *"length" of days – refers to how long you should go.* This speaks to the length of time it should take to accomplish or achieve something, or the time allotted or pre-delegated by God for you to establish, complete, fulfill or accomplish the assignment that He has given to you. Each season of your life has a designated time assigned to it. Therefore, what you do in that time sets the course for your next season. You must accomplish what God has mandated for you to do within each set time period.

- *"breadth" of days – refers to how wide you should go.* It relates to the magnitude and purpose of your existence and assignment on this earth. It further relates to how far you are going to go and speaks to your sphere or reach of influence. For example, you may share your gift with friends and family, your neighborhood or community or you can choose to expand it to your nation and the entire world.

- *"height" of days – refers to how high you should go.* This reveals how high and how deep you are supposed to go or the levels to which you should aspire and the degree of sacrifices you should be willing to make in order to achieve new levels. For example, fasting and praying to overcome challenges and spending much time in the Word to achieve greater encounters in God, determine the level of your success and achievements in life. *(The quality of your character and attitude will help to determine your altitude in life.)*

These established dimensions are further governed by the system of times and seasons. It is important that you do not miss your seasons and times in God as He has ordained various moments in your life when something significant should happen. Various moments indicate pivotal occurrences which may mark seasons of maturity, promotion, transition, elevation and more. These seasons can also be identified by various age periods.

For example, at eight (8) days old, Jesus was taken to the temple to be circumcised, according to Jewish customs. At the age of twelve (12) years old he went to the temple to preach, because He knew His purpose in God throughout His life.

Missing your "divine coordinates" in life can lead to disorientation confusion and frustration!

The ages twelve, sixteen, eighteen, twenty-one, twenty-five, thirty, forty, fifty, and a few others all represent pivotal moments or turning points on your road to destiny.

Failure to recognize seasonal shifts, changes and the meaning of these significant years could adversely influence the fulfillment of God's ultimate plan for your life. When you do not accomplish your God ordained assignment within each respective season, this can breed frustration, irritation and even levels of dissatisfaction.

Hence, many people are battling with stress, anxiety, stagnation or vexation simply because they have missed moments, opportunities or *"coordinates"* in life which should have taken them to a blessed place.

Failing to understand the "when" in your life can lead to painful regret and agony!

For example some people did not move as prompted by the Holy Spirit; staying in relationships and on jobs much longer than they should; while others may remain bound in debt because they did not obey godly wisdom or counsel.

By the same token, some people impulsively leave good relationships and churches only to find themselves out of total alignment with God's plan.

This can lead to what I call the "Church or Relationship Hopping Syndrome" whereby many abort the purpose or intent for such connections. Further, they may advance through life dissatisfied and frustrated because no one and nowhere passes their "blue litmus test".

During your season of promotion if, for whatever reason, you have fallen short of your next dimension in life, it may be an indication that your "compass" has malfunctioned and your life is off course. This happens because you have not completely followed the blueprint that He has put in place. Without a doubt this is why many people find themselves headed in the wrong direction.

On the other hand, sometimes the enemy may attack your life, afflicting your mind, will, intellect and emotions in an attempt to divert you from the divine will of God. He uses various tactics and employs demonic spirits, like the spirit of death, to affect your coordinates by undermining your entire life. He tries to intercept your destiny by orchestrating traps and snares in your way.

Whenever your "coordinates" are manipulated by the enemy, you will continue to miss your appointed seasons in God. Your progress becomes hindered by a spirit I call *"the spirit of arrested development." (See more in book by author, "IT'S MY TIME TO LIVE!")*

UNDERSTANDING YOUR DIVINE PURPOSE

By definition, the word *"purpose"* is the original intent for which something has been created. Understanding your purpose allows you to discover, operate in and accomplish what you have been predestined to do. This leads to overall fulfillment, contentment and peace. Many people in today's world have not yet discovered or embraced their true purpose in life and, therefore, they are dissatisfied and ill-accomplished.

I believe that a person who genuinely finds his purpose has found a cause, principle or belief outside of his own "little" world for which he is willing to work, sacrifice and even die.

If you have not yet identified that *"thing" that keeps you up late at night, consumes your mind, your prayers, your finances* or even *your conversations,* then I propose that *you have not yet found your purpose in life.*

"ACTIVATING YOUR GIFT HELPS YOU TO FUND AND ULTIMATELY FULFILL YOUR PURPOSE IN LIFE."

The completion of your assignment is the fulfillment of your purpose. Some people's gifts will take them before kings or great men. Once you move beyond the boundaries of your families, neighborhoods and communities this will be a sign that you have fully activated your God-given gift.

When you cultivate and activate your gifts, talents and abilities you become a viable and valuable commodity. The demand for what you are carrying increases and, will eventually "set you before kings, in high seats of prominence." *(Proverbs 18:16; Proverbs 22:29)*

The fulfillment of life is discovering and rediscovering your divine purpose while seeking means to accomplish it.

Your divine purpose is the all-encompassing, conceptualized thought that God had concerning you before he created you. Your true identity lies in the innate characteristics which God placed within you before your conception *(Jeremiah 1:5).*

Who you have become is the sum total of your God-given characteristics coupled with what you have experienced. Many people miss their God-given purpose in life by settling for what they have become rather than pursing what God has divinely called them to be.

Also, the enemy seeks to prevent every believer form ever coming into the fullest measure of God's design for their life. Therefore, you must make a decision that you will fulfill your divine assignment, live out your fullest purpose and never give up!

In **John 10:10** the Word of God says, *"The thief cometh not but for to steal, and to kill and destroy:..."* The "thief" here is the adversary, the devil, whose three-fold assignment against your life is:

1) to steal – one of his missions is to "steal" your joy, peace, praise, worship and your "worth-ship" or value. He seeks to do everything in his power to devalue you.

2) to kill – Satan also wants to "kill" your zeal. He further seeks to subvert your desires and affections away from the things of God.

3) to destroy – another goal of the enemy is to destroy any indication of what the will of God is for your life. His relentless mission is to totally annihilate God's divine purpose and destiny for you.

People who understand their divine purpose in life and know that they are destined to be great usually have a plan. Once you identify your divine purpose in God, you should seek His face and plan the way to your destiny. Planning is a gift from God, and should be used as a vehicle to take you to your blessed place.

"He that fails to plan, plans to fail!" – Benjamin Franklin

GIFTS AND ASSIGNMENTS
"A man's gift maketh room for him, and bringeth him before great men." (Proverbs 18:16)

It is important to understand that every person has been given a gift and an assignment by God to fulfill while here on earth. Your gift is the innate ability or talent you possess that helps to equip you in fulfilling your assignment for God. *(See more in Chapter Four)*

Your assignment is the mandate given to you by God to accomplish a specific task. This mandate cannot be negotiated, bartered or bargained; it must be completed. Your gift can further be identified as the talents, skills and abilities that you perform well in with very little effort and operate in at will. On the other hand, your assignment is a divine command by God that you must obey and is structured according to God's desired will and timing.

Rediscovering Your Purpose, Power, Potential & Destiny

People who operate in mediocrity have not yet realized their purpose. Mediocrity is failure to excel beyond the boundaries of that which is ordinary. A person operating in mediocrity knows what needs to be done but fails to do it. These are people who make excessive excuses and struggle with a victim, helpless or limited mentality.

You must remove yourself from mediocrity if you are going to begin to function in the purpose for which you were created and if you are ever going to experience the God-kind of life that has been purchased for you through Jesus' death.

"YOU MUST SEEK TO DISCOVER WHO YOU ARE, WHY YOU ARE HERE AND, MOST IMPORTANTLY, WHERE YOU ARE GOING!"

Also, in *John 10:10* Jesus tells us that He came that we might have life and life more abundantly. I believe the first stage of experiencing this life is being able to overcome all of the onslaughts of the enemy; this speaks to you being able to merely exist or survive. However, when He spoke of life more abundantly, I believe that He was referring to a prosperous life where there is nothing lacking and nothing broken in an individual's mind, body, soul and spirit.

In *3 John verse 2* Jesus' idea of prosperity was directly connected to the overall wellbeing of a person's soul. He died so that we could experience prosperity in every arena of our existence. It is not His will that we are sound spiritually but suffering financially, or that we are financially accomplished but mentally tormented. Jesus wants us to enjoy our lives; to be whole and totally set free.

FULFILLING PURPOSE, DESTINY & POTENTIAL

"You Have Been Pressure Tested And Approved!"

PURPOSE is the original intent for which something was created. Although you were created for a specific purpose, God has to form, fashion and "make" you into the vessel or tool He envisioned so that you can fully function in the way that He intended. This is why He allows tests and trials to come your way in an effort to cause you to be able to withstand the assignment that you have been given and to accomplish the purpose that He has pre-ordained for you.

Can God rely on you to do what He has called you to do and not compromise the gospel? Can He release you into your assignment and trust that you are going to obey His every word? The tests and trials in your life are there to ensure that your answer to each question is an affirmative "Yes!", not because of happenstance, but because you have been *"pressure tested and approved!"*

By definition, **DESTINY** is the inevitable or predetermined course of events beyond human powers or ability that takes you to the place of resolve. In other words, your *destiny* can be defined as the course of divine events which take you to your God-ordained destination!

God wants each of His children to reach their destination. He has pre-ordained "co-ordinates" for your life which are divinely inspired to bring you to a designated place within a specific time. His unique blueprint is specific to your molecular structure and spiritual DNA and His ultimate plan is to see you accomplish every goal, dream and idea that He has breathed into your soul. For this reason He formed and fashioned you with gifts, talents and abilities which act as catalysts to propel you towards your God-ordained destiny.

God is a Master Planner, a Clever Marksman and the Premier Strategist. I firmly believe that God's ultimate plan is to lead, guide and help you navigate through life. Further, *Jeremiah 29:11* states that His plans are to "give you an expected end". As the Supreme Teacher, He also desires to reveal more of His kingdom and, ultimately, Himself to you.

I have had the privilege of mentoring scores of individuals and observing thousands more. There were few people who could truly say that the pathway to becoming something in God was a straight and narrow road. On the contrary, many people who determined to go after their destiny have talked about the many days

Your potential will push you into your purpose; your purpose will give you the power to fulfill your destiny!

they wanted to give up, the many times when they made major mistakes, the people who disappointed, neglected, betrayed or abandoned them and the various difficulties they endured as they pursued the will of God for their lives.

I have spoken to many believers, pastors, ministers, Church leaders and have heard it all! The one recurring theme that I have also heard them confess is that if it had not been for God who was on their side, they never would have made it. They all attested to the reality of something on the inside propelling them to move forward when they badly wanted to give up. I believe that this motivation was breathed into their soul by the Spirit of God.

In *Genesis 2:7* the Bible reveals that God breathed into Man and he became a living soul. I believe that at the very moment of creation when God breathed life into Man, He also breathed into him the inner, gifts, talents, abilities, potential, purpose, motivation and inspiration which were all intended to cohesively propel him into his destiny.

This destiny or divine pathway is a road map designed, not only to teach powerful life lessons; it is also designed to lead every human being into divine revelations of who God is...*with every step taken!*

As you see God's will for your life you will inevitably discover and rediscover His divine purpose concerning you and finding the means to accomplish it. You cannot "box" God in; He is as unpredictable as He is infinite. I believe that God gave everyone a gift called potential.

Your *POTENTIAL* is simply the capacity or ability you possess to grow, develop and mature into something better, greater or more refined. Your potential is that unction in your spirit that says, "I can do more!" or "I can be better!" Your innate potential is what will drive you to "rediscover or, better yet, redefine your purpose.

When you discover something, you find out what it is or what it is about. However, when you re-discover something it indicates that you find something you once had but lost along the way. In the process of achieving your God-given goals and dreams, you can become disoriented as you are redirected by the opinions of others, insecurities within yourself, a lack of motivation, discouragement, and many other distractions.

When life becomes a "chore" and you are no longer excited to face your day, I propose that you may have lost your purpose. This place of struggle may indicate that it is time for you to "rediscover" your purpose, rekindle your zeal for your assignment and "reset your coordinates."

> *You have been predestined and anointed by God to fulfill your destiny and win!!*

I sincerely believe that there is nothing greater in life than fulfilling the call of God. It may cost you some sleepless nights, financial challenges, lost relationships, disappointments and "missed turns" along the way; however I believe that, in the end when you are holding the prize in your hand, you will look back at "all the way you came" and realize that, although it was not easy, it was worth it!

"....I FIRMLY BELIEVE THAT ANY MAN'S FINEST HOUR – HIS GREATEST FULFILLMENT OF ALL THAT HE HOLDS DEAR – IS THAT MOMENT WHEN HE HAS WORKED HIS HEART OUT IN A GOOD CAUSE AND LIES EXHAUSTED ON THE FIELD OF BATTLE – VICTORIOUS." – VINCE LOMBARDI

PREDESTINED FOR GREATNESS

Whenever you have been earmarked for greatness or divinely pre-destined to accomplish something great, the enemy comes after you with a vengeance. Great men and women of the Bible such as Joseph, Esther, King David and the man on his way from Jerusalem to Jericho are all testaments of this truth.

Several years ago the Holy Spirit revealed to me that there were many believers being defeated in their walk with God because of five main challenges:

- they did not know the enemy they were fighting
- they did not know how to fight
- they did not know how to deal with the wounded
- they did not know how to heal themselves
- they did not understand their kingdom assignment

(Excerpt from book by author,
"Breaking The Chains, From Worship To Warfare")

God wants you to know Him and the very essence of who He is while also gaining insight on the enemy you are fighting. In particular, He wants every believer to get a better understanding of how Satan uses the spirit of death to try and destroy our lives. Many people are not only experiencing the physical death of a relative or loved one, they are also encountering spiritual, mental, emotional, financial, relational deaths, and so many other atrocities in their daily lives.

Moreover, I believe that it is of great importance for people to understand that neither salvation nor the call of God exempts anyone from being attacked by the enemy. In fact, it is because you are anointed and called of God to do a work that the enemy will pursue you and pose a constant threat to your life. Regardless of what comes your way, know this: his diabolical weapons will be formed but they will not prosper. *(Isaiah 54:17)*

THE SIGN OF GREATNESS
"¹Now when Jesus was born in Bethlehem of Judaea
in the days of Herod the king, behold,
there came wise men from the east to Jerusalem,

²Saying, Where is he that is born King of the Jews?
for we have seen his star in the east,
and are come to worship him". (Matthew 2:1-2)

The three wise men were able to follow Jesus' star directly to the place where He was born. They were able to distinguish his celestial representation above the others. His star, no doubt, had a characteristic that announced, the "King Is Here!" This was heaven's way of letting the world know that someone great was born. *Jesus was not just a star, He was a "supernova!"*

DEATH SEEKS OUT GREATNESS
"Beware of the Spirit of Herod!"

Death always seeks out greatness and goes after those who have been earmarked to shake the enemy's kingdom. In *Matthew 2:3-8, 16* we can see this in the life of Jesus, from the time of His birth.

Jesus' parents were warned in a dream that King Herod, the ruling monarch of the day, had sought to kill Him. Although Jesus was just a baby, King Herod knew that He was anointed with a kingly assignment. This greatly intimidated Herod who immediately became Jesus' archenemy and, subsequently, the hired agent on earth through whom the spirit of death sought to assassinate Jesus before He came into the fullness of His destiny. Unbeknownst to Herod, due to his own jealousy, hatred and suspicion, he was "employed" by the devil in an attempt to stop Jesus from fulfilling His divine assignment in the earth.

In Acts 12 we can identify the same spirit operating through another King Herod who killed James, one of Jesus' disciples, and imprisoned Apostle Peter with the intention of also executing him. The biblical account highlights that when King Herod saw how killing James had pleased the people, he sought to kill the Apostle Peter as well.

However, when the church heard the news prayer was lifted for Peter until he was miraculously released from jail. Today this same spirit of Herod seeks to assassinate the leadership of the church. This demonic spirit seeks to target modern day Apostles and Prophets in an effort to stop the preaching of the gospel of the kingdom. The Body of Christ must position itself to pray and cover our frontline leaders so that the kingdom of God can continue to advance equally or in the same manner as the faithful saints in Acts 12.

YOU ARE DESTINED FOR GREATNESS

Again, it is important to note that everyone has been born with a specific assignment. Heaven has marked it with a celestial sign and the earth anticipates your life's contributions *(Romans 8:19)*. Some people are destined to bring about a godly change in their families, some in their communities, and others are destined to make a global impact. Whatever scope or degree of influence is your destiny, know that it is an assignment given to you by God. For this reason alone the enemy does not want you to fulfill your assignment.

"THE ENEMY IS NOT AS INTIMIDATED BY YOU, AS HE IS INTIMIDATED BY THE KINGDOM ASSIGNMENT THAT GOD HAS GIVEN YOU."

You may agree that it appears as though an adversary has been assigned specifically to resist you since the day you were born. This is why some of you may have experienced warfare from the time you were in your mother's womb and throughout different seasons of your life. You may have been attacked by a particular childhood illness or experienced some other life-altering tragedy. Whatever strategy the enemy used, it was his intention to destroy you before you came into the fullest revelation of who you are.

I want to encourage you today that if it appears as though all "hell has broken loose" in your life and the enemy is after you, this could be an indication that you are earmarked for greatness.

Nevertheless, do not be discouraged; before you were born your co-ordinates were set and God has an appointed time when you shall become all that He has created you to be. However, you must survive the warfare and make a resolute decision that you are not going to die before your appointed time or before your assignment is fulfilled.

I can remember seasons of testing and trials when *"I Refuse To Die!"* became the very "anthem" for my life. I loved God so much and all I wanted was to see His purpose and plan for my life come to pass, but the enemy of my soul was determined to do everything he could to stop me. I realized that if I was going to fulfill the call of God on my life, I had to fight.

As a servant of the Most High, I believe that God has not only called me to prophesy but He has fashioned my life so that I would, in effect, become the prophecy; i.e. I learned how to prophecy into my own circumstances until the plans of darkness were defeated and the power of God manifested in my life. I am alive today because of this and I am honored to attest to this fact.

You can also become the manifestation and fulfillment of prophecy by yielding yourself to the will of the Almighty God, activating the prophetic words spoken over your life and initiating all that God said concerning you. As you begin to "voice activate" the will of God and bring His purpose to pass in every area of your life, you then become the fulfillment of the prophecy and an agent of greatness. *(See more in book by author, "IT'S MY TIME TO LIVE!")*

PROPHETIC PRAYER NUGGET (PPN)

"Stand and pray this prayer, taking authority over every demonic assassin that would seek to sabotage or subvert your destiny in Jesus' name!"

Father God in the name of Jesus, I pray that every purpose in my life will be completed and that I will not die prematurely or unfulfilled. I come against every demonic principality of Herod that would seek to assassinate my life, in Jesus' name. I stand on the Word of God which says that greater is He that is in me than he that is in the world. I am who I am by the grace of God and I will do everything that God has called me to in this present life, in Jesus' name, AMEN!

CHAPTER TWO

THE NATURE OF DEATH

"WHO" IS DEATH?

"Death By Definition!"

"Death" as defined by Webster's Dictionary is the "absence of life." Further, when we hear the word death, this encapsulates the word *"cessation"*. "Cessation" means to naturally or normally come to the end of life or "to come to its final end as a matter of course without external input or influences."

> *The spirit of a "thing" carries the nature and characteristic of that "thing!"*

On the other hand, to "cease" means to interrupt, abnormally stop, or cause to come to an end. Therefore "cessation", relative to death, is different from "to cease". Whenever someone's life has stopped abruptly or abnormally, they cease to exist, function, produce or manifest. *It is the ultimate plan of the spirit of death to cause your dreams, visions, ideas and ultimately your life, to "cease".*

"DEATH...THE LAST BREATH"

"There is no man who has power over the spirit to retain the breath of life, neither has he power over the day of death;..."
Ecclesiastes 8:8 (AMP)

In *Genesis 2:7* the Word of God tells us that when God breathed into man *"...man became a living soul (Hebrew- nephesh; pronounced neh'-fesh)".* This simply means that the very essence and purpose of who Man was and would become was activated when God breathed the breath of life into Man. It is said that, *"breath"* is sometimes used as a metaphor for life itself. The cessation of inhaling and exhaling can be an indicator that a person is dead.

Some people may never appreciate the importance of breathing until they encounter a near death experience, such as suffocation, almost drowning, an asthmatic attack and the like. Unfortunately, unless some people encounter or can relate to any of these types of experiences, they may never truly celebrate the gift of breathing.

We respire without fully understanding how important the respiratory system is to the overall function of the body. When we release our *"last breath",* this is one of the most obvious signs that death has occurred.

UNDERSTANDING THE SPIRIT OF DEATH

The spirit of death comes after everyone and everything that has a divine mandate from God. During the seasons when I believed the spirit of death came against my life, it was the principles of God's Word and precious promises that He made to me that empowered me to survive every attack and onslaught of the enemy.

Whenever there is prayer on the altar, it will always foil the plans of death against your life.

It is important to both define the spirit of death and examine how it works. I believe that this spirit is the principal enemy that fights against and tries to cripple the believer and the Body of Christ at large. For this reason, I also believe it is imperative to not only expose this destructive spirit, but to also show how you can gain the victory over it.

Always remember that the spirit of a "thing" carries the nature, characteristics, representation and mannerism of that "thing". Therefore, the spirit of death carries the very nature and characteristics of "death" itself.

Further, it speaks to the invisible force that propels movement. It is the hidden element not visible to the natural eye or in natural form, but the results of its presence can be seen, demonstrated and, in many instances, manifested. For example, you may not be able to see the spirit of rejection, but you will be able to identify its characteristics, mannerisms and manifestations.

"The wind bloweth where it listeth, and thou hearest the sound thereof, but canst not tell whence it cometh, and whither it goeth: so is every one that is born of the Spirit." (John 3:8)

The spirit of death that I will be discussing in this book, refers to a demonic force that is *"characteristic"* of death. There are a number of factors which determine when the "spirit of death" may be in operation in your life, family, organization or community.

There are times when a spirit comes into a person's life, representing a particular demon. It should be understood that this spirit may not necessarily be the actual demon itself but acts as an agent representing that particular cluster of demons and this may be the case in any demonic category. For example, many people contract cancer, however this disease may originate from various sources, be they physical or from the demonic realm. A construction worker may contract a form of cancer called *"mesothelioma"* due to asbestos exposure. In that case, you would understand that the origin of this type of cancer is asbestos.

On the other hand, you may encounter a perfectly healthy person who eats well and exercises, but is afflicted with a debilitating cancer that cannot be medically explained and where there is no evidence of such illness in this person's family line. It may be concluded that this form of cancer originated from the demonic realm. In such cases one must seek out the counsel of God as to how to address this problem.

For the person who contracted cancer as a result of asbestos exposure, you would pray a prayer of healing. For the healthy person who unexplainably contracts cancer, you would pray the prayer of deliverance.

It is important to note here that whenever I make reference to the "spirit of death", it is different than when I refer to *"Death"*, itself. Adding the qualifier "spirit" to "death" indicates that it is not the principality of *"Death"* itself; rather, it is the *spirit of death* that is merely an agent acting on behalf of *"Death"*. Whereas *"Death"* is the strong man, the spirit of death is the hired agent working on behalf of *"Death."* This diabolical spirit carries out a mission and mandate *like death* while acting on its behalf.

For example, a demonic *spirit of death, acting as a death agent* may come into your life, representing all of the qualities and characteristics of death, such as: depression, disease, distraction, discouragement and the like. Although it may not be *"Death"* itself, if you "let your guard down" to entertain it, embrace it or come into agreement with it, you have then surrendered your power to it and now it has the authority to destroy you.

"SATAN HAS NO AUTHORITY IN OUR LIVES, EXCEPT THAT WHICH WE GIVE OVER TO HIM!"

As long as you remain oblivious or ignorant to the will of God or the work of the enemy in your life, the enemy can and will superimpose his ill-wishes and desires upon your life. In this regard, people who are ignorant are those who fail to acknowledge the truth.

I have noted on numerous occasions that people go from doctor to doctor seeking answers for their vexing problems and leave disappointed because there was no medical resolution or remedy for their issue. The same people come into my prophetic deliverance services and, immediately, the Spirit of God will reveal to me that they are suffering from a spiritual attack. He will also reveal to me the name of the demonic spirit that is in operation. Once the person is willing to be set free, deliverance becomes easy. *(See more in Chapter Five: THIS IS MY STORY!)*

Demons are very territorial and stake aggressive claim to their dwelling place; they do not easily give up or willingly surrender their habitation. For this reason, Jesus instructed us to first bind them and then cast them out. You should not try to negotiate with, tolerate or pacify a demon. Further, you cannot medicate or counsel them out of your life; *DEMONS MUST BE CAST OUT!*

Over the years I have realized that you cannot see the spirit of death with your natural eyes, but by the spirit of discernment I can identify its code of conduct and modus operandi. The spirit of death does not naturally identify itself but it overshadows a person and works closely with the spirit of heaviness; leaving persons despondent. Jesus died so that we could have the victory over every attack from the enemy, including the spirit of death.

THE PROCESS OF NATURAL "RIGOR MORTIS"

When a body dies, within a few hours the process of *"rigor mortis"* begins to set in and becomes one of the most obvious or visible signs of death. This occurs after the heart stops and the final breath leaves the body. Rigor mortis is a biochemical process that causes muscles in the body to constrict, becoming rigid and stiff due to a lack of the chemical ATP.

ATP is a biochemical responsible for causing the muscles in the body to relax. When you die, this chemical is no longer produced and the muscles remain contracted. In Latin, this process is known as the "stiffness of death"

- **Rigor** – stiffness
- **Mortis** – derived from the Spanish word *"muerte" WHICH means "of death"*

Therefore, *rigor mortis* can be defined as all of the unpleasant physical factors associated with the death process. Within the initial stages of death, the joints of the body stiffen and become locked in place. This process which starts within four (4) hours after death may begin in the face, and spread throughout the entire body within forty-eight hours.

Rigor mortis is temporary and its process is generally influenced by environmental conditions. For example, in cold climates rigor mortis occurs at a slower rate than in hotter climates.

Other physical signs, which occur during "rigor mortis" are:
- all vital organs shut down
- the body becomes "unpliable", stiff and cold as blood circulation ceases

- breathing stops
- the body swells because it can take in air (or inhale) but it cannot expel it (or exhale)
- the body emits a foul odor as it decays

Once the process of "rigor mortis" is complete, the body begins to decay and there is no more hope of life left. Eventually, the body turns to dust, reverting to its original state prior to when the breath of life was breathed into it.

SPIRITUAL RIGOR MORTIS

As rigor mortis occurs in the physical body it can, similarly, occur in your spiritual walk with God. "Spiritual rigor mortis" takes place when an individual is void of the presence of God. This simply means that this person has lost his joy for the things of God and is no longer "pliable" in the hands of God. When spiritual rigor mortis occurs, this is one sign that the spirit of death is in operation in your life.

There are times that you can become so preoccupied with the affairs and "cares" of life that this "preoccupation", in and of itself, can be used as a weapon or vehicle to drive you far away from the presence of God. Your life can become so "cumbered" that you no longer pray, read the Word, or witness the way you should.

I propose that the spirit of death may be trailing you when you can no longer feel the conviction of the Holy Spirit and you may be in danger of succumbing to the destructive nature of "spiritual rigor mortis."

SIGNS OF SPIRITUAL RIGOR MORTIS

Many people suffer from spiritual rigor mortis, unawares. You can identify if you may be suffering from "spiritual rigor mortis" when:

- there is no breath, no spirit or presence of God in your life; in other words you become carnal
- you have lost your excitement for the things of God
- you become "numb" to spiritual things but somewhat alive to the things of the world
- you feel as though you have lost your joy and become overwhelmed with spirits of hopelessness and despair; there is no warmth in your spirit and you become "cold"
- there is no spiritual "flexibility" and it becomes increasingly difficult to respond to the Spirit of God
- you may abandon your dreams, visions and ideas or leave your kingdom assignment
- you may abandon your family
- businesses that were once thriving close down
- you backslide and walk away from the church with no desire to return

In *John 10:10*, Jesus promised us life and life more abundantly. It is not God's will that you should live in any level of distress or defeat. You must rise up immediately; engage in spiritual warfare and strategic prayer to launch a counter-attack against this spirit in Jesus' name.

You can use the weapon of the Word and declare, according to *Psalm 118:17*, that you shall not die but live to declare the works of the Lord. Life and death are in the power of the tongue; release a Word in the atmosphere against this spirit of rigor mortis in Jesus' name and begin to live.

THE WALKING DEAD
Defeating The Spirit of "Comatosa"

I have had numerous encounters with demonic spirits, during times of ministry. One such spirit that I commonly found in the Body of Christ is *the spirit of "comatosa"*. As someone's life is affected physically by a natural coma, likewise someone's life may be affected spiritually by *the spirit of "comatosa"*.

Some people exist in a non-responsive *"spiritually comatose"* state as it relates to the things of God just as someone may be physically unconscious or non-responsive. This demonic spirit seeks to put people in a spiritual state of despondency, apathy, weariness or discouragement.

People in this condition do not have the desire to read the Word or pray. These types of people go about their daily routine and are living outside of the will of God for their lives. They are not physically or clinically dead but, due to various circumstances, they have no enthusiasm for life or the things of God.

When a person is in a natural coma, they depend on a life support system for survival. Just as a physical coma is considered to be a medical emergency, a person in a spiritual state of *"comatozation* is a spiritual emergency.

It is important to note that the spirit of death is working behind the scenes, in conjunction with the spirit of sleep and slumber, in order to keep a person in a *"spiritual coma"*. When a person is in a natural, medical or even a "spiritual" coma, their survival depends on their strong desire to live.

The Bible declares in ***Ephesians 5:14***, *"**Wherefore he saith, Awake thou that sleepest, and arise from the dead, and Christ shall give thee light.***"*

Sleep is a form of partial consciousness or sub consciousness. God admonishes us to shake ourselves out of a state of being ***partially*** conscious or ***"spiritually asleep"***. He wants us spiritually alert, ***fully*** conscious and aware. Whether in a natural or *"spiritual coma"*, a person must fight for survival.

DIMENSIONS OF DEATH

At some point in time we may experience death on various levels, either physically, spiritually or eternally. What many people do not realize is that they can be alive physically but dead spiritually. In other words, they appear to be alive but they are, figuratively, in a "deep sleep."

That is what I refer to as the state or condition of *"spiritual comatosa."* It is also possible to experience "eternal death" which is separation from God throughout eternity.

Figuratively speaking, "death" in the Word of God means a separation from the divine purpose of God for which you were created. However, the redemption that Jesus bought for us through the shedding of His blood on Calvary remitted our sins and saved us from the judgment of eternal death.

Let us look at some of the basic aspects of death, which are as follows:

- **Physical Death:** Physical death occurs when the final breath is released and the soul leaves the body. In ***Hebrews 9:27***, the Word of God reveals that, ***"...it is appointed unto man once to die, but after this the judgment."*** We may all, at some point experience this form of death. This simply means that everyone is destined to die.

Understanding the process that takes place during physical death, will help you to better comprehend what occurs during spiritual death.

- **Death to the Flesh** *(Psalm 66:10–12; Isaiah 48:10; Isaiah 54:16):* This type of death leads you closer to God and His divine plan for your life.

It is important to understand that although you may have accepted Jesus Christ as your Lord and Savior, your mind may still be *"unrejuvenated."* This type of mindset is one that is not fully alive to the Spirit of God. Therefore, as a believer, you must go through the necessary process of "dying" to an ungodly mindset or system of beliefs so that you can begin living the life that Christ has for you.

"Death to the flesh" also speaks about dying to your own selfish ways and ambitions. It is the process of consecration and sanctification from a carnal mindset in order to embrace the mind of Christ. Very few people continue this "death" process as it requires personal sacrifice, total commitment and dedication to God.

This type of death process allows the spirit of Christ to be formed in you. *"...if ye live after the flesh, ye shall die; but if ye through the Spirit do mortify (kill) the deeds of the body, ye shall live." (Romans 8:13)*

During this process there are tests and trials that can occur which may make you feel as if you are dying. These "fiery trials" are not designed to kill you but, rather, they are designed to perfect you.

> *"Beloved, think it not strange concerning the fiery trial which is to try you:..." (1 Peter 4:12)*

It is important to understand that each believer must endure some level of testing and trial in order to develop your spiritual endurance and forge the godly character which equips you to remain faithful to the call of God. Even the Apostle Paul declares in *1 Corinthians 15:31, "I die daily!"* It is the "death to the flesh" to which he refers.

Further, God knows that opposition would come your way, so He has to prepare you for what He is calling you to do by taking you through the furnace of affliction. This "purging experience" is a type of "death" which strips away everything in you that is not like God.

In *Hebrews 5:8* the Word of God reveals that although He was the Son of God, Jesus *"...learned obedience (through) the things He suffered."*

- **Spiritual Death** *(2 Samuel 13:19, 20; James 1:14)*: Spiritual Death occurs when the spirit of death launches an attack against your life as a believer in order to remove you from the presence of God. This demonic spirit launches missiles of hurt, pain, despair, rejection, abuse, neglect and more at your soul, all in an effort to bring oppression, confusion, discouragement, frustration and ultimate separation from God and the things of God.

Spiritual death can also occur when a seducing spirit comes and seeks to lure you, as a believer, entirely out of your kingdom assignment. This subtle spirit comes to separate you from the divine plan of God for your life *(Judges 16:16–20)*.

- **The Spirit of Death:** *(Revelation 6:8; 1 John 3:8; 1 Peter 5: 8–9; Ephesians 2:1–2)* The spirit of death is an enemy which relentlessly pursues the lives of the people of God. This demonic nemesis seeks to destroy your life as a believer separating you from your divine purpose. Its plans are to discourage, derail or demote your progress with the intent of frustrating you out of your kingdom assignment, or to cause you to die before your time.

  The primary mission of this spirit is to drive you away from the presence of God. In some cases, its relentless pursuit leads the believer to giving up and eventually backsliding. It was the spirit of death that I rebuked when I made the declaration that *I refused to die!*

- **Eternal Death:** *(Matthew 25:46; Revelation 2:11; Luke 16:22–23) As we saw earlier, there is physical death, spiritual death, the death of the flesh and the spirit of death.* It is also important to know that there is also an eternal death. Eternal death occurs when a man chooses to remain separated from God in sin and then dies physically. With no more possibility for reconciliation, this separation is eternal and is referred to as the *"second death."*

THE AVENUES OF DEATH

Over the years, I discovered that there are other avenues through which the spirit of death attacks people's lives in order to destroy them. Some of the ways include:

Accidental death – this occurs when someone's life is taken by an unforeseen circumstance or mishap.

Mental death – this occurs when the spirit of death attacks you in your mind. The mind malfunctions and the person experiences what is called a nervous breakdown or the loss of their capacity to think, reason or function normally. This type of death may have occurred as a result of some trauma, tragedy, incident or accident which may have taken place in that individual's life.

Emotional death – The spirit of death may diabolically attack your soul in order to deliberately shatter you and bring about emotional death. This occurs when you experience something so tragic and heart-wrenching that you no longer have a desire to live. Trauma to the soul occurs when the soul has been scarred and wounded to the point where you lose all hope. Emotional death causes a great deal of loss, including the loss of a person's spiritual zeal for God and the things of God. Further, their love for God is diminished, they become lethargic and non-responsive to spiritual environments. They may also become introverted or even detached from society.

Further, you may become numb and non-responsive as you build internal walls in an effort to protect yourself from any future hurts or disappointments. You may grieve for extended periods of time which, if not properly handled, can lead to the death of your emotions. The death that I am referring to here is where you are so emotionally fragile and unstable that the slightest event can negatively alter your entire state of being. You may cry for no reason and live in a constant state of depression.

Relational death – this occurs when you are betrayed by a trusted loved one or friend. In some cases it may occur as a result of infidelity in a marriage, betrayal in a business partnership, disloyalty in a friendship or disappointment in a parent-child relationship.

As a result of relational death, some people fear ever trusting again, getting married again or re-entering business partnerships. I have seen relationships with Pastors and other associates destroyed because of misunderstandings and minor incidences that could have been resolved, if only they were willing to defeat the spirit of death. Satan takes every opportunity to rob God's people for he knows that good relationships are very important and can contribute to your overall development.

A spiritual-relational death – takes place between a spiritual leader and his members.

This type of death occurs in two basic forms:

1) A pastor may be betrayed by members or a trusted servant. It can wound the pastor to the point that he leaves his assignment. In America alone approximately 1,500 pastors leave their pulpits each month, many of them suffering from this type of hurt.

2) On the other hand, members can be hurt or disappointed by their spiritual leaders or by other members of their local assembly. If these persons become offended and leave the church, this not only creates a void in the kingdom, it also brings about a spiritual death and the abandonment of their kingdom assignment.

"SPIRITUAL-RELATIONAL DEATHS MAY SOMETIMES BE PERPETUATED BY SPIRITS OF PRIDE, OFFENSE AND JEALOUSY."

Social Death – This occurs when a person loses influence in a society or their reputation becomes marred or tarnished. For example, someone can be alive but experience a form of social death. This type of death is experienced by persons who are incarcerated, separated from society; a public figure who "falls from grace"; an entertainer who no longer produces a product that the public desires, and more.

Financial/Economic death (a sudden loss) – This occurs when a person misappropriates, funds, experiences financial and economic loss, failure to embrace doors of opportunity and the like. Financial or Economic death may be experienced in various forms such as, bankruptcy, the loss income; the loss of investments *(stocks, bonds, businesses, 401K plans, etc.)*, the loss of a home *(foreclosures, by natural disasters, etc.)* and loss of insurance coverage. Financial distress can cause you to become so overwhelmed by your economic state that you become dysfunctional and may be distracted from your kingdom assignment.

There are many other death experiences that will seek to overwhelm your life as a believer. Remember, the enemy's primary goal is to separate you from the will, the purpose and the plan of God for your life. He knows that if he is successful, you will not live the fullest life that God has for you. The only way you will defeat the enemy is to refuse to die!

THE NATURE OF DEATH

When "death" is present, it can manifest in but is not limited to, any of the following ways:

DEATH AS THE ABSENCE OF LIFE:

- **Immobility** – the lack of movement; the inability to move or progress forward
- **"Monumentalism"** – a spiritual condition where you may become stagnant, remaining focused on triumphs and accomplishments of the past while not experiencing any current victories; generally speaking, you can only identify with what has happened and what you once did that was successful, lucrative or prosperous. Death as the absence of life is also experienced in the church when the Body of Christ goes through seasons of **"mechanicalism" (programmed worship; having to be primed, prompted to give, sow, praise, worship, etc.)** and **"monumentalism."** *(focusing on*

past victories; tied to tradition and religion, not willing to change and holding onto monuments) However, it is the will of God that His Church becomes a spiritually evolving **"movement"** *(this type of church is not stagnant; operating like a river that is lively, active and vibrant, functioning in demonstration and the power of the kingdom of God)*

DEATH AS THE ABSENCE OF PRODUCTIVITY:

- **Unproductive** – not being able to produce or accomplish anything; the loss of one's zeal and passion to perform
- **Useless** – no specific function; inoperative

DEATH AS THE ABSENCE OF GROWTH:

- **Stunted growth** – growth with restrictions
- **Retardation** – lack of growth; extremely/unusually slow growth; delayed or impeded growth; obstructed/hindered growth
- **Regression** – retreat; go backward, to lose ground
- **Insanity** – desiring to grow but not willing to change. Albert Einstein said, "Insanity is doing the same thing over and over and expecting different results"

DEATH AS THE ABSENCE OF STRUCTURE/ORDER:

- **Anarchy** – lack of government; a state of lawlessness; political disorder due to the absence of governmental authority and leadership
- **Disorder** – the presence of chaos, confusion, turmoil and mayhem because of a lack of order. The Word of God lets us know that God is not the author of confusion, He moves and flows in precise order

DEATH AS BEING NON-RESPONSIVE TO YOUR ENVIRONMENT:

- **Numb** – unfeeling; when you have no thoughts, feelings or concern toward others or what is going on around you
- **Apathetic** – when you become disinterested, indifferent or unconcerned about others or what is going on around you; you observe what is happening but you do not become involved
- **Unconscious** – being totally unaware of what is going on around you
- **Insensitive** – when you are aware of what is going on around you but you choose to ignore it or your response lacks compassion, concern or care
- **Lethargic/Sluggish** – lacking energy, enthusiasm and drive; slow moving
- **Dispassionate** – remaining mentally and emotionally detached from a particular situation or lacking the appropriate passion or drive

DEATH AS THE DEPARTURE FROM LIFE/ACTIVITY:

- **Divorce** – the separation of a union between yourself and another individual; to separate or distance yourself; to no longer be connected or identified with; you can also divorce places, ideas, etc.
- **Reclusive** – keeping to oneself; willfully remaining isolated
- **Isolation/Separation** – moving away from something that should bring life; turning away from what God has given or called you to do; staying away from family and friends

DEATH AS THE END OF SOMETHING (INVALIDATION):

- **Expiration**- a coming to an end; the finish of something; to lose validity and relevance

SOME OTHER WAYS TO IDENTIFY THE SPIRIT OF DEATH :

Murder, Suicide, Divorce, Miscarriage, Oppression, Gossip, Slander, Character Assassination, Stigmatization, Betrayal, Diseases/Terminal Illnesses, Morbidity, Jealousy, Isolation, Grief, and so many more.

As you have seen, death can occur in so many ways. However, you must be willing to resist the plans of death and make a resolute decision that you are not going to die. If you begin to see the signs and symptoms of death in your life, you must do everything you can to defeat this spirit. You cannot allow what God has placed on the inside of you to die. You must be prepared to do whatever it takes to live!

DEATH IS THE "NIGHT" OF PURPOSE

Do you know that before you were *conceived* in your mother's womb you were first *conceived* in the mind of God? It is true! It is important for you to understand that before you were born, you were in the imagination of God. He thought about you before He released you into the earth realm.

Therefore, all of your unique attributes and qualities, such as your gender, race, nationality, personality, gifts, talents, abilities, passions and more were predetermined by God. Subsequently, He envisioned a creation that was fearfully and wonderfully made, a *"Designer's Original."* Now He wants you to become everything that He imagined you to be. *Wow! What an awesome God.*

Along with your external characteristics and internal qualities you were also born with a specific purpose. Your God-ordained purpose is the original intent and reason why you were born. However, before He released you, He "breathed" His Word into you. *(Genesis 2:7)* This Word sealed the "divine coordinates" of your destiny and nothing can stop or alter what God created you to do.

"Before I formed thee in the belly I knew thee; and before thou camest forth out of the womb I sanctified thee, and I ordained thee a prophet unto the nations." (Jeremiah 1:5)

Although, the enemy may not be able to change your destiny, he seeks to stop you from coming into the fullest measure of who you are. In most instances, he deploys the spirit of death and all of its cohorts in order to sabotage your divine purpose in God. The enemy knows that the fulfillment of your purpose defines the reason why you are alive and helps to identify your true worth and value. You must continue to fight against the spirit of death if you are going to accomplish everything that God has for you.

Similarly, if you are not living out God's preordained intent for your life, I propose that you are dead already. Therefore, death being the "night" of your purpose means that if you are not fulfilling your God-given destiny, then you are in "darkness" or void of understanding who you really are and what God has called you to do.

You may go through this life living other people's dreams while your divine purpose remains buried in a "valley" somewhere. This is not God's idea; neither is it His will for your life.

When you are in a position where you do not understand your reason for existing or living, you are spiritually dead, *disconnected from the life that God intends you to live.* You "die" spiritually because your true identity in God is absent and you are therefore void of accomplishing the things that you were created to become.

Further, if you are actively functioning in what you believe God has created you to do and you become somewhat despondent, ineffective or indifferent, then I submit to you that you may be exhibiting signs of spiritual death. Your God-ordained purpose defines your reason for living. You must seek to do all that God has assigned for you in order to experience His abundant life.

DEATH AS THE ABSENCE OF VISION

In *Proverbs 29:18* the Word of God reveals that *"...where there is no vision, the people will perish:..."* There are many dreams, visions, business ideas and the like that you may have launched at some point in your life. However, they may not have endured because there was no "specific plan in place" to maintain the vision. "Vision" is the ability to see beyond where you are and it equips you with the insight you need to prepare for where you are going. Where there is an absence of "spiritual vision and insight", "spiritual death" is inevitable.

If you are going to successfully fulfill the plan of God for your life, you cannot have "sight" only, but you must also have vision. Pray and ask God for wisdom, knowledge and understanding so that you can maintain whatever He has given you.

"THE ONLY THING WORSE THAN BEING BLIND IS HAVING SIGHT BUT NO VISION!" – HELEN KELLER

NO ONE JUST DIES!

It is my opinion that no one just dies! In some instances, what appear to be unusual occurrences or unexplainable behaviors are in fact, signs and symbols that death is imminent. This type of prophetic unction can be further qualified as spiritual discernment given by God. In the world, this type of "foreknowing" is referred to as "instinct", "intuition" or "premonition." It is also important to understand that this foreknowing is not merely happenstance but that the "spirit" being

---

of an individual becomes more alert or sensitive when the "time of death" is near and knows that it is transitioning.

Although, some people may not know exactly when they are going to die, I believe that people enter a "perimeter" or "spirit realm" when they are about to leave the earth. For the most part these premonitions are unexplainable but should not be ignored when they are perceived.

In other words, if you really think about it, even naturally there seems to be a process leading to death, unless it happens suddenly or tragically. Even then, there are times that an individual has some type of dream, spiritual encounter or other indicator to warn them of impending death.

As it is in the natural, so is it in the realm of the spirit. People do not just wake up one morning and, for no reason, make a decision to "give up." There is always a successive accumulation of factors which indicate that a person is becoming discouraged, even to the point of disgust. When they inevitably get to the point where they become hopeless, despondent and extremely apathetic, these are some of the indicators which suggest that the process of spiritual death has begun.

No one just dies! As you begin to see the signs of death, I believe that God uses these as opportunities to prepare each individual.

CHAPTER THREE

DEATH NEVER ACTS ALONE

"FACING LIFE OR DEATH!"

In recent years I have noticed that unexpected deaths are occurring more frequently. To "die" simply means that "life" has come to an end; the heart has ceased to pulsate, the brain no longer functions and there is no more breath left in the body.

Although "death" is imminent, meaning that one day we will all die, I still believe that there are persons who did not have to die when they did. This, I am sure, may raise some eyebrows, but I believe it to be true.

In some instances, I believe that you have a choice in the matter. Your overall outlook, mindset and attitude to your situation, all tend to have some influence over the result of your affliction. I have seen circumstances where two people were faced with the same dilemma and one succumbed while the other overcame.

Similarly, when faced with life or death circumstances it is vitally important to have the right people around you, as any inappropriate action, movement, thought or word can cause you to slip into an ensuing battle of discouragement, doubt and unbelief.

This may only intensify the warfare that you are facing. If you have decided to live, you must make every effort to do so by creating the right atmosphere around you. This determines if you will live or if you will die.

Your outcome will sometimes depend on three (3) basic factors:

1. Having the right people around you
2. Creating the right environment around you
3. And most importantly, ***maintaining*** the right mindset

I have spoken to many people who were *"on their death beds."* In most cases, the doctors had told their loved ones that nothing more could be done and to start making plans for a funeral.

However, some of those same people who were "once near to death's door" are still alive today. *"What exactly happened?"*, you may ask. Although I do not claim to have ***all*** of the answers, I do believe that somewhere in that person's soul they made a resolute decision that ***they refuse to die!***

As their "trial of life or death" continued, their faith activated a miracle from heaven and God intervened. The angels in heaven, therefore, altered their "death" verdict, initiated a "stay of execution" on their behalf and their life was spared.

Raising A Loved One From the Bed Of Affliction

I believe that as long as there is breath in your body, you are still alive. Whenever someone is on the bed of affliction, whether they are conscious or comatose, the way we care for them is very important. I have seen people who were in a coma, with no hope of recovery, be suddenly revived because of the love, care and attention given to them.

I can vividly recall when my father was in the hospital battling for his life due to an alcohol-induced coma. By the time I arrived at the hospital there were a number of family members and friends who had already assembled near his bedside. Taking in the scene, I could not believe what I was seeing.

As he lay there, the curtains in the room were closed, people were literally mourning his death; crying loudly and shaking their heads, others were standing there singing funeral hymns as if he was being eulogized. But there was one major problem with this whole scenario: *he was not dead yet!*

On advancing into the room, I was overtaken by righteous indignation. These people were acting as though he was already dead, despite the fact that he was still living. I felt that they should have been doing everything they possibly could to keep him alive.

I demanded that they stop and leave, immediately. I flung open the curtains and let the sunlight come in. I called for a vase to be filled with water and placed some flowers in it. I brought a worship CD and allowed the music to fill the air. I went to his bedside and began praying for him. I let him know that I loved him and that I did not want him to die. I told him that he had too much to live for and that there were other people who loved him as well and were not ready for him to die. I was fighting for his life!

"ATMOSPHERES CREATE CLIMATES AND SUSTAINED CLIMATES ESTABLISH YOUR BELIEF SYSTEM, LIFESTYLE AND CULTURE."

Shortly thereafter, my father regained consciousness and in his usual humorous manner he looked at me, smiled and said, *"Hey Mattie ... it's hard to keep a good man down!"* I was so grateful to God for bringing my father back to me. God graciously granted me a few more years with him. Within that time, he gave his heart to the Lord and also released a blessing upon my life and told me to "Never forget the children."

To this day, I remain convinced that God has given me a mantle for this generation. It was an assignment given to me by God and endorsed by my father.

Here are some strategies that I recommend when seeking to revive your loved one:

- prayer
- worship
- play soft instrumental music
- play empowering and encouraging sermons
- keep fresh flowers by their bedside
- open the windows to let fresh air and light in
- gently touch or kiss them on their hands, forehead, etc.
- groom their hair, while talking to them as if they were conscious
- read poetry or the psalms to them ... and more

On the other hand, there are some things that we should not do:

- Sing hymns or other songs of death or dying
- Speak words of death or dying
- Leave them in darkness
- Burden them with bad news (for example, the amount of the hospital bill, the death of a pet, or the like)
- Blame them for unresolved issues
- Do not overbear them with condemnation or guilt

It is understood that Man is a triune being – a spirit, possessing a soul and living in a body. While in a comatose state, an individual's subconscious remains aware. If you begin to speak life to him, this could revive the spirit of the individual and ultimately his soul.

While your loved one is unconscious, I believe that you should attempt to find ways to encourage them to stay alive by employing means such as: playing soft music, bringing them fresh flowers. Continuously speak Words of Life over them like, *"You shall live and not die!"*; *"You have so much to live for!"*; *"You are important to God!"* ; *"Your life is not over!"*

Some people pray and their loved one still dies. This does not mean that these people did not have faith. It is merely an indication that no one has absolute control over death. There are many times we do not understand the divine providence of God.

We may not know why someone who loves God was not raised from their bed of affliction, but we do believe the Word of God that all things are working together *for* good, even if they do not always *feel good* **(Romans 8:28)**.

We have to believe and accept that God's grace is extended to us as His sovereign will is accomplished in every area of our lives, even when we are faced with life or death experiences.

WHEN DEATH COMES ...
"The last enemy that shall be destroyed is death."
(1 Corinthians 15:26)

In *1 Corinthians 15:26* the Word of God states that "death" is the last enemy that shall be destroyed. I truly believe that it is one of the greatest enemies you will ever confront as a believer.

There were times when the spirit of death attacked my life so severely I knew that it was only by the grace of God that I survived. I also believe that God led me through all of these experiences because He wanted to reveal more and more of Himself to me.

When the spirit of death came against my life, I had to use every spiritual weapon available to me in order to conquer this destructive enemy. At first, this seemed like a very intense test but, deep inside, I knew that I had to pass it in order to go to another level in the Kingdom.

When death comes, you must make a conscious decision to either fight or surrender. I made a decision to fight because I did not believe that it was my time to die.

"WHENEVER YOU ARE AT A CROSSROAD, YOU MUST CHOOSE WHETHER YOU WILL DIE THERE OR PICK UP THE PIECES OF YOUR LIFE AND MOVE ON."

I further understood that, if I survived, God would get the glory out of my situation and empower me to show others how to overcome this demonic adversary. Jesus defeated the spirit of death when He died and rose again with all power in His hands, taking the "keys" of death, hell and the grave.

That same resurrection power is available to everyone who believes in Him. You do not have to succumb to the schemes of the spirit of death once you make a decision that you are going to live.

YOU HAVE A CHOICE IN THE MATTER

I know exactly what it feels like to go through something extremely devastating and want to give up; it *feels* so easy to just let go. Whenever intense tests and trials come against you, you have to choose if you are going to persevere. The word "choice" means the act of making a decision when faced with two or more options.

> *"I have set before you (this day) life and death, blessing and cursing: therefore choose life, that both thou (you) and thy (your) seed may live. (Deuteronomy 30:19)*

As you endure various challenges, it is vitally important to understand that even your hardships sometimes fulfill purpose in your life. While going through them there may be much pain, confusion and frustration involved in what you are facing.

However, it truly takes spiritual strength and courage to trust that God has a divine purpose in what you are going through. Life and death are in the power of your tongue. Your trials should "press out" the Word of God that is in you.

When you find yourself going through, you must begin to declare:

- "Though He slay me yet I will trust Him!" *(Job 13:15)*
- In all things I will give thanks for this is the will of God concerning me! *(1 Thessalonians 5:18)*
- Yea, in all things I am more than a conqueror through Jesus Christ who loves me! *(Romans 8:37)*
- No weapon formed against me shall prosper! *(Isaiah 54:17)*
- I shall not die but live to declare the works of the Lord! *(Psalm 118:17)*
- This poor man cried and the Lord heard him and delivered him out of all of his distresses! *(Psalms 34:6)*

These and other "power" scriptures will help you make it through your difficult seasons. No matter what comes your way, you must make up in your mind that God is greater than any challenge you may be facing.

You have a choice whether you will speak the Word of God or if You are going to speak defeat as you endure your trial. You have a choice to come out better or become bitter. You choose to come out mentally, emotionally, financially, or even physically stronger. God says that He will always make a way of escape with the temptation – so you have a choice to make in every situation with which you are faced – speak the Word and live! *(1 Corinthians 10:13)*

DEATH – THE "TERMINATOR"

Jesus reveals how the enemy uses the spirit of death to work against your life as a believer. This demonic spirit comes, like a "thief" to steal, kill or destroy you. In *John 10:10* Jesus exposes the plans of our archenemy. He specifically reveals that satan is a murderer, a thief and a destroyer.

In other words, he is a "terminator" called the spirit of death. Jesus wanted us to know that no matter how the enemy disguises himself, his greatest goal is to bring death and destruction.

"Be not ignorant of satan's devices, for your adversary the devil walketh about like a roaring lion seeking whom he may devour." (2 Corinthians 2:11; 1 Peter 5:8)

The spirit of death has two main functions:

1) *it will either seek to bring about spiritual death in your life, where your soul becomes wounded and broken; you become totally separated from the presence of God or simply give up and abandon your kingdom assignment.*

or

2) *It will seek to drive you to a point of physical death, where you actually die before your time without fulfilling the will of God for your life.*

One of the greatest strategies of the spirit of death is that it works in subtle ways. As you go through your daily routine, this demonic spirit typically seeks an opportunity or place of vulnerability in your life in order to totally consume you.

IDENTIFYING HOW THE SPIRIT OF DEATH WORKS

As a result of the numerous experiences and situations in my life, I believe that God allows me to discern or recognize when the spirit of death is trailing someone.

I am not at liberty to reveal everything regarding this ability, however, what I will say is that He allows me to see what I can best describe as a dark film that overshadows and covers the person's face. I can further define it as a looming, dark presence that covers the person's countenance.

Another clear indication that the spirit of death is present occurs when the strong man of heaviness, through spirits of lethargy and apathy, seeks to oppress someone. Whenever a person becomes "dry", "lifeless" or "indifferent", this is a clear indication that the spirit of death seeks to overwhelm this person's life, driving him or her to a pre-mature demise.

"Death" can occur in any aspect of your existence, including your business, marriage, finances, dreams, relationships and more. *Therefore, when death is present, life is absent, and vice versa.*

As we consider "death" in the physical sense, there are a number of indicators or "signs" which can be used to determine whether a person is physically dead:
- the absence of breathing or respiration
- the absence of a pulse or heartbeat

- the lack of responsiveness to touch, sound, sight, smell and taste
- the lack of warmth in body temperature, which indicates that blood is not flowing

One of the functions of the blood is to carry oxygen throughout the entire body, especially its organs. Whenever blood is not flowing, this means that the organs such as the brain, heart and lungs are not receiving necessary oxygen.

> *"For it is the life of all flesh; the blood of it is for the life thereof:...for the life of all flesh is the blood thereof:..."*
> *(Leviticus 17:14)*

Further, there is a decrease in the blood pressure that typically regulates the blood flow in the body. Therefore, vital organs begin to cease their function and the body experiences heart failure. As it is in the natural body, so is it in the spirit. These same signs can also indicate what happens when a person is dying spiritually.

SUBTLE WORKINGS OF THE SPIRIT OF DEATH

The spirit of death is a destructive, relentless spirit sent by the enemy on an all-out mission to destroy your life. This destruction is not only designed to take place physically; it may also seek to cause you to die spiritually.

As mentioned earlier, spiritual death occurs in someone's life when they are void of, or separate from, the presence of God. Whenever some tragedy or trauma comes to a person's life, the initial or natural response may be to "shut down", respond in anger or demonstrate some other emotional reaction.

The spirit of the thing speaks to the characteristics or nature of the thing.

66

Some people can become so consumed with their pain that they lose their desire for the things of God. The Word of God says in *Proverbs 18:14, "The spirit of a man will sustain him in his infirmity; but a wounded spirit (soul), who can bear?"*

Many people have experienced numerous traumatic experiences such as: rape, hurt, neglect, abandonment, rejection, abuse and others. In other instances, some people may have been disappointed by someone they trusted or respected.

Whatever the scenario, the enemy launches a diabolical attack against your life in an effort to wound your soul. It is his intent that this wound would be so devastating that it leads to your ultimate "spiritual death".

In other instances, the enemy may also seek to create contentious struggles and challenges in your interpersonal relationships. During intense arguments, disputes and disagreements, the enemy subtly masterminds the strife which exists in many relationships.

The enemy further seeks to create the deceptive belief that your problem is the person standing in front of you. He seeks to keep you at odds with other people when he is the real enemy, subtly working behind the scenes.

"For we wrestle not against flesh and blood, but against principalities, against powers, against the rulers of the darkness of this world, against spiritual wickedness in high places." (Ephesians 6:12)

You must understand that because you are in spiritual warfare, your fight is not with the person that you see in front of you but it is the spirit that is operating inside of the person that is the true source of your warfare.

Whatever the tactic or strategy, his ultimate intent is to create so much chaos in your life that you no longer know who you are in God. Neither do you have the mind, the will or the desire to go after the things of God. This is the spirit of death at work, seeking to keep you frustrated, distracted and, thus, void of the presence of God.

THE STRONG MAN OF DEATH AND ITS COHORTS

When spirits of discouragement, hopelessness and despair begin to attack you, this means that the strong man, which is the spirit of death, is after your life.

The strong man of death is a spiritual assassin that works along with other demonic spirits in order to bring you to a place of destruction, seeking to stop you from living as God has designed for you to live. Further, this spiritual predator works with a number of cohorts in an effort to remove you out of your kingdom assignment and eventually destroy your life.

It is the *"spirit"* of each of these cohorts which seeks to operate in your life. For example, although all may be going well with you, there are some times you may feel that you are a failure. There is no natural evidence to support the way you "feel"; however, the feeling is so strong that you are engaged in a literal fight against *the spirit of failure.*

Some of these demonic cohorts are "devouring spirits" which seek to consume or destroy your substance, health or peace of mind with the intent of causing you to experience total loss or devastation.

Whenever the spirit of death attacks your life, the enemy will try to affect you in three (3) main areas:
1) Your health
2) Your wealth
3) Your relationships

Almost everyone can attest to the fact that at some point in their life they were afflicted in at least one of these areas. However, for some reason, the area of your wealth or finances is always, somehow, affected by the other two.

The enemy releases a devouring spirit which is symbolic of a locust, caterpillar or palmer worm that can eat and destroy crops more quickly than a bulldozer. You must be in a spiritual position to be able to identify when the spirit of death or any of its cohorts are attacking your life.

Some of the cohorts and conspirators of the spirit of death are:
- **the spirit of limitations** is a stifling spirit that works along with the spirit of hindrance; the main function of this spirit is to keep you restricted and constrained, perpetually falling short of the will of God for your life.

- **the spirit of the parasite** is a leech-like spirit that sucks and drains the very life out of you or an organization. Similar "sucking" creatures include: leeches, ticks, vampire bats and even snails. People who are under the attack of such spirits find themselves inexplicably losing weight at a rapid rate until they become frail and deteriorate.

- **the spirit of the octopus** is a seducing spirit which works along with the spirit of deception that seeks to attack and restrict your mental functions, through the use of mind control. It is a tormenting spirit that plagues your life with incessant mind battles, with the intent of manipulating, controlling and deceiving you as it spawns confusion and contention in your mind, bringing you into bondage and adversely affecting those around you. Its ultimate goal is to cause you to give up on what God has blessed you with or to draw you away from what God has called you to do.

- **the serpentine spirit** is a criminal spirit which uses its poisonous venom to infect and fatally afflict your life; it uses the snake-like tactics of the deadly cobra; viciously smiting and causing the womb or abdomen to become an incubator for numerous "birth defects" and can also cause various female disorders such as: fibroids, cysts, incompetent uterus syndrome, cancer and barrenness while causing abdominal defects in men, such as ulcers, pancreatic cancers and stomach disorders. It is also known to afflict the reproductive organ in men, causing prostate cancer and even erectile dysfunction.

- **the spirit of the python** works by wrapping itself around you with the intent of suffocating, restricting and constricting, ultimately causing you to asphyxiate, as it seeks to squeeze you to death; its ultimate goal is complete strangulation; it seeks to bring discouragement and causes you to give up to some degree.

- **the spirit of leprosy** is a devouring spirit that brings decay to your dreams, visions, ideas and even your life, until you eventually abandon what God has given; this spirit also causes things to decay and fall off.

- **the spirit of famine** comes to bring extreme lack and want into your life; it brings with it a lack of resource and supply; it causes great deficiency.

- **the spirit of pestilence** directly attacks your life; these are deadly plagues and viruses that continue to poison your spirit; it is similar to being overtaken, overwhelmed or overrun by a swarm of issues; a culmination of many different maladies.

- **the spirit of miscarriage** comes to bring death to something that God has placed in your spirit; you either give up on the dream before it manifests or you fail to do what is necessary to bring it to pass

- **the spirit of abortion** comes to cause you to become discouraged and prematurely rid yourself of or destroy what God has birthed in your spirit, and also works with a spirit of frustration to cause you to walk away from your God-given assignment, which may be your ministry, business, marriage, etc.

- **the spirit of the "bastard child" or "black sheep"** works closely with a spirit of rejection; this diabolical spirit seeks to make you feel as though you are cursed and marked for hardship, oppression and rejection; this spirit will follow your life and where others are being blessed, will seemingly have you in a repetitive cycle of being cursed, rejected, declined and denied; *this spirit comes in the life of an individual because of a strong man in the form of an authority figure that permits this to happen to you or opens the door to this spirit in your life.*

- **the spirit of violence** sends strong, aggressive resistance to your life with the intent of bringing you much harm or pain, and works along with blood-thirsty spirits which seek your ultimate demise.

- **the spirit of murder** is sent to take your life, either spiritually or even physically; the ultimate goal of this spirit is to destroy your character, dreams, visions, ideas and eventually your life.

- **the spirit of suicide** overrides a person's mind and drives him to a state of helplessness, hopelessness and despair; it is a deep-seated desire to give up, leave, or throw in the towel; it makes you feel as if it is the end of the road; it torments and drives a person to his demise.

- **the spirit of failure** is an enemy of success; it is released in your life in order to cause you to fall short of your intended goals and objectives; this spirit also works along with the spirit of fear so that you do not attempt to do what God has called you to do.

- **the spirit of poverty** seeks to attach itself to your life to drain you of necessary financial resources; this spirit seeks to cause you to become destitute and suffer extreme lack of basic human needs. It causes you to become deprived of food, clothing, shelter, finances, etc. Statistics indicate that there are 1.2 billion people, worldwide, who live in abject poverty.

- **the spirit of lack** is released in your life in order to stop the necessary resources from coming to you. It creates insufficiency and causes you to "not have enough" in various areas of your life such as, good/healthy relationships, financial empowerment, motivation, passion, drive, etc.

- **the spirit of grief** comes to "weigh" you down; it seeks to generate feelings of sadness, despair and hopelessness due to the loss of something or someone valuable.

- **the spirit of discouragement** makes you feel that nothing is working, as if God has forgotten you, and you want to give up. At times you struggle or have no desire to pray, worship, read the Word, go to church or work. This spirit seeks to deter you from completing your kingdom assignment or may even cause you to backslide.

- **the spirit of depression** makes you feel a deep sadness or loneliness. It may make you feel unwanted or unloved, driving you into isolation. You may become numb, neglecting your health, appearance, surroundings and even other people.

- **the spirit of sabotage** comes to intentionally cause things in your life to malfunction or fail; it is a counter-productive spirit which seeks to interfere or disrupt your life with the purpose of destroying your destiny or the thing you have been called to do.

- **the spirit of dereliction** is a destructive spirit which comes after you in order to destroy everything you have and causes everything to "break down" around you.

- **the spirit of "ambushment"** are subtle "spiritual predators" which seek to attack and destroy your life by surprise; these methodical spirits study their targets carefully, strategically planning their demise.

- **the spirit of slaughter** is sent out to brutally attack your life, your dreams, visions and ideas; this spirit will hire individuals who are filled with jealousy and hatred to come up against you. They want to viciously destroy everything in your life.

- **the spirit of slander** is released against your life in order to destroy your character through lies and a false witness; because it wants to kill you, it will defame you.

- **the spirit of lies** releases statements about you that are not true; further this spirit works with a spirit of illegal representation and seeks to bring accusations against you, falsely in an effort to destroy you.

- **the spirit of assassination** works along with the spirit of murder. This high-ranking, crafty demonic spirit will go to great lengths to destroy you by targeting your character or reputation.

- **the spirit of ignorance** will cause you to be devoid of necessary information and knowledge; being uninformed and unaware.

- **the spirit of fatigue** attaches itself to your life in order to cause you to remain in a state of unrest, extreme tiredness, exhaustion and lethargy. The ultimate goal of this spirit is to hinder you or slow you down so that you miss your times and seasons in God.

- **the spirit of weariness** brings despair and heaviness to your life; this spirit pushes you to a point where you either want to give up or stop pursuing the will of God for your life.

- **the spirit of slumber** works with a slothful, lazy spirit; It will cause you to procrastinate and stifle your dreams, visions and ideas; it causes delays in your life.

- **the spirit of crime** seeks to rob you. Further, it seeks to kill, steal and destroy the promises of God for your life.

- **the spirit of worry** comes to wear you out; it causes you to be so overly concerned or troubled about your situation that you do not take the time to pray about it.

- **the spirit of fear** seeks to produce anxiety, panic, terror and agitation in an effort to cripple you. It is the ultimate goal of this spirit to cause you to become immobile and hinder your progress in the things of God. This spirit also works to cause you to be afraid to trust anyone, even God.

- **the spirit of doubt** attacks you and causes you not to go after the things that God has promised you; it causes uncertainty, hesitation and indecision.

- **the spirit of infirmity and disorders** seeks to afflict you with prolonged or cyclical bouts of sicknesses. It is the overall goal of this spirit to slow you down and eventually hinder you from moving forward. This spirit comes to attack your physical body with various ailments and diseases.

"YOU HAVE TO DEFEAT EVERY ATTACK OF THE ENEMY BY REFUSING TO ALLOW THE SPIRIT OF DEATH OR ITS COHORTS TO CAUSE YOU TO GIVE UP ON THE PLAN OF GOD FOR YOUR LIFE."

As the cohorts of the strong man of death are exposed, just know that you have the victory over every demonic spirit the enemy sends your way. If you are wrestling with any of these spirits pray this prayer and continue to take authority over them, in Jesus' name.

PROPHETIC PRAYER NUGGET (PPN)

"Stand and pray this prayer, taking authority over every demonic cohort in Jesus' name!"

Father God, in the name of Jesus I stand before you right now under the blood of Jesus. I declare that Jesus is exalted far above every principality and power. I come against every demonic spirit tied to the spirit of death. Your Word declares that he that dwells in the secret place of the Most High shall abide under the shadow of the Almighty!

I give you thanks and praise and come against every spirit of death and its demonic cohorts which seek to bring my life into bondage and declare that I have the victory, now in Jesus' name! AMEN!

DEATH NEVER ACTS ALONE
"Exposing The Spirit Of Death"

Although "Death" may be considered to be one of the most powerful and impacting forces on earth, it still does not act alone. In fact, it is very important to note that whenever or wherever the spirit of death shows up, it shows up with a confederation of other demonic spirits in order to complete its lethal mission.

One of its chief cohorts is the *spirit of fear*. This is one of the deadliest and most subtle spirits that has crippled many people in the Body of Christ for countless years.

The enemy (satan) will allow the spirit of fear to dominate your life because he wants you to become ineffective and ill-accomplished in the kingdom of God and, ultimately, in every area of your life.

Whatever result the enemy desires, he launches a diabolical attack using the spirit of fear, which can be manifest in various degrees:

- **Fear** – a terrifying state of panic where you lose the ability to think or function. The spirit of fear will cause you to react inappropriately or become overwhelmed by an adverse situation, either real or imagined, causing you to become fearful or timid
- **Anxiety** – a state of extreme worry, uneasiness and unrest in your mind and emotions, which negatively affects your nervous system
- **Phobia** – a phobia is a condition where you experience a debilitating fear related to something specific and only manifests when that "thing" or experience is present. For example, some people have a fear of flying, heights, spiders, snakes, etc.

- **Panic attack** – a sudden surge or rush of fear that attacks your mind or emotions, which adversely affects your nervous system
- **Terror** – a state of being that keeps you bound in heightened fear or continual torment and panic. A spirit of terror is generally motivated by the fear of something negative, painful, or devastating happening to you. In some instances, this spirit can enter your life after you have experienced some form of tragedy or trauma and perpetuate the emotional state of fear long after the negative experience has ended. For example, at night some people may dread the dark and are afraid to turn out the lights because they may have once been attacked, robbed or violated at night. Although these persons may have never been afraid of the dark, after their negative experience, they now struggle with the spirit of terror created as a result of the fear of enduring the same experience again.
- **Torment**– an agonizing state which produces nervousness and stress beyond normal levels. This demonic spirit may cause you to suffer from a lack of sleep and bring you into a perpetual cycle of confusion, unrest and turmoil. You may also experience degrees of distress, discomfort and total disarray. In some cases, people can become totally *"discombobulated"*.

"DECLARE YOUR VICTORY OVER THE SPIRIT OF FEAR RIGHT NOW AND BELIEVE GOD TO MANIFEST HIS POWER THROUGH YOU R LIFE, IN JESUS' NAME!"

Regardless of the form in which the spirit of fear comes, you have to win the battle over it if you are going to advance in the kingdom of God, and even in your everyday life. God reminds us in 2 Timothy 1:7 that He has not given us a spirit of fear: but of power, love, power and a sound mind. *(See more in this Chapter)*

BATTLING THE SPIRIT OF FEAR

Battling *"fear"* is one thing but when the *"spirit of fear"* attacks your life, it will cause you to become afraid of everything, even if it is related to your kingdom assignment.

Fear can drive you to do something destructive. This demonic spirit can also paralyze you so that you do not move forward or advance in the things of God. You may also miss opportunities to be blessed, promoted or progress.

Many people, overcome by the spirit of fear, were driven to take their own life or the lives of others. Therefore, every effort should be made to wage relentless war against this spirit. Other forms of fears and phobias include, but are not limited to:

- the fear of responsibility
- the fear of commitment
- the fear of being deceived
- the fear of losing a loved one
- the fear of being hurt
- the fear of being abused

- the fear of new relationships
- the fear of success
- the fear of failure
- the fear of being alone
- the fear of losing
- the fear of heights
- the fear of snakes
- the fear of bugs
- the fear of the dark
- the fear of change

- the fear of being taken advantage of
- the fear of losing your mind
- the fear of poverty and lack
- the fear of the future
- the fear of germs
- the fear of flying
- the fear of dying unaccomplished
- ...*and more.*

THE NATURE OF THE SPIRIT OF FEAR

In *1 John 4:18* the Word of God declares, *"There is no fear in love; but perfect love casteth out fear: because <u>fear hath torment.</u> He that feareth is not made perfect in love."*

To *"torment"* means to cause agony, distress, suffering, anguish and more. Fear can terrorize and plague you, as it opens the door to other demonic spirits. In *2 Timothy 1:7* the Word of God states:

"For God hath not given us the spirit of fear; but of power, and of love, and of a sound mind."

If we look at the converse of this scripture, we will see that this text exposes the true purpose and intent of the spirit of fear. If God has not given us the spirit of fear then fear is of the devil. Whenever fear is present, then power, love and a sound mind are absent.

Therefore, when the spirit of fear comes against your life, it will weaken and cause you to become void of the love of God. Again, *1 John 4:18* highlights, *"There is no fear in love."* However, I also believe that *there is no love in fear.* In other words, fear and love cannot coexist. You cannot operate in the *spirit of love* while you are bound by the *spirit of fear.*

This is why the enemy seeks to dominate your life with the spirit of fear. He knows that once this spirit is in operation in your life, you will function ineffectively in your kingdom assignment. He also knows that love is the ultimate foundational premise upon which the kingdom of God thrives.

Fear cripples, weakens and demobilizes you. It keeps you locked *in* vicious, destructive cycles and locked *out* of the presence of God. You must make every effort to defeat the spirit of fear.

THE ENEMIES OF FEAR
"Faith, Hope & Love!"

"And now abideth faith, hope, charity (love), these three; but the greatest of these is charity (love)." (1 Corinthians 13:13)

According to *1 Corinthians 13:13*, faith, hope and love are three powerful forces which drive the kingdom of God. However, it further states that, "Love" is the greatest of the three. Similarly, in *1 Corinthians 13:1–3 (AMP)*, the Word of God affirms that without love you are a "noisy gong", a "useless nobody", or are in a position where you gain nothing from what you do for God:

" 1 If I [can] speak in the tongues of men and [even] of angels, but have not love (that reasoning, intentional, spiritual devotion such as is inspired by God's love for and in us), I am only a noisy gong or a clanging cymbal.
2 And if I have prophetic powers (the gift of interpreting the divine will and purpose), and understand all the secret truths and mysteries and possess all knowledge, and if I have [sufficient] faith so that I can remove mountains, but have not love (God's love in me) I am nothing (a useless nobody).
3 Even if I dole out all that I have [to the poor in providing] food, and if I surrender my body to be burned or in order that I may glory, but have not love (God's love in me), I gain nothing."

Without love, everything that you endeavor to achieve is in vain. All of your actions, behaviors and functions in the kingdom of God mean nothing if you are not motivated by the spirit of love. Your service becomes "church work" and your words become loud sounding cymbals. Everything that you are doing has no eternal value and is not recognized by the courts of heaven.

This is why the spirit of fear seeks to destroy your access to the love of God. It seeks to keep you locked into outdated and obsolete seasons from which God has already promoted you. For example, God may have called you to be an entrepreneur. However, because you may be bound by the spirit of fear, you remain on a "dead-end" job.

This tormenting spirit acts as a demonic gate-keeper, which is trying to keep you living beneath your privilege and outside of the blessings of God.

You cannot allow your life to be consumed by the spirit of fear. Therefore, you must make a decision to take authority over this spirit and accomplish everything that God has called you to do.

Your greatest defense against fear is your faith. If you are going to defeat this demonic spirit, you must begin to stir up your faith, even now. Stirring up your faith will cause you to move in the direction to which God is taking you. You may be fearful and feel afraid but you must begin to move.

As you move, in faith, you will begin to slowly weaken the grip that the spirit of fear has over your life. Eventually, you will see that fear is just a deception of the enemy and all it represents is **False Evidence Appearing Real!**

"THE SPIRIT OF FEAR IS A SUBTLE DEBILITATING ENEMY WHICH SEEKS TO PARALYZE YOUR ABILITY TO THINK, FUNCTION AND TAKE ACTION."

THE F.E.A.R. FACTOR

I was never considered to be a "fearful" person. However, in retrospect, I realize that the spirit of fear had crept into my life unbeknown to me. As I began to assess where this spirit originated, I recognized that it initially gained access to me during my childhood. Although it did not completely "cripple" me, I knew, as an adult, that I had to confront what had become a "full-blown" enemy.

In *Chapter Five, "This Is My Story!"*, I share about a time in my life when I had become so sick that I could not even walk. The doctors could not determine what was wrong with me and I had become a modern day medical enigma.

I became so disfigured that, as I looked into the mirror, I could hardly recognize myself. It was then that the spirit of fear really gripped and sought to demobilize me.

It was the strong man of fear that stood as a demonic gatekeeper over my life, giving access to other spirits, such as infirmity, depression, oppression and disorders. Week after week, the doctors were constantly finding something else wrong with me.

During this season of affliction, I decided to obey the instructions of the doctors and did everything I could to get well. I knew that I would also have to close the door to the spirit of fear if I was going to overcome.

Although the diseases had disfigured my body, it was the spirit of fear that had disfigured my soul. Again, in that season I found the courage and strength to rebuke the spirit of fear because I was determined that I was going to live.

DEATH AND ITS TERRORIST MOVEMENT

Can you imagine being tormented and feeling as if you were being stalked by someone or something but you were not sure what it was? That was me several years ago.

One of my spiritual sons would usually visit me when I returned home from traveling. In some cases, he would ask me for cooking tips. At other times, he asked me to help him understand the scriptures better.

One evening while we were speaking, he showed me a huge bird that was looking through my window. He wanted to know if I noticed that almost every day this particular bird would suddenly appear from out of nowhere. Distinctly, *I did!*

I went through a season where huge birds, approximately two feet tall, would show up at my poolside every evening. I had never seen these types of birds in my entire life. No matter how much we chased them away they would always return, settling in the same position. They would stand there and just stare. There was one occasion when we literally saw other birds attacking them, but they stayed their position, just sitting and watching. During that season when I would go to the beach, it seemed as if the same birds had followed me there.

I soon discerned that this was no casual encounter and that I needed to pray for divine protection against any evil plan or intent against my life. It was the Word of God and particularly the scripture in *Psalm 91:3–6*, to which I referred for comfort and God's divine protection:

"³Surely he shall deliver thee from the snare of the fowler, and from the noisome pestilence.
⁴He shall cover thee with his feathers, and under his wings shalt thou trust: his truth shall be thy shield and buckler.
⁵Thou shalt not be afraid for the terror by night; nor for the arrow that flieth by day;
⁶Nor for the pestilence that walketh in darkness; nor for the destruction that wasteth at noonday."

To some people, this may seem like an unusual position for me to take; however, I discerned that there was a greater significance to the presence of these birds that I could not ignore. One of the things that I always teach my students is: just as God has given you the ability to discern good, you also have the ability to discern the presence of evil.

For the most part, when people are under a spiritual attack that cannot be seen by others, it is very difficult to explain or even understand. Although you cannot explain to everyone what you may be going through, it is imperative that you aggressively fight for your life. In truth, most people will never understand the nature of the warfare that they are experiencing.

As I encountered numerous attacks from the spirit of death, many people had no idea of my level of warfare. In order to survive I began taking authority over every demonic spirit of death in Jesus' name, praying the Word of God every day.

I did not care whether it manifested in the form of a bird or an evil force of darkness, I clearly understood that all of the demonic visitations I received were from the spirit of death, but it was not my time to die...and I was prepared to fight!

"For we wrestle not against flesh and blood, but against principalities, against powers, against the rulers of the darkness of this world, against spiritual wickedness in high places." (Ephesians 6:12)

You should take every measure to fight against every demonic opposition that comes against your life, regardless of what it is. *Death or the devil, by any other means, is still death ... or the devil!*

ISOLATION
"Satan's Death Trap!"

At times, many people succumb to the destructive vices of the spirit of death because they are either too weak or too passive to fight. In other cases, because they are going through so much, they seek to isolate themselves or conceal what they are going through ... *this is a big mistake!*

Isolation is a satanic set up for the enemy to "take you out!"

Some people isolate themselves and may find comfort in being alone. This is not always good as the enemy sometimes uses this "knock-out" plan to bring about their demise.

Some people stay home from church and their jobs, locked in with the windows closed to isolate themselves from a world they feel they can no longer live in. Often times the enemy will use this tactic to perpetuate deadly demonic cycles of depression, grief, fear and discouragement.

We can see one such example with the Prophet Elijah in the account in *1 Kings 19*. He had just called down fire from heaven and killed over eight hundred false prophets of Jezebel. However, just a few verses later we find him running from her, the enemy he had just defeated; hiding under a juniper tree and wanting to die.

How did this happen you may ask? Satan uses the *"weapon of isolation"* to lure you away from people, especially those who are willing to encourage, celebrate and help you. He seeks to discourage you from surrounding yourself with family and friends who truly love and support you. He knows that your strength lies within this strong network of people.

I discovered over the years that it is always safer to go through a battle with people praying, fasting and covering me than going in as a "lone ranger" with no backup plan or protection.

Praying for yourself is good; however, when you are called on the frontline of battle to impact entire cities, nations and regions you must seek out strong spiritual reinforcement. I encourage you to solicit a battalion of prayer warriors and intercessors who only have one motive, mission and mandate, which is to pray for you.

When people come under an attack from the enemy, they may become fearful, anxious or withdrawn. In some instances, they begin to worry and may even become overly consumed with what people would think if they knew what they were experiencing.

For this reason, I want to share my numerous encounters with the demonic spirit of death and what God has done for me. I believe that my transparency will give others the boldness they need to identify, expose and defeat the workings of the enemy in their own lives.

If you are going through hardship, I believe it is important to let others know that you are in distress. The enemy wants you to believe the lie that you are facing your struggle alone. As you begin to seek out your spiritual support system, you will begin to realize that there are more with you than against you! *(2 Kings 6:16)*

I strongly believe that many people who are being trailed by the spirit of death, will agree that they experience various signs that the spirit of death is trailing them. Most of these people will testify that they have had some prophetic foresight or indication that they were going to die.

Therefore, for the most part people have either had a dream, flash or vision where they saw themselves in a place or state of death. These people sometimes begin speaking the language of death such as, "I'll soon be gone!" or "I won't be here!" and in some cases they go to the extent of making plans and putting measures in place in preparation of their own funeral.

I believe that if we would become more discerning about when somebody is being attacked or affected by the cold grip of the spirit of death, then we should be able to pull him away, especially if it is not his time to die. You can do this by praying and speaking the Word of God over his life. *(2 Kings 20)*

TRAILED BY THE SPIRIT OF DEATH

Although I realized that I had the victory over death in a previous season, I soon learned that this demonic spirit was relentless in its pursuit against my life. The thought of giving up and dying escalated to the point that I not only began feeling a strong presence of death, but I began experiencing symptoms of it. Many nights when I could not sleep, I would leave the house and drive for hours. In some instances, I found myself in some very dark places.

After driving for a while one night I found myself at the base of the Paradise Island Bridge. It was around 3:00 a.m. in the morning and many homeless people were under the bridge that night abusing drugs and engaging in other unscrupulous activities.

I asked myself, *"What am I doing here?"* I became perplexed in my mind as I wrestled with the overwhelming thought of "giving up". Then I started walking to the top of the bridge.

To this day I cannot remember how or when I climbed over the edge of that bridge but the thought came that this was a good time to jump. I had never before entertained the thought of killing myself. However, that night there was a strong impression that came to my mind. It was simply, *"just jump."*

I believe that most people who foolishly end their lives do not really believe that they are going to die. The enemy places them in a gross deception that all they need to do is *"jump";* once they *"jump"* then everything will be alright!

Standing over the top of the railing, I could not help but notice that there were multi-million dollar yachts docked in the nearby harbor and, at a glance, I could see luxurious hotel resorts in the distance. I was in "Paradise" but going through what I considered to be one of the darkest moments of my life.

Up to that point, I had only heard the audible voice of God once in my life and this would have been the second time. He said, "Mattie, I love you, but if you jump, before you hit the ground, I will have someone else in your place to do what I have called you to do."

I was shocked because that was not what I had expected to hear. I was looking for sympathy, comfort, or better yet, I was looking for God to feel sorry for me. Instead, I heard a voice that sounded like a father reminding his child to get up and *"do their house chores."*

"WHEN YOU STOP BELIEVING AND TRUSTING IN GOD, YOU WILL BECOME OVERWHELMED AND TRULY FEEL AS THOUGH YOU WANT TO DIE!"

Although He spoke to me in a stern tone of voice, for some reason I felt so much love and compassion. If I never knew that He loved me before, in that moment, I experienced the overwhelming power of the love of God. That day I left assured that my Heavenly Father loved me beyond what I could understand ... *and I realized that I was in love with Him too!*

I HEARD THE VOICE OF GOD

That day on the bridge, I had one of my most memorable encounters with God that I will never forget. However, for that moment, I was so embarrassed. *What was I thinking?* I knew within myself that it could only be the enemy that would cause me to do such a thing.

I began climbing back over the rails of the bridge. I suddenly realized that climbing back over was proving to be extremely difficult. It seemed as if there was an evil force, stronger than I was, pulling at my legs, making it nearly impossible for me to safely return to the other side. This was so difficult, as by that time, the wind was blowing very hard and I was crying, uncontrollably.

I began to fight desperately and call on Jesus for help. By supernatural intervention, I was able to finally climb back over the rails, falling flat on my back, giving God praise for rescuing me. I told God that I was sorry and needed help to defeat this nagging spirit of death. The Spirit of God spoke to me again and said, "You already have the victory through the blood." The only way that you will defeat this spirit of death is that you must ***"REFUSE TO DIE."***

This was the "Word" I had been waiting for ..."*Refuse to Die!*" That one "Word" from God changed my life forever. That was exactly what I needed to hear. I sat up on the sidewalk, weeping and worshipping. Then something very simple but strange happened. Out of nowhere, a one-dollar bill blew right in front of me.

I picked it up and began running as fast as I could off of that bridge. I bumped into a few people on my way down but kept running until I got back to my car. I sat in my vehicle, trying to make sense of everything that had just happened. I offered up a quiet prayer of thanksgiving and sped home as fast as I could.

As I was driving, I kept thanking God for His love that had rescued me from the spirit of suicide. By the grace of God, I survived! I later realized that through these experiences, I was being equipped with the necessary tools to teach and empower others to overcome their adversities in life.

"YOUR DIVINE PURPSOE GIVES YOU AN ETERNAL REASON WHY YOU SHOULD LIVE!"

EXPOSING THE SPIRIT OF SUICIDE

The overwhelming challenges of life had pushed me to a point where I literally wanted to die.

"Suicide" is the weak "way out" that people take who:

1. do not trust God enough to see them out of their problems
2. are not willing to wait on God
3. are not willing to try again
4. have already decided to "give up"
5. have already decided to take the "cowardly" way out of their dilemma

Tormented by the spirit of hopelessness, some people attempt to take the easy way and, as they perceive it, the only way out. Yes, I was at a point where I had allowed myself to become depressed by everything that was going on around me. I was so overwhelmed with the cares of life that I literally wanted to die.

I was tired physically, mentally, emotionally and spiritually. It seemed as though I was in a constant battle as the enemy sought to destroy my life. I had a wonderful husband, beautiful children who loved me and so much to live for, but I found myself overworked, frustrated and vulnerable to the attack that had been launched by the enemy.

The word *"Suicide"* comes from the latin word *"suicidium"*, which comes from the word *"sui + caedere"*, which means, *"to kill oneself"*. Suicide is the act of intentionally causing your own death or the act of taking your own life.

Most people who commit suicide feel hopeless and overwhelmed by life's challenges, thinking that things will never get any better. They simply resolve within themselves that there is no way out. I firmly believe that the spirit of suicide is governed by the spirit of death which works with the demonic spirit of heaviness.

DRIVEN BY SPIRITS OF HEAVINESS AND SUICIDE

Once the spirit of heaviness takes over a person's life, it uses other spirits such as, oppression, depression, grief, sorrow, hopelessness and despair to carry out its "death" mandate.

What truly amazes me is the number of people who live in mansions, drive luxury cars, wear expensive designer clothes and work on high profile corporate jobs, but still have to "pop" pills to wake up in the morning and go to sleep at night. Some of these same persons leave their corporate high-rise office every day and go home to drown their sorrows in a bottle of alcohol; all in an effort to feel better. This is the demonic working of the spirit of heaviness, which has no respect for persons.

This demonic spirit, working along with the spirit of death, has driven many people to succumb to various self-destructive acts, the most detrimental of which is committing suicide.

People are driven by the spirit of death to commit suicide due to:
- undue stress
- gross anxiety

- poor interpersonal skills
- dysfunctional relationships
- financial hardship
- drug and alcohol abuse
- mental disorders such as acute depression, bi-polar disorder, schizophrenia...
- and more

It is believed that over one (1) million people worldwide commit suicide each year. It is further believed that it is more than likely the tenth (10th) leading cause of death worldwide and the rates are generally higher in men than in women.

SUICIDE: THE FACTS

According to the *Centers for Disease Control*, studies indicated that males are three to four (3 to 4) times more likely to kill themselves than females. For example, for every one hundred (100) suicides that are committed, it is likely that twenty (20) of them were committed by women, whereas approximately eighty (80) of them were committed by men.

Further statistics indicate that, amongst teenagers, SUICIDE is the third (3rd) leading cause of death, following Accidents and Homicides.

The enemy uses demonic tactics in order to mislead people into believing that committing suicide will end the torment they are experiencing. However, the Word of God teaches that every man is a spirit-soul being who has an appointment with death and will live and be judged beyond the grave. He will be judged for the deeds he has done in this earthly body and will receive an eternal reward of heaven or an eternal punishment of hell. *"The soul that sineth (sins), ... it shall die!" (Ezekiel 18:20).*

It is my firm belief that your life belongs to God. You become a "thief" or a "murderer" when you take or kill something that belongs to someone else.

If you feel as though the spirit of death, by way of suicide, is tormenting you, I strongly encourage you to resist that spirit by calling on the name of Jesus and asking Him to help you.

"For whosoever shall call upon the name of the Lord shall be saved." (Romans 10:13)

Further, if you are plagued with thoughts that nobody cares about you or if you feel as though you have been pushed to the limit and are facing what seems like an impossible situation, please know that *God Cares About You!* The enemy lies and tries to convince you that nobody cares about what you are going through. God loves you so much that He made you who you are and gave you a special assignment that only you can fulfill.

Your friends may leave you. Your family may not be in a position to help, but the one thing that will always validate you is your divine purpose and worth to God. You are worth so much more than you realize because you were uniquely created by Him. Take up strength and rebuke that spirit of suicide and death. God loves you and wants you to live!

BY THE GRACE OF GOD I SURVIVED!

Grace is Jesus Christ! It is God's supernatural enablement given to you in order to perform and to do that which He has purposed and mandated for you. Grace is a gift that does not cost you anything.

It is not by your works, nor is it limited because of your mistakes or wrongdoings, it is unmerited favor from God. I survived and overcame, not because of my name, but I survived because the Spirit of

God reminded me of my purpose; the reason He had created me and my reason for living. The spirit of death was defeated that day because the Spirit of God reminded me that I had not fulfilled my kingdom assignment as yet and I still had too much to live for.

Could it be that many people are giving up because they have not discovered their kingdom assignment, which represents their eternal reason for living? Or could it be that some persons have lost sight of why they were ultimately created by God? Remember, you were created by Him, for Him. In *Isaiah 43:7* it says, *"Every one that is called by my name: ... I have created him for my glory..."*.

In Isaiah 43:7, God is talking about you! YOU were created to display the glory of God.

If you allow yourself to become encumbered with the cares of life and what people think about you, or what they are saying about you or how they have hurt you, then you will begin to lose sight of the God who is greater than anything He has created.

The purpose that was breathed over your life even before you were born gives you an earthly assignment designed to keep your eyes fixed toward a heavenly prize. God does not want you to get caught up in the cares and affairs of this life.

More than anything else, seek to build your relationship with God. Nothing or no one else should come before Him. He wants to be your ultimate joy. There should be nothing more important to you than pursuing the presence of God in your life.

Remove yourself from the realm of frustration; seek to find peace in your mind and make a decision that you are going to live.

PROPHETIC PRAYER NUGGET (PPN)

"Pray this prayer and take authority over every spirit of fear in Jesus' name!

Father God, in the name of Jesus, I give You praise for who You are. There is none like You. You reign above all kings and powers. You are sovereign God. I stand on the authority of your Word and declare that you have not given me the spirit of fear but of power, love and of a sound mind.

Now, I bind the spirits of anxiety and fear from over my life and I declare that every demonic stronghold is broken, in the name of Jesus. I plead the blood Jesus and I engage war angels to fight against the enemy on my behalf, in the name of Jesus. I decree and declare that I have the victory through Christ who always causes me to triumph. In the name of Jesus! AMEN!

CHAPTER FOUR

OVERCOMING THE REALM OF DARKNESS

SPECIAL NOTE

In this Chapter we will seek to expose more of the realm of darkness and show how the enemy works with the spirit of death in an effort to bring destruction to the life of God's people. It should be clearly understood that there is no power in this world greater than the power of God. As long as you remain steadfast in your faith and maintain a pure heart, no weapon of darkness formed against you will be able to penetrate your life.

"DON'T BE AFRAID OF THE DARK!"

"The heathen are sunk down in the pit that they made: in the net which they hid is their own foot taken. .... the wicked is snared in the work of his own hands.... The wicked shall be turned into hell, and all the nations that forget God."
(Psalm 9:15, 16b, 17)

We live in a beautiful world and there are beautiful people everywhere. Unfortunately, amidst all the splendor that we see, there are some people who choose to live in rebellion against God's divine purpose and plan. These are wicked men and women who insist on operating in all that is evil and demonic with no regard for the innocent or the weak. They operate out of the realm of darkness, are power-hungry and will go to any lengths to obtain more power.

Over the years I have seen many lives destroyed by wicked people who are involved in evil practices. They heartlessly use the powers of darkness, through witchcraft and sorcery, carrying out their demonic assignments to destroy marriages, children, businesses, nations and even churches. These demonic workers practice various forms of their craft, leaving vulnerable people in total confusion, trying to make sense of the chaos that has just "hit" their lives.

It would seem as though more and more people are "dabbling" in the "realm of darkness" and are defiling their hands with occult practices. These "once-upon-a-time" customs which were thought to be restricted to smaller countries and regions have made their way to the mainstream arena and have crossed borders transcending racial, cultural, political and religious divides.

The idea of occult activities has seemingly been made acceptable through movies and television programs which depict "evil" as good, and the practice of magic as "normal."

The entertainment arena is showing more and more glorified images of psychics and mediums as normal, everyday people who have a "gift". However normal they appear to be, because of their involvement in the occult, they subject themselves to the consequences of their actions, unless they are willing to change. *(Romans 6:23)*

People's appetite for more information about "paranormal" and "supernatural" encounters is also increasing their interest and desire to tap into the realm of darkness. It is now becoming the norm for people from every arena and sector of society to consult with mediums for answers to their past, present and future. What they fail to realize is that whenever they consult with a psychic, soothsayer, sorcerer or a witch, they are opening up their lives to a demonic realm.

These wizards are tapping into the spiritual realm outside of the blueprint created by God and are operating totally against the set plan of God for humanity. They are tapping into the realm of the unknown but it is through the use of the powers of darkness rather than the power of God.

EVIL SHALL SLAY THE WICKED
"...neither shall wickedness deliver those that are given to it ..."
(Ecclesiastes 8:8)

You must understand that there is no such thing as good evil or bad evil–all evil is bad. The scriptures highlight that anyone who willfully engages in demonic practices such as necromancy, soothsaying, divination or other forms of witchcraft will be judged by God:

"9 When thou art come into the land which the LORD thy God giveth thee, thou shalt not learn to do after the abominations of those nations.

10 There shall not be found among you any one that maketh his son or his daughter to pass through the fire, or that useth divination, or an observer of times, or an enchanter, or a witch. 11 Or a charmer, or a consulter with familiar spirits, or a wizard, or a necromancer. 12 For all that do these things [are] an abomination unto the LORD: and because of these abominations the LORD thy God doth drive them out from before thee." (Deuteronomy 18:9-12)

Many times people are suffering under curses because they opened a door to the enemy, by involving themselves in evil practices and various forms of occult activity

Again I say to you that "dabbling" in these practices will open the door to curses over your life and, in many cases, these curses continue throughout your generational line, affecting your children, your children's children and, sometimes generations later. You do not want to curse your bloodline. Do not entertain witchcraft practices. *There is a high price to pay.*

"TO EVERY ACTION, THERE IS AN EQUAL AND OPPOSITE REACTION." – SIR ISAAC NEWTON

THE RISE AND FALL OF THE WICKED
"When The Wicked Die!"

God gave His Only Son, Jesus Christ, to die *for* our sins so that we would not die *in* our sins. Whenever you do not accept Jesus Christ as Lord and Savior before you die, you die as "the wicked".

"¹⁷The wicked shall be turned into hell, and all the nations that forget God.
¹⁸For the needy shall not always be forgotten: the expectation of the poor shall not perish for ever." (Psalm 9:17–18)

One of the greatest tragedies of our human experience is to reject the gift of salvation that has been freely given to us. Unfortunately, many people lose out because they are unwilling to change. God desires that the wicked, or the unbeliever, would turn from their evil ways so that they can receive the benefits of the true life He has prepared. It is not His will that anyone should perish, but that we all come into the knowledge of His love. *(2 Peter 3:9)*

If you are, or have been involved in any dark practices, take some time to ask the Spirit of God to come in and take full control of your life. Sever any ties, pacts, allegiances or soul-ties to the demonic realm and begin confessing the power and blood of Jesus in your life.

"Have I any pleasure in the death of the wicked? says the Lord, and not rather that he should turn from his evil way and return [to his God] and live?" (Ezekiel 18:23 AMP)

PROPHETIC PRAYER NUGGET (PPN)

Pray this powerful prayer of repentance in Jesus' name!

Father God, in the name of Jesus, I acknowledge that you are Lord of my life. I repent of every sin I have committed and ask that you set me free right now from every wicked way in me. Drive out every root of bitterness and deceitful thing that will separate me from knowing you and receiving your eternal plan of life. Thank you for Your grace, mercy and eternal, unmerited favor, in Jesus' name! AMEN!

"EVIL WORKS IN THE DARKNESS!"

Wherever there are strong occult and witchcraft practices in an area or home, there will be an increase in demonic manifestations. Some of these ungodly practices may include, but are not limited to: palm, tea leaf and psychic readings, necromancy, reading horoscopes, soothsaying, Ouija board, astrology and more. Such demonic manifestations may include: people being tormented or "hagged", children who cannot sleep or objects moving on their own accord.

Whenever people begin to activate and stimulate the realm of darkness, they run the risk of increasing other demonic activities in that environment or region. Wherever there were strong demonic activities taking place, there was also an increase in demonic oppression over that region. In essence what these wicked people are doing is "conjuring up" evil spirits, giving them the legal right to operate.

For example, when there is an increase in witchcraft or occult practices, there are increases in unexplainable tragedies, violent activities, crime, child abductions, fatal accidents and more. This happens because something may have been sent to attack that home, business, church or community or it may indicate there is someone in that area involved in demonic practices.

Whenever demonic manifestations are accepted or embraced as a lifestyle, way of life or daily practice, this establishes a demonic stronghold. Such strongholds can generate spiritual and social issues which may include: gross depression, suicide, drug addiction, poverty, torment of the mind, perpetual violence and more.

At times "blood thirsty" spirits are also released, increasing violent crime and even death. Please understand that I am speaking in reference to *unexplainable* tragedies and misfortunes which are subliminally motivated by demonic activity.

102

If we, as the Body of Christ, are going to revolutionize our communities and region, we must preach the kingdom of God in demonstration and power. Just as Jesus is the light of the world we, as believers, are also the light of the world and have been called to dispel the darkness. The more "light" we shine in our cities, communities and countries, the more we will diminish the powers and influence of the realm of darkness.

The Spirit Of Murder

Whenever you see a history of violence prevailing in a land or country, this is an indication that the strong man of murder is in operation. The spirit of murder is a "blood thirsty spirit" that seeks to violently take the life of another person. It works for, and along with, the spirit of death spawning tragedies and traumas, causing grief and pain to those left to mourn. It further seeks to divide and weaken a society by inciting fear, terror and reclusion. The ultimate goal of this spirit is not only to bring death but also to generate crime, poverty and lack in a region.

The spirit of murder is heartless and works along with, but is not limited to:

- **principalities or demonic assassins** such as *Jezebel, Ahab, Hamen, Herod, Pharaoh, Hitler, Athaliah, Absalom;*

- **ungodly spirits** of *greed, selfishness, rebellion, violence, bloodshed, torment, hatred, racism, pride, anger, rage, retaliation, torture, brutality, resentment, jealousy, envy, strife, covetousness, rejection, abuse, pain, divorce;*

- **ungodly people such as** *wicked leaders, authority abusers, thieves;*

- **ungodly acts/behaviors,** *such as bullying, robbery, revenge, rape, terrorism, brutality; and*

- **demonic entities such as** *the mob, the Mafia, gangs, and much more.*

A police officer killing an unarmed suspect, a gunman robbing a store and shooting customers, rebels storming onto school campuses and killing students or a brother taking the life of his family members are all senseless acts of violence.

The blood of innocent people cries out from the ground for justice every day in a world where few people seem to care, especially if it is not "knocking on their own doorstep". None of these senseless acts are logically or morally justifiable and we must now begin to look deeper to seek out the real culprit behind these heinous "death" crimes.

Whether or not it is an aggravated assault with a lethal weapon or death by stabbing or strangulation, the sad fact is that someone died prematurely without completing their divine assignment or living a full life.

The Blood Speaks

In the book of Genesis when Cain killed Abel, it immediately got God's attention. God heard Abel's blood crying out from the ground and judged Cain for his deliberate actions, telling him that he would be a vagabond, wandering from place to place in the earth. In other words, God did not condemn Cain to a "death penalty" because he had killed Abel but He punished him severely for his wrongdoings.

The blood of the innocent always speaks out. In other words, the Spirit of God always hears the silent cry of everyone who has been wrongly hurt or distressed in any way, even by death. Although their body is buried, I believe that the spirit of the victim cries unto God like a child lost in a vast forest crying out to a parent for help.

God hears that silent cry and judges the wicked, especially if they do not repent. God imputes His mark on the unrepentant aggressor even as He placed a mark on Cain and instructed that anyone who murdered him would be cursed. God's punishment to Cain was allowing him to live a very long life haunted by the misery of knowing that, although he wanted to die he could not, and no one was permitted to kill him.

God, Himself judged during the days of Cain and Abel, prosecuting men's misconducts. Today, God has raised up judges; giving man the right, by power of attorney, to judge and execute judgment in His stead.

One of the methods used to execute judgment is the modern day Legal or Judicial system. It is through this system that every man's actions is weighed and judgment fairly imputed based on the laws and bi-laws established in society. The laws of the land should stand in accordance with the Word of God and should, in no way, unjustifiably heal one while unjustly harming another.

Racism – The Demonic Prejudice

It is so amazing how the enemy has craftily convinced people that they are better than others based on their socio-economic status, culture, ethnicity, nationality, or educational background. In my opinion it is rather absurd for anyone to think that they have the power to abuse or mistreat someone because of their skin color or that they belong to a minority.

What is a minority in the eyes of God? I really do not think that He has one because in the beginning, God said, "Let us create man (mankind) in our image which implies that all men are the same, despite the "external packaging".

As a matter of fact, the term "minority" was attributed to a group or race of people that were numerically smaller than others. However over the years, the word "minority" evolved into a term used by people of one race to classify a race as inferior. I do believe that there are marked social, mental, emotional and physical differences among races. However, I also believe that difference does not denote inferiority or superiority. It simply denotes...*difference!*

Racism is a demonic spirit bred out of spirits of hatred and pride. These spirits seek to overtake a person's mindset and deceive them into believing that anyone who is not a part of their "group" is of a lower class or quality and should be treated as inferior.

In Luke 10 Jesus illustrates the essence of brotherly love in the parables of *The Good Samaritan*, one of the greatest stories ever told. This story was actually a sharp rebuke to the religious Jews of that day. In Bible days, the Samaritans were a mixed breed of people who were considered inferior to the Jews, a "pure" race. In this powerful account, Jesus speaks of the Samaritan as a hero who helps a man who was robbed, beaten and left for dead.

Jesus was careful to highlight the Samaritan's kindness and compassion more than his social, religious or ethnic status. Jesus reminds us that whenever someone is in need, we are to be our brother's keeper regardless of the religious sect, nationality or race to which we belong. God is not racist. He never stated that His Son only died for a "superior" race of people, but He died that *all* flesh might be saved.

Whenever racism is tolerated in our society or within the walls of our church community, we are operating in direct contravention to the Word of God and we empower spirits of demonic prejudice and death. Paul wrote in *Galatians 3:28* that there is neither Jew nor Greek, bond nor free, male or female; God loves us all. He clearly pointed out that we are all one in the eyes of God and should treat every human being as God treats us, not as a lesser class.

Far too often we classify or prejudge others based on something as superficial as the color of their skin, where they live or their financial status. This prejudice may be based on the other person having what we classify as a "menial" job. In our prejudice we tend to despise someone. Jesus' viewpoint directly opposes this mindset.

In **Matthew 20:16** He said that *"...the last shall be first and the first shall be last."* He also stated that "...he that is greatest among you, let him first serve." After all, someone has to clean windows or else we will not be able to see through them clearly; someone has to drive the bus or else we will never make it to our destination; someone has to clear away the snow or we would not be able to drive on our streets. Regardless of a person's gift or contribution to society, we should learn to appreciate and celebrate every person and his gift. *(Continued from Chapter One "Gifts & Assignments")*

The Power To Be Different

As a woman, I can remember suffering from gender biases. For the most part, I grew up in a culture which dictated that if you were a quiet female then you were deemed as passive and weak. However, if you were "loud" (expressive) and progressive then you were labeled as an aggressive, overbearing Jezebel. Many criticized my

> *Not because a man collects garbage or cleans toilets for a living means he is a bum. Great people actually help to "clean up" the lives of others.*

zeal to fulfill the assignment that God had placed on my life and felt as though I was advancing too rapidly. While others, on the other hand, condemned my style of ministry because, in their eyes, I was different.

Through all of this I realized early in ministry that this is how God made me, so I found no other choice but to be who God had created me to be. I would encourage anyone who is being targeted or ostracized for the "gift" that God has given you, to be what He has created you to be. You may not be liked, accepted or appreciated but you will, at least, be true to yourself and true to your God.

It is important for persons who perpetrate such prejudice to note or understand that God uniquely created everyone for His glory. Everyone is not going to look like you, sound like you or communicate like you – allow people to be who God has called them to be. I suggest that you learn how to celebrate other people's "differences".

Let us not create our own interpretation of evil, but let us also not create our own interpretation of what is good and righteous. All of our beliefs and moral ethics should be based on the Word of God written in the Holy Scriptures. This should hold true, not only relative to marriage, fornication, and money but also in how we treat our neighbors. As cliché as it may sound, what the world really needs is more love. The only thing that will eradicate racism spawned from a spirit of hatred is a spirit of love. Genuine love truly "covers a multitude of sin". *(Proverbs 10:12)*

A DEMONIC ENCOUNTER
"Face Like A Snake"

Throughout my entire life I had many encounters which were anything but common to the typical pastor's wife. I had to quickly come to the realization that there was a unique call of God on my life and swiftly embrace the assignment.

I can distinctly remember being in a prayer service where a demonic spirit manifested in one of the young men. I began hearing the "hissing" sound of a snake and, to my surprise, his face began to contort and literally take on the appearance of a snake. I immediately demanded that this demon spirit identify itself. *"Who are you?"*, I demanded. The demonic spirit continued hissing as the young man's tongue extended longer than was normal. The other young men who were present tried to subdue him but he threw them all around the sanctuary as if they were rag dolls. By this time the demonic spirit had totally overtaken him.

I took authority over that spirit, in the name of Jesus and commanded it to identify itself. By this time the men were able to restrain him and I continued to interrogate him.

"Who are you?", I demanded again.

He said, *"My name is Coba; I am he who breaketh the east wind."*
"What are you doing here?", I asked.

"I have come to bring hatred between brothers", the demon responded.

As he was overtaken by this demonic spirit, the young man's posture changed to that of a dog. He began to run and crawl like an animal, violently overturning all of the chairs as he moved with "lightning speed" from the front to the back of the sanctuary. A few of the men pursued and subdued him again. At this time I commanded the demonic spirit to come out of the young man.

After I finished interrogating the demons, one by one they left and eventually I commanded *"Coba"*, who was the strong man, to leave. As these demonic spirits left, the young man lay on the ground tired and thirsty, but totally set free by the power of the Holy Spirit. I later found out that this demonic spirit entered him because his family had been heavily involved in the occult and witchcraft practices.

In an effort to pull him away from the church, they had placed something in his food to control him. After ingesting what they had given him, the door to demonic possession was opened in his life. I have had many encounters with demonic spirits and in every situation I have learned that no two manifestations or deliverance sessions are ever the same. However, in every instance, I have seen the power of God literally set the people free.

INDECENT AND UNLAWFUL EXPOSURE

Many people inadvertently practice various beliefs, customs and traditions based on what they understand to be their culture. These practices have been embraced as a part of their social heritage based on their upbringing, what they were exposed to and what they have come to believe. Some of these traditions represent indoctrinated belief systems which have been interwoven in the fabric of common religious observances and secret orders.

Several years ago, a young lady named "Wanda" gave her life to Jesus and joined our local church. She was fifteen years old at the time. Whenever she came to church, she always appeared to be extremely tired but never wanted to go home. One day we asked her why and she began crying uncontrollably. She said her parents had migrated from another country and were heavily involved in the occult. During the time she converted to Christianity they were still conducting weekly séances at their home. They would become very angry when she returned home after each church service because she now represented "light." She would be tormented all night and got little to no sleep. Eventually, she graduated from high school and moved out of her home to live with some Christian friends.

I do not believe that it is right for parents to expose their children to these or any form of demonic occult practices. Rather, children should be raised to reverence and love God.

"Train up a child in the way he should go: and when he is old, he will not depart from it." (Proverbs 22:6)

As a parent God expects you to raise your children in the "nurture and admonition" of the Lord. *(Ephesians 6:4)* There is a thriving kingdom culture that He wants you to understand and then impart to your children. You must spend time studying the Word in order to effectively fulfill this God-ordained responsibility in the lives of your children.

COMING OUT OF THE DARKNESS

During my years of ministry I have had the opportunity to minister to numerous people who were involved in occult or witchcraft practices. In most cases, these people were innocently "groomed" into such practices, and were exposed to these ungodly crafts by people they either trusted or knew.

People who are actively involved in such practices are tapping into the realm of darkness, thus attracting demonic visitations to their lives and, in some cases, the lives of their children. Further, I also learned that every witch pays a price for consorting with the realm of darkness.

In *Isaiah 1:16* the Word of God says, *"Wash you, make you clean; put away the evil of your doings from before mine eyes; cease to do evil;..."* I believe that Jesus loves everybody and it is not His will that any should perish. If you or anyone you know are involved in such activities you must immediately renounce your involvement, ask God to forgive you and seek out His true plan for your life.

THE WITCHES' LAMENT
"Thou shalt not suffer a witch to live." Exodus 22:18

I can vividly remember a woman named "Geraldine" who was on an assignment to work against God's people, including me. She had done much evil over the years and had caused many people tremendous pain but now she, herself, was in a place of suffering. One Sunday morning she came into my service in a wheelchair. She was much older now, grossly disfigured and miserably tormented.

While weeping uncontrollably, she begged for prayer and asked me to forgive her for all the wicked things she had done. She firmly believed that this was the only way that she would no longer be tormented. I forgave her and began walking her through the process of deliverance. Subsequently, the word began to spread about our deliverance services as people from all walks of life came to receive help.

I can also remember when another lady by the name of "Beverly" came to my office because her child became ill and had to be rushed to the hospital. Although she came seeking healing for her son, I informed her that I needed to pray for her as well. The Holy Spirit revealed to me that He was going to heal her son, but she needed to repent and turn away from her involvement in the occult. She was a practicing witch for many years and had a large clientele which included some church people. While sitting in my office, she began shaking uncontrollably and started weeping as I began to call on the name of Jesus.

Eventually, barely speaking above a whisper, I heard a voice say, *"I hate you Mattie Nottage! I hate you!"* I immediately recognized that this was the voice of the enemy speaking and not this woman. I told her that Jesus loved her and wanted to set her free. She continued weeping and begged God to help her.

I told her to renounce her involvement in the occult by surrendering all of her satanic emblems to Him. Slowly, she opened her handbag and removed her tarot cards and other paraphernalia, laying them on my desk. As she looked at me, the Spirit of God revealed to me that there was still something else that she was holding on to. I later discovered that it was a satanic pentagram necklace. It had been given to her when she was inducted into witchcraft at the age of twelve, and since then, had never left her neck. This she reluctantly surrendered.

Upon removing it, I noticed what appeared to be a thick line forming around her neck which looked like a snake. When the necklace was removed she fell off the chair, gasping and said she felt as if something was choking her and she could not breathe. I immediately took authority over that demonic spirit, in Jesus' name. From the moment she accepted Jesus Christ as Lord she and I encountered relentless warfare because the people of her sect were not willing to let her go. In spite of this, we embarked on a journey towards her deliverance.

When someone decides to turn away from the kingdom of darkness to serve God, it is not always an easy process. In Beverley's case, this involved a season of prayer, fasting and walking her through the Word of God. I can vividly remember her receiving the Baptism of the Holy Spirit and the joy it brought to her life.

Today she is an Evangelist, preaching the gospel and leading others to Christ. ***All glory belongs to Him!*** The Word of God says in ***Proverbs 16:7, "When a man's ways please the Lord, he maketh even his enemies to be at peace with him."***

A CALL TO REPENTANCE
"From Darkness Into Light"

As I continued to remain faithful to my kingdom assignment, God used me to bring healing and deliverance to many people. I eventually came to understand that my experiences occurred as a direct result of the divine assignment and mandate God had given me.

I also recognize that I have been called to the ministry of healing and deliverance so that the glory of God can be revealed. If you desire to break free from the powers of darkness, know that God is willing and able to set you free. The Spirit of God is calling for you to repent. He is calling you to come out of darkness and walk into His marvelous light. *(1 Peter 2:9)*

"THE POWER OF GOD WILL ALWAYS BE GREATER THAN THE POWER OF THE ENEMY!"

Further, this is the season that God will raise up Prophets and Prophetic Seers to bring to light the power of the matchless kingdom of God. I firmly believe His kingdom, in demonstration, will prove to be more powerful than the kingdom of darkness.

"And he shall reign over the house of Jacob forever; and of His kingdom there shall be no end." (Luke 1:33)

PROPHETIC PRAYER NUGGET (PPN)

"Pray this powerful prayer right now and take authority over every spirit of the works of darkness in Jesus' name!"

Father God, in the name of Jesus I plead the blood of Jesus over my mind right now. I stand in the power and authority given to me by my Lord and Savior, Jesus Christ.

I prophetically declare the victory against every spirit of the occult that will seek to come against my life and the life of my family, in Jesus' name. I break every pact and renounce every tie to every power of darkness and declare, from this day forward, that I will be open to the Holy Spirit and His divine will for my life.

I refuse to succumb to any plans of the enemy that would seek to control, manipulate or dominate my life and I activate the life of Jesus Christ over me right now in Jesus' name. I plead the blood of Jesus over my life right now. I break free from every demonic influence of the spirit of murder, demonic prejudice, divination, or soothsaying in Jesus' name. I come against every blood thirsty spirit that would seek to attack my home, family, community or region and release a spirit of peace and godly love, in Jesus' name! AMEN!

DEMONIC "AMBUSHMENTS"

Although satan tries to perpetrate everything God does; satan's ultimate goal is to satisfy his own evil intent. There are times the enemy will set up what I call *"demonic ambushments"* in your life. An "ambush" is a surprise terror attack that an enemy launches in order to gain an advantage. His ultimate goal is always to bring destruction to the life and, ultimately, the testimony of the believer.

Satan has become famous for the numerous "surprise" attacks he has launched against the righteous and will seize every opportunity he can find to sabotage your life; especially when you are weak, experiencing pain, hardship or distress. It is your duty to be aware of his devices and make every effort, through strategic prayer and spiritual warfare, to destroy them in Jesus' name.

"And when they began to sing and to praise, the LORD set ambushments against the children of Ammon, Moab, and Mount Seir, which were come against Judah; and they were smitten."
(2 Chronicles 20:22)

In *2 Chronicles 20* Jehoshaphat was surrounded by his enemies. However, God sent "ambushment" in the midst of the enemy's camp causing them to become confused. As a result, Jehoshaphat's enemies destroyed themselves.

"They meant it for evil, but God allowed it for good."
(Genesis 50:20)

This is how the enemy sometimes seeks to attack your life. For example, if you suddenly become ill and the doctors are unable to diagnose what is really wrong, it is very important that you begin to assess and analyze what may be the origin of this attack.

You should not ignore any sudden, untimely, unexplainable or reoccurring attacks or circumstances which you may deem to be strange encounters. If there is no viable cause for such experiences, then this could be the result of a *"demonic ambushment"*. If this is the case, then it is necessary to engage your spiritual warfare artillery and seek God for His divine assistance.

In other cases there is a combination of factors which may cause you to become sick or succumb to an affliction. For an example, some people smoke and drink excessively and later develop liver or heart problems. Some people experiment with deviant sexual behavior with multiple partners then wonder how they contracted a venereal disease. Others develop bad eating habits with little to no exercise and wonder why they suffer from poor health.

On the other hand, some people become overly zealous and stressed out by everything in life, including the need to succeed or rescue everyone. *These are not what I refer to as demonic "ambushments". These are examples of poor choices people make over which they have control.*

A demonic "ambushment" occurs as the result of the enemy suddenly infiltrating your life with some affliction, suffering, difficulty or hardship. These are the demonic traps from which you should seek to break free!

Historically, the enemy has been known to launch surprise attacks against the righteous. However, in 2 Chronicles 20, God decides to "flip the script" on the devil and releases a demonic ambushment in the midst of Jehoshephat's enemies, causing them to destroy themselves. *To God Be The Glory!*

DEMONIC VISITATIONS

As I share in *Chapter Five: "This Is My Story!"*, I endured a season where I was greatly afflicted in the area of my health. In the midst of all of this I began to have strange visitations, not only naturally but also in my dreams. I can specifically remember an encounter where one moment I was lying on my bed asleep and the next I was on the inside of a house in the midst of a local village. I could see people standing around a fire wearing hoods and chanting my name.

For a moment it seemed as if I was unable to move. However, an angel appeared in the dream and began praying with me. I was then able to break free out of that house and run for my life. As I ran away people began firing bullets at me, but I escaped, unharmed. I could literally feel when my spirit returned to my body and I was back in my bedroom. Even in my dreams I had to be strong and very courageous because I had to make a decision to continually break free from the "traps" and "snares" of the enemy.

On another occasion I had a dream where I can remember taking a flight. Somehow I knew that everyone on this plane was automatically going to die. When I looked around me there were dead bodies everywhere. I tried desperately to get a flight attendant's attention to find out why I was on this plane. However, as I looked a little closer, I realized that the flight attendants were not real people. Instead, they were demonic spirits in disguise.

The plane was moving at an alarming speed towards its destination. Immediately I knew within myself that I was not supposed to be on this flight. The temperature on the plane was so cold that I literally felt as though I was in the Arctic Ocean. I began praying in the spirit and somehow God took me off that plane.

Although I had made declarations that I was not going to die, after each of these demonic dreams I did notice that I received another disturbing diagnosis. I was in constant warfare and found myself fighting while I was awake and also while I slept.

I realized that if I did not take authority over what was happening, even in my dreams, then the enemy would have gained grounds in that area of my life; weapons were formed, but they did not prosper. *(Isaiah 54:17)*

THE NIGHT WATCHES
"Discerning Your Dreams!"

Sometimes the enemy will seek to intensify his attacks against your life during the night watches. In other words he will wait until you go to bed to invade your mind.

Whenever you are going through a difficult season you must ask God for wisdom to discern the dreams you may have. This is important because the enemy will seek to invade your dream realm and use demonic dreams as an affirmation or suggestion of his demonic plan for your life.

Further, he may send dreams to other people as a false confirmation of his demonic plans concerning you. I can remember a few occasions that I felt as though my dreams were invaded. I saw dreams which depicted what was supposed to be my own funeral. Eventually, other people began having the same dream. I not only felt that the enemy had invaded my dream life, but he had also invaded the dream life of some of the people who knew me.

The enemy was determined to cloud my mind with fear. I knew that if I was going to survive, I would have to position myself in the presence of God to overcome these relentless assaults.

Seeking the face of God and lying before Him turned these demonic invasions into heavenly visions. The Spirit of God began speaking to me in my dreams as He showed me the plan He had for my life, and death was nowhere in that plan. According to His Word, the plan He had for me was to live a bright future and not die, prematurely. *(Jeremiah 29:11; Psalm 118:17)*

God will give you the power to overcome the vices of the enemy even if they show up in your dream. Dreams reveal the will of God for your life, and can also expose the enemy's plans.

Once you are able to discern that your dream came from a demonic realm, your first position is to not ignore the dream but to engage in strategic prayer and spiritual warfare to cancel it. Take authority over the dream by fasting, praying, declaring the blood of Jesus and the Word of God against it, God will turn it around for you!

"...thanks be unto God, which always causeth us to triumph ..."
(2 Corinthians 2:14)

DREAM ASSASSINS AND NIGHT RAIDERS
"While You Slept!"

Several years ago the Spirit of the Lord revealed to me how the enemy sometimes waits until you fall asleep to set demonic traps and snares in your way. It is a known fact that the wicked plan their attacks between midnight and 3:00 a.m. It is during this time period that the demonic realm is most active.

In a vision, I saw people who had no idea of what was going on being represented in a courtroom by demonic spirits. During these court proceedings charges, curses and allegations were placed on them without their consent and they were subsequently being sentenced to periods of hardship and difficulty.

As the vision continued I noticed that when those who had been falsely accused awoke the next morning, they felt as if they had been in a boxing match. They could not explain what had happened to them during the night. These demons are *"dream assassins"* sent to sabotage the divine destiny of the person they claimed to have been representing. This is also what I call *"illegal representation."*

Upon awaking from the vision, I realized that God was giving me a revelation of what takes place in the invisible realm. I then understood how the enemy seeks opportunities to take advantage of you whenever you are in a vulnerable state. He has no legal right to do so, especially if you are sleeping.

I became further concerned when the Lord revealed to me that in the spirit realm these court cases take place almost every night. It is the enemy's ultimate plan to diabolically subvert or circumvent the purposes of God from coming to pass in your life.

It is therefore of paramount importance that you, as a believer, consecrate time in prayer and the Word of God, especially before going to bed. It is further important that you anoint your children and cover them under the blood of Jesus so that no spirit of torment *"dream intruder"* or *"demonic night raider"* can attack you or your household while you are sleeping.

Dream Intruders seek to infiltrate your dreams just like a thief who breaks into your home at night. These demonic intruders invade your dreams; holding the door open for Dream Assassins to enter. These assassins, seek to subvert your dreams and shift your life into a demobilized or demoralized state.

In *Matthew 13:24–29* Jesus tells the parable about the wheat and the tares:

"²⁴Another parable put he forth unto them, saying, The kingdom of heaven is likened unto a man which sowed good seed in his field:
²⁵But while men slept, his enemy came and sowed tares among the wheat, and went his way.
²⁶But when the blade was sprung up, and brought forth fruit, then appeared the tares also.
²⁷So the servants of the householder came and said unto him, Sir, didst not thou sow good seed in thy field? from whence then hath it tares?
²⁸He said unto them, An enemy hath done this. The servants said unto him, Wilt thou then that we go and gather them up?
²⁹But he said, Nay; lest while ye gather up the tares, ye root up also the wheat with them."

As indicated in this parable, there may have been some *"tares"* or *"ungodly seeds"* sown in your life, unbeknown to you. However, through the power of God you can uproot and cancel every one of them in Jesus' name.

In *2 Corinthians 2:11* we are warned, as believers, not to be ignorant of Satan's devices. In other words, whether or not you believe that there is an evil or demonic realm does not negate the fact that one exists. However, the truth is the power of our God is, and always will be, greater than the power of any demon or devil.

"... because greater is he that is in you, than he that is in the world..." (1 John 4:4)

WHILE YOU WERE "SLEEPING"

While you are sleeping, if you dream that something negative is happening to you, I admonish you to immediately take authority and cancel it in Jesus' name. For example, if you dreamt that a stranger was trying to give you something to eat or drink which had a foul odor, do not accept it; the enemy is trying to poison you. When you wake up, take authority and cancel every demonic poison in Jesus' name.

This type of dream invasion represents what can happen when you fall asleep in the natural. Just as the enemy seeks to take advantage of you when you are physically sleeping, he also tries to take advantage of you when you are "spiritually sleeping."

Spiritually speaking, "sleeping" here can also represent:
- a season in your life where you were void of the knowledge of God or the truth
- when you, as a believer, cannot discern the times and seasons of your life
- when someone is disconnected from the "fold" or fellowship of believers
- a place or time where you were spiritually naïve or vulnerable
- a time when you were ignorant of the activity of the enemy in your life
- a season of weakness when you were not strong enough to handle some of the experiences that you encountered
- a time when you operated in generational curses and did not realize what you were doing

The enemy seeks every opportunity to sabotage your life and keep you in bondage. This can occur during periods of weakness, ignorance or vulnerability. You do not have to remain bound. Jesus has come to "destroy" the works of the enemy and set you free.

"For this purpose the Son of God was manifested, that He might destroy the works of the devil." (1 John 3:8)

THE DEMONIC SPIRIT HUSBAND & SPIRIT WIFE
Night Visitors!

Over the years during numerous deliverance services, one of the many demonic strong men I encountered in the lives of people were the demonic spirit husband and spirit wife. The demonic spirit husband and spirit wife are territorial, "death demons" known to destroy intimate relationships and "spiritually" terminate the life of an individual. Their primary function is to "marry" you in the spirit realm for the sole purpose of destroying your life. These demonic destroyers attempt to manipulate you to make bad choices, erroneous decisions and cause destructive behaviors, making it difficult for you to remain committed or "married" to anything or anyone in the natural realm.

This is also one of the reasons why some people cannot commit to functioning in their local church for any long period of time. The spirit husband and spirit wife works with a spirit of Jezebel and does not want you to be committed to God or anything godly, especially your assignment in the kingdom. It causes spiritual disloyalty and unfaithfulness. For example, it allows you to pledge or volunteer your time, gift, or talents to the work of the local church but causes you to become unable to remain committed for an extended period of time although you made a faithful promise to your Leader. This is due in part to your being influenced, manipulated or controlled by the demonic spirit husband or spirit wife. *(See more in book by author, "IT'S MY TIME TO LIVE!")*

Married or Single

If a demonic spirit husband or spirit wife has soultied with your life, you will eventually become unfaithful in relationships, dysfunctional on your jobs, inconsistent in completing assignments, apathetic towards fulfilling your God-given purpose and more.

In marriages, it can render the male impotent and the female barren. If they do have children, no love or care is given to them. These spirits seek to bring frustration and dissatisfaction with assignments, activities, relationships and especially marriages.

If you are a single person these demonic spirits seek to prevent you from ever being married or cause you to attract the wrong people to your life. Additionally, if they allow you to marry, the marriage is viciously sabotaged or short lived and you may be driven from one relationship to another, breaking hearts or becoming heartbroken.

On the other hand, in the lives of married couples these demonic nemeses seek to create a masquerade, allowing the couple to marry and live together, however in name only, as both individuals continue to lead separate lives.

These perverted spirits sometimes force their victims to live an independent lifestyle or embrace false perceptions of success and fame, only to later discover that they are actually miserable and alone. Hence, they not only seek to destroy relationships, career goals, businesses marriages and more, but demonic spirit husbands and spirit wives also seek to destroy lives. These spirit husbands and spirit wives can also work with other evil spirits commonly known as the incubus and succubus.

Incubus and Succubus

Incubus and *succubus* are demonic spirits which seek to incite sexual immorality. These unclean spirits tend to invade your dreams seeking to torment, oppress and eventually overwhelm you through perverted thoughts and images. They attempt to have sexual intercourse with you while you are asleep and may even cause demonic nightmares.

Upon awakening, you may find yourself driven by a spirit of lust, battling thoughts of infidelity and even seeking to end your marriage or intimate relationships. These evil spirits can invade a person's life through witchcraft spells, sexual sins and curses of lust. They wreak havoc in intimate relationships and destroy godly marriages.

Once their destructive assignment manifests in the form of your divorce, severed relationship, isolation or other malady, they abandon you, they leave you battling spirits of guilt, shame and condemnation while heartlessly seeking out another victim. The *incubus* typically attacks females while the *succubus* attacks males.

They will "drive" you to engage in immoral activities and will even cause you to open the door to spirits of infidelity, pornography, masturbation, same sex relationships, husband/wife-swapping, swinging, bestiality and more. These spirits usually gain access to an individual's life through the doorway of abuse, neglect, rejection, hurt, lust, perversion, inordinate affections, immorality, family or ancestral curses, occult practices and the like.

To gain the victory over these unclean spirits you will need to break every ungodly soultie with them. God has His anointed apostles and prophets equipped to cast out every demonic spirit. His power is available to everyone who seeks to overcome these demonic spirits. You must be prepared to seek God until you overcome their destructive control.

DEFEATING THE REALM OF DARKNESS
"Mind renewal positions you to see in the realm of the spirit."

Although the spirit realm is real, it is a realm that cannot physically be touched or handled with the natural senses. It exists totally beyond this earthly realm where we dwell.

The best example of this I can give is that it is similar to the blowing wind that you experience in the natural. You can feel the wind, which indicates that it does exist even though you cannot see it; rather, you see its effects. So it is in the realm of the spirit that runs concurrently with the natural realm: demons and angels are both moving in that invisible world. You can recognize some of the manifestations of the demonic spiritual realm when you see people out of their minds, addicted to alcohol, "strung out" on drugs, consumed with a spirit of lust or perversion, and other ungodly vices.

I can remember one of my spiritual sons coming to me seeking answers for an encounter he had while in prayer. He had begun his prayer by speaking in tongues, his heavenly language, which he continued to do for a few minutes. Eventually, he was unable to breathe and it seemed as though something had its hand around his throat. As he gasped for air, he began to call on the name of Jesus and plead the blood of Jesus until that "thing" loosed the choke hold that it had on him. For a few minutes he was very confused. He had worship music playing in his home, he had settled himself for a time of prayer, and yet he had come under a demonic attack.

As he shared the experience with me, the Lord gave me revelation knowledge of what he had encountered. He had just begun to pray and had broken through into the realm of the spirit; however he had not identified who he had come to worship, whether God or the devil. Whenever you engage in prayer or any level of meditation you should first give glory and reverence to God. In the spirit realm, this identifies who you have come to worship.

It was not until he began to call on the name of Jesus and identify that he was worshipping God that he was free to navigate in the realm of the spirit. I believe when he shouted *"Jesus!* he received angelic assistance that arrested and removed the demons which were trying to bind him. In that moment, God had sent angels to help him.

As you constantly train yourself to discern, perceive and "see" in the realm of the Spirit, eventually navigating in this realm will become like second nature to you. Anything that takes place beyond the power and control of man originates from the realm of the spirit or, better yet, the realm of the supernatural. You can see the godly influence from the spirit realm when you see marriages restored, relationships healed, addictions broken, demonic spirits cast out, Revivals breaking out and miracles manifesting everywhere.

DIVINE ENCOUNTERS

"This charge I commit unto thee, son Timothy, according to the prophecies which went before on thee, that thou by them mightest war a good warfare;..." (1 Timothy 1:18)

Despite the numerous demonic attacks that I had growing up, there came a season in my life where I had to remember that God had truly called me. As the enemy was trying to infiltrate and destroy my life by using various means to attack me, God began using divine encounters to protect and prepare me.

On one such occasion, while I was working at the bank I was invited to attend a mid-day prayer service at a local church. I remembered standing at the back of the room worshipping God. The prayer and worship became so intense that I and several others fell to the floor under the power of God. It was as if the glory of God had consumed the entire building. While I was on the floor, the Spirit of God transported me into a vision.

In the vision, I became a little girl about five years old. I was wearing a beautiful white dress with frills and layers, I had white ribbons in my hair, and I wore a pair of white shoes. I can clearly remember being very excited in the dream as this man, who appeared to be an angel, took me by the hand and led me up a huge, golden staircase. The angel was a very tall man with silver, silk-like hair and huge hands. He was also wearing all white.

As I got closer to the top, I could see a huge golden double door with a radiant light coming from beneath it. *"What was beyond that door?"*, I wondered. I was not sure; nonetheless, I was very anxious to see. The angel opened the door and I could not believe my eyes. I perceived that I was in heaven; it was a huge place filled with radiant, brilliant light. There was a throne located at the very front of the room. I could tell that there was someone sitting on the throne but I could not see His face. I know now that it was the Spirit of God sitting on the throne and there was a brighter light emanating from Him.

I could not see His face, but I could see His glory. What I saw was the glory of God and the brightest light I had ever seen before. The light I saw far exceeded the brilliance of any light I had ever seen on earth and there are no words in the human vernacular to covey its piercingly peaceful brilliance. I was in such awe that I started crying. The person on the throne told me not to weep but to go around the room and open the treasure boxes which were sitting on individual pedestals. Each treasure box was elaborately decorated on the outside with beautiful, precious stones and gems.

I can remember being reluctant to open the first one, but when I did, I could not believe my eyes. In each box I saw something so beautiful that, to this very day, it is still difficult for me to articulate or describe in the English language.

"What are these?", I cried, *"And who do they belong to?"*

Then the angel spoke to me and said, *"Mattie, these are gifts for you! These are treasures that were hand-picked just for you!"*

129

I began crying uncontrollably and in an instant became like a "little kid in a candy store". I began opening more of them and by the time I got to the fifth one, the angel said to me, *"Slow down! You do not need to open them all today, save some for tomorrow."* I remembered counting all of the boxes and, in total, there were nine.

This was my first trip to heaven and later I understood God was revealing to me that, in time, He would release various spiritual gifts into my life. Hours later I got up; by that time the service had ended. I was so overwhelmed by the divine encounter that I had to be driven back to work and could hardly stand up for the remainder of the day. That experience stayed with me for many years and, amidst the many demonic attacks that came against my life, I always remembered my angelic escort who led me into the presence of the King.

ANGELIC ASSISTANCE

As mentioned earlier, the spiritual realm does indeed exist. In this realm a perpetual war ensues between the kingdom of darkness and the kingdom of light. Each kingdom advances, perpetuates or duplicates itself by establishing its laws, rules, regulations, culture, practices and beliefs.

I believe that even as there are *"Dream Assassins"* which work on behalf of the kingdom of darkness to infiltrate your life and bring demonic oppression, there are angelic beings working on behalf of the kingdom of light which are assigned by God to guard and protect you.

According to the Word of God, you have been empowered to command these angels to work on your behalf. Not only do heavenly angels guard and protect you, they also fight to bring to pass the will of God for your life.

In *Psalm 103:20* the Word of the Lord declares, *"Bless the LORD, ye his angels that excel in strength, that do his commandments, hearkening unto the voice of his word."*

These angels are ministering spirits and God uses them to carry out His command on the earth, especially where you are concerned. Angels are here for your protection. The Word of God further states in *Psalm 91:11 that he will give His angels charge over thee to keep you in all your ways, they shall bear you up lest you dash your foot against a stone; a thousand shall fall at your side and ten thousand at your right hand, but it shall not come nigh thee."*

Do not settle for demonic spirits invading your dreams, interrupting your sleep and worse, wreaking havoc in your life. The angels of the Lord are there to lend their assistance, and are activated to move on your behalf as you command them according to the Word of God.

Angels were created by God for several reasons: *to shield you from danger, protect you, bring answers to your prayer and execute judgment.*

There are a number of classes of angels each of which have a specific function:
- The *Cherubim* protect the glory *(Genesis 3:22–24)*
- The *Seraphim* declare the glory of the Lord *(Isaiah 6:2)*
- The *Arch-Angels* are assigned to fight and do battle on your behalf *(Daniel 10:13; Jude 1:9)*
- The *Warring Angels* have similar assignments as Arch-Angels in that they are dispatched to fight or do warfare to bring to pass the will of God in your life *(2 Chronicles 20)*
- The *Worshipping Angels* are assigned to worship before the throne of God day and night *(Revelation 4)*

- The *Ministering Angels* encourage and uplift you according to the will of God for your life *(Hebrews 1:14)*
- The *Messenger Angels* deliver messages to you on behalf of our Heavenly Father *(Daniel 8:15–16; Matthew 1:20–21; Matthew 28:5–7)*
- The *Destiny Angels* are assigned to your life to bring the purposes of God to pass in your life
- The *Deliverance Angels* are assigned to set you free from demonic entrapments *(Acts 12:7)*
- The *Surgical Angels* are release to replace human body parts, such as limbs, organs, and the like; to fix medical conditions, especially those which are seemingly impossible in the natural realm.
- *Prosperity Angels* are assigned to bring wealth and supernatural increase to you which may also include favor. They open the doors to financial blessings
- *Business Angels* are assigned to bring you strategies and skills on how to do business successfully.
- *Athletic Angels* are released to empower you in the area of athletic pursuits, causing you to excel
- *Genius Angels* are assigned to bring you godly information, wisdom and understanding beyond your years or scope of your natural experiences
- *Media Angels* are assigned to the area of media to bring profound creativity or ingenuity in the area of audio-video production and broadcasting
- *Publications Angels* are assigned to bring you creativity, words, formats and ideas toward producing printed matter.
- The *Angels of Breakthrough, Miracles, Signs and Wonders* are released to carry out the supernatural work of the Holy Spirit by bringing to pass divine occurrences and events in the lives of God's people.
- *... and more.*

Angels are poised and ready to accomplish God's will in the earth as it is being fulfilled in heaven. As a matter of fact, I believe that there are angels who look like mere men. *(Genesis 19)* They hearken to your voice to accomplish the Word of God through supernatural acts that you declare into existence.

Similarly, as angels showed up while Peter was in prison to supernaturally release his bonds and lead him home, you also have the power to deploy angels to operate on your behalf. *(Acts 12:5)*

Regardless of which rank of demons the enemy releases, whether "ground level" or "regional", God has given us power over them. As we use our spiritual weapons we can activate even greater results. When we employ angelic assistance in our lives, this gives us total victory over ***Demonic Assassins, Dream Intruders and Assassins, Illegal Representations and Night Raiders.***

PROPHETIC PRAYER NUGGET (PPN)

"Pray this prayer right now and command the angels to operate on your behalf, in Jesus' name!"

Father God, in the name of Jesus I give you thanks and praise for your faithfulness towards me. I thank you that you have released angels to operate on my behalf right now. I thank you for angels that hearken to the voice of the command of your Word.

I release them now to operate on my behalf to bring to pass every godly prophetic Word you have released over my life. I thank you for angelic assistance that will help me to overcome in every area of my life. I give you thanks and praise, in Jesus' name! AMEN!

CHAPTER FIVE

THIS IS MY STORY!

REFUSE ...
"It's Not Your Time To Die!"

Having the innate desire to not only survive but truly live after any life-threatening ordeal is commendable, and should never be taken for granted.

The fact is this: many people died, gave up and walked away from the very thing which you decided to hold onto and for which you fought. To me, this is proof positive that you possess the ingredients needed to make what I call *"the perfect cake of life."*

Though colorful in nature, the *"cake of life"* survivors speak loudly through the voices of all cultures and ethnicities, crossing barriers and overcoming hurdles to be satisfied that they found, deep within the vicissitudes of their soul, the unction driving them to "Live and not Die."

REFUSE – To violently oppose; to wrestle or adamantly go against; to strongly resist

135

These are the storm survivors, last place marathon runners, high school drop outs, rape victims, AIDS victims, cancer survivors, entrepreneurs, Pastors, abandoned women and yes, even the ones labeled as the "bastard child" who have been repeatedly told that nothing good will come of their lives.

These are the people who refuse to quit and give up on life; or better yet, refused to allow life to give up on them. They fight back from obscurity, fiery trials and the very "claws of death", even if they have to walk away smelling like smoke, waving a red flag of victory while there was no one around to cheer them on. At the end of the day, I realize that *I am* one of those survivors, and this is a brief account of my true story.

THE HARSH REALITY

For the most part, whenever we tell our stories, we often relate them in a manner that points a finger in an effort to implicate someone else. We often fail to recognize that "we" are mostly responsible for what we go through in life.

The first step toward every deliverance is to acknowledge your own personal issues and mistakes. Secondly, you should be willing to deal with your issues, mistakes and poor choices on every level. Once you have done that, you receive what I call the *"rite of passage"*. You become free to now make the necessary adjustments for your overall survival and well-being.

Regardless of what comes your way, or what has happened in life, you should now understand that no one else can be blamed for the place where you presently find yourself. In other words, you will remain a victim when you allow others to hold the keys to your progress in life. I too came to that realization.

There was a season in my life when it seemed as if everything I touched turned to gold. I was experiencing success beyond my wildest imagination. I traveled everywhere, preached the gospel, led scores of individuals to Christ and enjoyed what I did. Even though I did not search for fame or favor, they inevitably came to my life as I did the work of the Kingdom.

Little did I know at the time that, in the very near future, my entire world was about to experience a drastic shift. This shift was so extreme that my literal survival demanded a resolute decision and a firm proclamation to the very gates of hell that it was not my season to die but, rather, it was my time to live. I had to make a decision that I was going to enjoy everything that God had in store for me in my "personalized life packet!"

> *"38For I am persuaded, that neither death, nor life, nor angels, nor principalities, nor powers, nor things present, nor things to come,*
> *39Nor height, nor depth, nor any other creature, shall be able to separate us from the love of God, which is in Christ Jesus our Lord." (Romans 8:38-39)*

Humble Beginnings!

As I begin to reflect on my life, I am fully persuaded it was nothing but the supernatural grace of God that has miraculously preserved me through the years. My beginning was very humble, as I grew up on a beautiful island in the Caribbean – Nassau, Bahamas.

I pray that those of you who grew up in a big city or perhaps in a suburban, wealthy or even middle class neighborhood are able to comprehend the full context of my story.

However, I believe that everything I experienced has equipped me to help others receive their deliverance and defeat the same spirit of death that came after my life. Further, I know that I am taking a big risk by being so transparent, but it is one that I am prepared to take.

THIS IS MY STORY...

I trust that you would embrace my story with an open mind and an open heart. Through sharing my testimony, I believe that you will begin to understand that the plan God has for your life was formulated even before you entered your mother's womb:

"Before I formed thee in the belly I knew thee; and before thou camest forth out of the womb I sanctified thee, and I ordained thee a prophet unto the nations." (Jeremiah 1:5)

You will also understand that, although the enemy may not know everything about you, he does know that you are destined to be someone great. Therefore, he will do everything to destroy you before you come into your divine, God-ordained purpose.

In *John 8:44* the Word of God reveals that the devil is a murderer, liar and the father or "originator" of lies.

"Ye are of your father the devil, and the lusts of your father ye will do. He was a murderer from the beginning, and abode not in the truth, because there is no truth in him. When he speaketh a lie, he speaketh of his own: for he is a liar, and the father of it."

It is the enemy's ultimate plan to drive you to your death because he is a murderer. If he is not successful in this endeavor, then he seeks to speak lies against you and label you with something that does not belong to you. I literally had to contend with the spirit of death and its lies in order to fulfill the call of God on my life and still be alive today.

It is said that how you start something is typically how you will end it. My life's story began on a small island in the Caribbean. I had no idea that the hand of God was upon me, neither did I know for that same reason there was an enemy who was seeking to stop me from becoming what God had ordained me to be.

It would seem as though I was engaged in warfare from the time I was born. Firstly, I was a premature baby born fighting for my life. Secondly, it seemed as if I always had to fight to survive the frequent attacks of the enemy. This continued to be the norm for my life. I was very active as a child and enjoyed playing outdoors as did most children of that day. Although I was very small in stature, even as a child my mother believed that God had called me to do something beyond the ordinary.

"The Weapons Were Formed - But They Did Not Prosper!" (Isaiah 54:17)

I was not too young to remember when many "interesting" things started happening in my life around the tender age of seven years. During this time, amidst all of the demonic attacks that I had encountered, I was sexually abused by a distant relative of the family on numerous occasions. These occurrences totally devastated me and opened a demonic door of fear in my life. *(See more in Chapter Seven: DEATH OF A RIGHTEOUS SEED)*

I was raised in a home where my mother, a devoted Christian, loved God with all of her heart. She worked hard daily and made sure we all went to church every Sunday. My dad, on the other hand, was an alcoholic who drank almost all of my life. Although he never went to church, he was one of the nicest men you would have ever met. I loved him with all my heart but I hated his addiction.

We lived in a small neighborhood in Nassau where people were generally friendly and made it their business to look out for each other. But as I got older, the way I viewed many of them began to change. Even though most of them went to church, some of them seemed to be very religious, occasionally speaking of God.

My firsthand encounters with the spirit of witchcraft began at an early age. As a result, I soon understood that witchcraft was more than just lotions, potions and powders.

There was one particular woman in my neighborhood who was known to do "favors" for anyone who needed something or someone "fixed." For some reason she took a dislike to my siblings and I and constantly threatened our lives. In my opinion she was very strange, hanging various objects and bottles containing dark substances throughout her yard. She was always very hateful towards us and would watch our every move. I can specifically remember on one occasion she almost strangled my sister to death for picking a sapodilla fruit from her tree. This was one of many similar experiences.

EXPOSURE TO THE OCCULT

It is important to understand that neither I nor my family have ever engaged in occult practices. However, I witnessed enough occult activity while growing up to help me understand how people who are involved in that practice operate.

In various places, whenever someone was said to have been "fixed", it meant that this person's life was being manipulated and controlled by a demonic spirit acting under the instructions of someone else. It is further believed that people use different forms of dark powers to affect the lives of others. For example, when wicked people seek to kill you, they will use various types of poisons to bring about your demise. However, if they want you to suffer while staying alive they will render you useless to yourself and others. In this case, they may use the tactic of releasing a demonic force to afflict your body and cause you to exist in a state of perpetual misery.

Whichever form of dark practices these wicked people are involved in, demon spirits are employed to carry out these ungodly attacks. People's lives are adversely affected at the hands of the wicked who craftily execute their agenda.

Many people are malfunctioning under demonic bewitchment and in many cases are unaware of what is happening to them. They may find themselves engaging in behaviors which are totally contrary to their normal conduct and character. They may be bound by demonic curses and spells unbeknown to them; carrying out activities under the direction and manipulation of demonic spirits. For example, many men find themselves in warfare with their wives to the degree of grossly mistreating them; failing to take responsibility for their role as husband and father of their own children while simultaneously engaging in extra-marital affairs. These men appear numb and catatonic to the cries of their wives and children while happily meeting the needs of the "other woman".

It is important to note that not every adulterous relationship is under the bewitching influence of witchcraft. Some of these behaviors are motivated by spirits of lust, perversion and other "un-regenerated" desires. However, in some cases, it should not be disregarded or ruled out as a driving force which has destroyed the lives of many people, including their God-ordained marriages.

Whenever you become dysfunctional in the physical or natural realm with no logical explanation as to what is wrong, it may indicate that someone has "fixed" you.

God has called each of us to be led by the Holy Spirit. It was never His intention that we live in bondage to the wicked dictates of evil men or women. If you believe that you are under the manipulation or influence of someone evil, seek to break free from this demonic control, in Jesus' name.

FINDING PEACE WAS ONLY A DREAM

Growing up in my neighborhood was the same as growing up anywhere else. We played and had fun but the torment never ceased. Finding peace of mind seemed to have only been a dream. My experiences became even more challenging as I started having frequent demonic attacks throughout my childhood. Almost every night I was tormented by demons walking in the ceiling of my house, dragging what sounded like a long, iron chain. I fought night after night, as "they" entered my room to "press" me as I lay in bed.

Whenever this occurred, I could not speak at all, not even for a second. However, this did not stop me from trying to break free from their stronghold. At times it seemed as though these occurrences lasted for hours. Eventually I would break away from them by shouting the name of Jesus.

At some point, no doubt, you may have had a similar encounter.
These attacks should confirm to you that:

- There is an invisible demonic realm
- Demonic spirits are on an assignment to torment and harass you
- There may be occult practices, like witchcraft, at work in your area or neighborhood

I know that some of you may be able to recall similar experiences. In many cultures around the world, this type of encounter is known as "hagging." The term was derived from the traditional practice of referring to a witch as a "hag." It was generally thought that when someone was hagged, a witch astro-projected or sent a demon spirit to torment them.

In other instances a "hag" was referred to as a demon, ghost, fairy, or imp that was given an assignment *by* a witch to torment a person's life during sleep. This is not the will of God concerning you.

If this is happening to you or someone you know, you must continue to rebuke these diabolical attacks and take immediate authority over them, in Jesus' name.

In my own life, these constant bombardments began in childhood and continued throughout my teenage years. Even after I gave my life to Jesus, the attacks were ongoing and, at times, they even appeared to intensify. In spite of the continual warfare I knew my survival depended on my faith, calling on God and, more importantly, getting to know Him personally.

PRAYER BECAME MY REFUGE

As time went on, I found myself praying all night. Eventually, I noticed that the attacks came but were different in nature. I can vividly recall being wide awake in my room and literally hearing eerie voices outside of my window calling and compelling me to go with them.

I can specifically remember an incident where I woke up after hearing a knock at the front door. My parents awoke at the same time and upon opening the door, to our surprise, we saw what appeared to be huge "globs" which looked like chicken fat spread all along our driveway and patio. My family and I had become so accustomed to seeing "strange objects" and unusual things happening around our yard that we grew up knowing that we had to pray. It was our constant prayer that whoever was doing this would stop or, better yet, that God would eventually stop them.

Prayer is definitely the weapon you will need to combat the forces of darkness. I learnt how to pray even when I was not sure what prayer was all about. Through the power of prayer God dispatched angels to protect my family and I from danger.

"PRAYING YOUR WAY THROUGH THE DARKNESS USHERS YOU INTO THE LIGHT!"

Prayer is one of the most powerful weapons against the enemy. It is communion with God, but, better yet, it is God communing with you. Prayer is also a gift from God and opens the channel for you to converse with Him.

As a believer, quality time should be invested in prayer and learning how to pray. Too often people waste time fighting the enemy in the natural realm rather than giving themselves over to prayer and fasting. *(See more in book by author, "Breaking The Chains, From Worship To Warfare")*

Here are some of the ways I prayed as I began to grow and mature in the things of God:

- **Praying in the Spirit** – there were times that I prayed for hours in my heavenly language or an unknown tongue because I could not articulate in English what was going on in my life. These were the times I felt certain that the Spirit of God was carrying me *"...who knows the mind of God but the Spirit of God". (1 Corinthians 2:11–13; Romans 8:26; Romans 11:34)*

- **Consistency in prayer** – prayer became my daily posture and I prayed consistently; several times a day. *(Daniel 2)*

- **Persistence in Prayer** – I was determined to persevere in prayer with the mindset that I was not going to give up, regardless of what I was going through, because I knew that persistence yields results. *(Luke 18)*

- **Insistence in Prayer** – I prayed with fervency and passionate conviction. And, although God never forgets, I reminded Him every day of His promises to me. *(James 5:16)*

- **Prayer of Faith** – I had to believe God despite what I felt or saw going on around me. I was confident that faith in God would move my mountains. *(James 5:15)*

- **Warfare prayers** – I was convinced that the weapons of my warfare were not carnal, so I had to engage spiritual weapons in an effort to combat the diabolical plans of the enemy. *(2 Corinthians 10:3–4)*

- **Agreement in prayer** – I was convinced that if I could find at least two or more people to agree with me in prayer, I would gain absolute victory. *(Matthew 18:19)*

Find people to agree with you in prayer, especially if you sense the call of God upon your life. It is imperative that you surround yourself with prayer warriors and intercessors. In so doing, a hedge of protection is built around you that will enable you to fulfill and carry out the assignment that God has on your life. *Prayer watches* can be established on your behalf to help build this hedge of protection.

"How should one chase a thousand, and two put ten thousand to flight, except their Rock had sold them, and the LORD had shut them up?" (Deuteronomy 32:30)

Intercessors are the "gatekeepers" and watchmen over your life. Their primary purpose is to "keep watch" or to protect you and your interests. They are able to assist you as they engage the spiritual weapons of prayer and intercession. Never start a business, a marriage, a ministry, a foreign mission or anything that is God-ordained without engaging a "prayer shield".

Every president, queen, premier or prime minister hires bodyguards to protect or guard them. As a Christian, you are no exception to the rule and should, likewise, employ the assistance of intercessors and gatekeepers to safeguard your life.

PROPHETIC PRAYER NUGGET (PPN)

Pray this prayer right now and take authority over every spirit of torment in Jesus' name.

Father, God in the name of Jesus, I give praise right now that every spirit of torment and terror is broken from over my life in Jesus' name. I bind and rebuke every diabolical plan of the enemy to incite fear and anxiety in my life and the life of my children.

I break every satanic power working through witches, warlocks and evil people. I decree and declare that no lotion, potion, powder or any form of intimidation working through the counsel of men will hinder me. Thank you for teaching me how to pray and wage a good warfare. AMEN!

ANGELS WATCHING OVER ME

Apart from the unusual demonic attacks, my childhood was a normal one. I particularly enjoyed the long, hot summers when we would play all day until night fell. Some of our summers in the Bahamas were spent with my grandmother on the little island of Exuma where my father was born. I have always enjoyed the beach and did my best to stay near the shoreline.

However, one day I went with a group of friends to the dock where the huge Mail Boats came in to deliver their weekly cargo. We were engaged in typical childhood fun as some of my friends dove off the dock. I had no intention of diving because, at that time, I was not a good swimmer. To my surprise, I was suddenly pushed into very deep water and had to fight for my life. To this day, no one has ever admitted to pushing me.

I can vividly remember how the current in the water started to pull me towards the bottom. I had no choice but to fight. I did everything I could to make it back to the surface and fought vigorously to survive. When my head finally emerged from the water, I screamed for help but everyone thought I was joking and began laughing at me. I went down for a second, and then a third time. By this time, I was sure that my life was over. Although I could not speak, I prayed and cried out to God in my mind as I was being pulled back to the bottom. I prayed continuously until suddenly I felt someone grip my hands. It felt like a huge hand was pulling me up to the surface and dragging me onto the shore.

As strange as this seemed at the time, I believe that God had sent an angel to rescue me. I did not see who it was that pulled me out, neither did my friends. They just said it looked like a man, but no one knew who he was and he was never seen again. I found comfort in knowing that I was now safe on dry land and very grateful to be alive.

From that day on, I realized that God had angels guarding and protecting me from the plans of the enemy.

I sincerely believe that God also has guardian angels watching over you, protecting you from satan's attacks. Take a moment and thank God for angelic assistance. Their assistance will always be with you.

STANDING IN THE FACE OF ADVERSITY

After my "near death" experience that summer, I felt myself getting closer and closer to God as I began to study His Word more and more. As my relationship with God grew stronger, I began to discern when the Spirit of God was speaking to me.

Soon after, I perceived that the Spirit of God was leading me to start a prayer meeting in my high school, which was no trivial matter. Firstly, this had never been done before at my Seventh Day Adventist School. Secondly, at the time I was a devout member of the Baptist Church. I knew that it would take much prayer and an "act of God" to get the support of my school's administration. I literally felt like *David* facing many *Goliaths*, I somehow knew that the Spirit of God was with me, and I was learning how to trust God and take Him at His Word. I quickly obeyed and launched one of the most successful prayer "movements" that my high school had ever seen. I called it "The Prayer Link".

By the grace of God, I watched this little lunch time meeting grow from one student to hundreds of students and staff members who, I might add, were all excited about prayer. By the time I was ready to graduate from high school, this prayer revolution had totally taken over my high school campus. To this day, I continue to celebrate the way that God has used me to bring transformation to the lives of so many.

148

DIVINE VISITATION – HOUSE #9

As a young teenager I had developed a consistent prayer life. Although I did not fully understand everything about fasting or prayer, I often felt compelled to do both. Soon after I began to experience the manifested presence of God in phenomenal ways. I somehow knew that I needed "supernatural" help if I was going to survive, both literally and spiritually.

A Divine Encounter

One day after school I went home and decided to spend some time in prayer in my bedroom. I am not sure how long I had been in prayer and worship but I knew it was for several hours. I became totally overwhelmed by the Spirit of God. My room was suddenly filled with the glory of God. It was the most peaceful presence that I had ever felt. I began to weep uncontrollably. It seemed as if I was totally immersed in His presence and I felt as though I was in another place.

Even more unusual, the Spirit of God began to move throughout my room and I felt what seemed to be a blowing wind, although all the windows were closed. I remembered that the pages of my Bible began turning and for a brief moment I became very afraid thinking that this was another demonic invasion. However, this time I realized that the unusual presence was actually the Spirit of God. As soon as I recognized His presence a peace came over me again and I was no longer afraid.

In that moment He spoke two scriptures to me; the first from Isaiah Chapter 61 and the other from Jeremiah Chapter 1. He revealed to me that He had called me as a Prophet of Deliverance and that He wanted me to preach deliverance to everyone who was in any form of bondage or captivity.

At that time I felt that I was ill-equipped for such an assignment and could not fully comprehend why God wanted to use me in this way. Instantly, discerning my thoughts and hesitation, the Holy Spirit reminded me of all the spiritual warfare that I had experienced as a child and how He had delivered me. He began to reassure me that just as He had done it for me, so would He anoint me to help set others free. I felt highly "unqualified" for this assignment but I knew, beyond the shadow of a doubt, that this was what God had called me to do.

I later shared this experience with my grandfather who confirmed that it was truly God calling me. I kept this to myself for many years, uncertain about what others would think about me and somewhat uncertain, myself, of what this assignment would require of me.

GOD BEGAN USING ME

During my childhood I was immersed in a religious church setting. At the time, my local church rarely spoke of the existence of angels or demons.

At the age of sixteen, I can remember preaching one of my first sermons in my grandfather's church. I spoke about how important it was for believers in the Body of Christ to "get their house in order". I preached about how God is looking for a glorified church, without spot or wrinkle. This message was so powerful that many people came crying to the altar, weeping and repenting. However, a few short days later, this same "powerful" message caused a major disturbance in the church. I was threatened by members of the Deacon Council and was told that I would never preach again.

I learned very early that not everyone wanted to hear the truth, even in the Church. I eventually realized that many of the "religious" people, especially those who were living a duplicitous lifestyle, did not want to be compelled to the next level in God. It was at that time I began to have a strong burden to pray for the Body of Christ.

I believe that God wants to do so much more in the lives of His children but so many times people become satisfied with just going to church on Sunday and living any kind of life on Monday. That was not for me. I wanted so much more from God.

FULFILLING THE CALL OF GOD

Throughout my teenage years, my desire for God increased and I continued preaching the gospel. Because of my deep hunger for God and yearning to pursue Him more, the attacks of the enemy intensified. As a result of the levels of warfare I experienced, I realized that my prayer life also had to intensify. I knew that the only way I would be able to endure that season would be to engage in *"concentrated, strategic prayer"*.

I was young, a female and I soon became known as a "radical" preacher. Although many people did not know how to receive me, and others did not understand me, I continued to preach and teach as the Spirit of God anointed me. Through the years, the Lord has continued to use me in what I view as unconventional ways. I have seen miracles of healing and deliverance in the lives of His people and continue to be amazed by the power of God.

ANSWERING A GREATER CALL

After being employed as a banker for almost twenty years I answered the call of God. Together, my husband and I entered into full-time ministry. We had to believe God each step of the way. We prayed and fasted for months in order to receive direction and instructions for the Ministry.

Eventually, doors began to open and not only were local churches calling for me but I began to receive international engagements. I travelled everywhere, preaching the gospel and became one of the most sought after conference speakers, both locally and internationally. I received invitations from various regions such as Europe, Africa, South America, the United States of America and the Caribbean.

As we continued in ministry, my husband and I hosted numerous conferences and revivals. I received even more speaking engagements as God began opening mega doors everywhere, even on Christian television networks and radio stations. I was in a season where I was blessed to minister the gospel to tens of thousands of people worldwide.

I came to realize that I could preach tirelessly for hours, jump over chairs, cast out devils, pray for the sick, lead scores to Christ, counsel after the service then go home and cook a scrumptious meal for my family. I was traveling almost every week and was seeing God move in powerful ways. Despite my radical style of ministry in the pulpit, I enjoyed being a "princess" in my home when the dust settled. I was walking in my divine purpose and loving every moment of it.

"SHOCKED, AWED AND AMAZED BY THE POWER OF GOD!"

Seeing the Miraculous

During this time, whenever I took the microphone it seemed as though deliverance would take place almost immediately. People were miraculously delivered and set free as chains began to break off their lives. I saw scores of people healed and delivered from various diseases and demonic oppression. Women and children, in particular, were healed from lumps, tumors and various forms of cancer.

I can recall that in 2006 a woman diagnosed with a type of stomach cancer flew in to attend one of my services. We prayed for her, rebuking the spirits of infirmity and death. To our surprise the tumor was dislodged and a mass the size of a grapefruit was expelled from her mouth. This was truly amazing as God continued to work these and other types of miracles in our services.

I can remember conducting a revival in South Florida where a young woman, named Minnie, came to the altar for prayer to be healed of a brain tumor. The Spirit of God told me to take authority over the spirit of infirmity and command every curse of the enemy to be broken off of her life. When I called out tumors and cancers, Minnie fell to the ground. Several days later, she went to the doctor and, to her family's surprise, it was confirmed that the brain tumor was gone.

I began to realize that the enemy was releasing curses over the lives of these women and even the doctors, themselves were shocked and amazed at how they were miraculously healed. I can relay countless testimonies of miracles and how God healed many people in my services. However, there is one young woman I could never forget.

Gerry was diagnosed with an aggressive type of brain cancer that required immediate surgical intervention. As we prayed for her, the Spirit of the Lord gave me a Word of knowledge and I told her that God was going to reverse the doctor's report. The following day, after undergoing emergency brain surgery, to the doctor's amazement, Gerry was sitting up speaking to the nurses and everyone else that came into her room. There was no need for chemotherapy or an extended period of recovery. Today, Gerry is a walking medical miracle.

I still cannot fully explain what happens in my revival services, but it is obvious that the Spirit of God deploys angels to enter the sanctuary and shift the entire atmosphere. It is then that healing and deliverance take place. God was using me in these miracle revivals to administer healing and deliverance to His people. Little did I know that one day I would have to fall on the same grace for myself.

As the demand for the deliverance ministry grew, I continued receiving ministry engagements. I am grateful that the Lord has blessed me to preach in so many different places. One of these places was a beautiful little island located in the Caribbean Sea called Curacao of the Netherland Antilles. I must admit that I had somewhat underestimated what would happen during that ministry engagement and decided to travel with only one assistant. I had already anticipated that when I took the microphone the Spirit of God would move in the service. However, what I had *not* anticipated was that mass deliverance would have ensued immediately throughout the entire church.

The building was filled to capacity with thousands of women who were all desperate for a touch from God. People began falling under the power of God throughout the entire sanctuary while others were crying incessantly as they received their deliverance. The Spirit of God took control and I watched in total amazement as people were set free!

Mass Deliverance

I had never seen that many people receive deliverance all at once – without me even laying hands on them. This was a pivotal moment in my ministry and these kinds of experiences continued to happen almost everywhere I went. In Africa, Brazil and everywhere people were hungry for God, He would move in this manner; revival would break out and people began calling me a modern day Revivalist!

As time passed the demand for the deliverance ministry increased. More and more people were seeking to be set free from oppression and demonic strongholds. I had no idea what I was getting into at the time, but I continued conducting deliverance sessions on a daily basis, and revival services every week. We administered deliverance to everyone who wanted help, including people involved in various forms of the occult and other demonic practices.

In that season I was simply doing what God had called me to do. What I did not realize was that I was causing such a "stir" in the demonic realm that the enemy had devised a diabolical attack, not only to stop me from advancing in ministry, but also to literally take my life. I began receiving more threatening letters from wicked people warning me to stop casting out demons. However, I was completely sold out to the call of God and was not about to stop for anyone. This bold resolve resulted in both friends and enemies.

It is important for every believer to take a righteous stand in doing the work of the kingdom. Jesus, througout the New Testament, healed the sick, the lame, cast out demons and even raised the dead. *(Mark 16:17)* He also said in *John 14:12, "the works I do, greater works than these shall you do."* I believe that this is the hour of the greater works!

THE SPIRIT OF DEATH COMES WITH A VENGEANCE

As a result of answering the call of God on my life, I have endured much over the years, from demonic visitations to near-death experiences. I am neither easily intimidated nor fearful because I know that God is with me and I can feel Him leading and guiding me.

Whenever you decide to do what God has called you to do the spirit of Jezebel gets angry.

I do not consider myself to be a part of an exclusive class or elite group of people. I believe that anyone who decides to take a bold stand for righteousness becomes a likely candidate for such levels of spiritual warfare.

Just as with the Prophet Elijah in *1 Kings 18*, the spirit of Jezebel attacks and seeks to silence every prophetic voice that rises up against her. I soon learned that the spirit of death does not compromise, negotiate or "broker deals", but it is on a relentless mission to fulfill its deadly assignment for your ultimate demise. This spirit will seek to destroy you physically, mentally, financially, emotionally, as well as, spiritually.

Whatever you do, it is incumbent upon you to don yourself in the whole armor of God. This can be done by praying a simple prayer every morning by asking God to cover you in His whole armour according to *Ephesians 6:10–18.*

THE ASSIGNMENT CONTINUES

In addition to the Church that was steadily growing in the Bahamas, God also blessed my husband and I to raise up a following in the South Florida area. Through our youth programs we were able to go into the inner cities and establish a college club in one of the largest universities in that area, leading scores of young people to the Lord.

The South Florida followers and college students became a significant part of my "whys" and the reason for my labor of love in that area. I am glad I did not give up on them. Inadvertently, the students also became the "glue" that kept me there. No matter how I tried leaving, they would text and call me all hours of the day and night for help. Whenever, I answered, their first words would be, *"Dr. Mattie, you were the only person I could call!"*

I became someone they could trust and their college became my new mission field. I was trying to do so much and help so many people, without realizing that I was slowly depleting myself of much needed personal resources. Nevertheless, God still provided.

Whenever you are called to do something bigger than yourself, you may feel discouraged some days, but you must hold on to the reason "why" you are doing it and not give up.

In the next season, God revealed to me that He had strategically placed me in that area in order to "mother" and "mentor" the students for that time.

All too often, people want the "glitz" and the "glamour" of ministry without the "challenges". God will test you with a small assignment before blessing you with "mega glory!" The Bible states that Joseph worked in Potipher's house faithfully completing housework, Jacob tended to Laban's flocks and the great Moses took care of Jethro's herds before being promoted to "Chief Executive Prophet" (CEP).

Make a determination that you are not going to give up or give in; greater is He that is in you than the devil or any spirit of death that is in the world *(1 John 4:4)*.

MY SEASON OF AFFLICTION

As soon as one season of affliction concluded, another began. My body began shutting down and I became extremely ill to the point where I was unable to walk. I was in and out of emergency rooms and the doctors could not explain what was happening to me. Within six months, my body had unexplainably swollen to over two hundred (200) pounds, which greatly exceeded my normal weight of one hundred and twenty-five (125) pounds. I could no longer wear shoes because my feet had also swollen from a size seven to a size ten wide width and my dress size went from a size 4 to a size 18W.

My skin tone turned two shades darker than my normal complexion. All of my fingers were swollen to the point where, eventually, the doctors had to cut my wedding rings off my fingers to allow for proper circulation. My entire body, including my stomach and abdomen, became so swollen that people started asking me if I was pregnant and when I expected to have "the baby".

My health deteriorated as my condition became progressively worse. I spent months in bed because I was unable to walk due to the pain and fatigue I felt. I had to be transported in a wheelchair. At other times, I had to use a walker to move about. Whenever I was able to preach, I was literally lifted to the pulpit and had to be carried back to my seat when I was finished. Many nights I could not sleep and it was during the night watches that the enemy began to torment me with demonic visitations.

Many people die or totally give up when facing such levels of warfare. I believe the one thing that kept me in those dark hours was my commitment to prayer and worship. I began noticing that whenever the presence of God showed up in my room, the demons would leave. They could not stand the anointing or bear hearing the name of Jesus.

I went through a season of total embarrassment and humiliation. I was totally disfigured and refused to look at myself in the mirror. Whenever I did, I wept inconsolably. I could not stand for long periods of time. I was experiencing extreme dizziness most of the day and was in constant, tormenting pain. At first, the doctors had no answers so they insisted on performing a series of tests in an effort to diagnose my condition.

If you are ever confronted with any level of spiritual warfare or attack from the enemy, be it against your mind, health, wealth or relationships, you should take immediate action to launch a counter-attack against the vices of the enemy using prayer, the Word and worship.

The Diagnoses

Soon thereafter, the medical diagnoses began rolling in. Within a six-month period I was diagnosed with over seven (7) major debilitating disorders which included: *Acute Hypothyroidism, Auto Immune Disorders, Lupus, Multiple Sclerosis, Cancer, High Blood Pressure, Stage Two Diabetes, Anemia, Chronic Fatigue Syndrome, Insomnia, an Abdominal Hernia, Abdominal Cysts, Fibroids and more.*

I could hardly believe what the doctors were saying to me. Even now, it is still difficult for me to comprehend the magnitude of the enemy's attack against my life. Immediately I was given a number of prescriptions and began treatments. I was sent home with bags and bags of medication in order to treat the various ailments and their side effects. The medications and treatments made me extremely nauseous, causing me to vomit constantly. I continuously prayed for relief. My hair started breaking and falling out. My skin also began to itch unbearably.

To make matters worse, during this period I started losing my memory. I had a mental "meltdown" and did not even realize it. At times, I felt extremely lost and battled the confusion that plagued my mind to the degree that I could not identify the day of the week.

I must admit that I had an excellent team of doctors and I believe that they were doing what they were trained medically to do. However, I recognized that as they diagnosed me, they also prescribed more and more medications, some of which were making me increasingly ill and dysfunctional while "the disorders" were becoming worse. This led me to conduct an in-depth study on the word "diagnosis".

Discernment Is Necessary!

I discovered that the word, *diagnosis* comes from the Greek word *"DIA-GIGNOSKEIN"* meaning a discerning or distinguishing. In the medical application, *"dia"* means apart and *"gnosis"* means "to learn" (or knowledge). Therefore, in this context, I believe the word *"diagnosis"* represents a two-fold understanding of any given sickness. In other words, there are at least two possibilities as to why something is happening in your body. I believe that one is from a natural realm and the other is from a spiritual realm. Therefore, according to the Greek definition, you must discern the source of your situation.

I had to fight to stay spiritually sound, even if I did nothing else. I decided that my relationship with my One True God had to remain secure. I had mentally resolved that if this was a test, just like Job, I was going to pass it.

It was in that season I began to learn about demonic sicknesses and how the enemy can afflict your body with a disease or disorder. I had to discern the difference between what was natural and what was a demonic attack.

I quickly learned that just as each demon had an assignment, they all also had distinct personalities. Demonic spirits, within their specific ranks, will do whatever they must in order to carry out various functions. At times, if they wanted to afflict you, they would consult with other demonic spirits which are "familiar" with your ancestral lineage and discover a common illness in your family line in order to carry out this assignment. For example, a spirit of infirmity may consult with an ancestral spirit who will reveal to it that diabetes is prevalent in your family line. Then the spirit of infirmity assigns a demonic spirit of diabetes, which attaches itself to your life. His "intelligence" reveals that you have diabetes in your family and that you may, at some point, accept this diagnosis, based on the fact that your mother, grandmother and aunt have all had diabetes.

"IT IS NOT GOD'S WILL FOR YOU TO BE AFFLICTED BY OR RECEIVE ANY DEMONIC SICKNESS THAT THE ENEMY SEEKS TO RELEASE IN YOUR LIFE."

One of the biggest tricks of the enemy is to convince people that he is not real. Ignoring something does not mean that it is not there. Many "faith-walking", "tongue-talking" people who go to church have died because they believed that as long as they did not acknowledge the name of the sickness or disease then it would not harm them – *wrong move!* Satan is a deceiver and demons love hiding behind ignorance. *(2 Corinthians 2:11)*

Jesus cast demons out of people, calling them by their title, class, group, name and sometimes their manifestation. Although I did not know the name of every demon that was seeking to attack my life, I learned to deal with them based on the symptoms that were manifesting.

Identifying, Acknowledging, Exposing, Confronting, Confessing are **The First Five (5) Laws Of Deliverance** which must be adhered to if you are going to be totally set free from anything. *(See more in book by author, "IT'S MY TIME TO LIVE!")*

DEMONIC SICKNESS

Whenever the enemy presents symptoms of illnesses, his purpose is to penetrate the core of your being. The plan is to cause you to conform to a restricted, lower or disadvantaged way of thinking, believing and living.

I unconsciously began to wear dark clothing. I darkened my hair color and began to feel deeply discouraged. I subsequently canceled preaching engagements and felt isolated from ministry circles. I was plagued by constant thoughts of giving up. Strange things also began to happen, including the fact that my health eventually began to deteriorate. I was diagnosed with seven major debilitating disorders within a six-month period and was, literally, in and out of the hospital.

None of the three seasoned specialists to whom I had entrusted my health, knew what was really wrong with me or what was causing the complications in my body. I did not know whether I would live or die. I then realized that many of the people who were dying prematurely with no reasonable or justifiable cause of death were, in numerous instances, being afflicted by what I call "demonic sickness." *(Luke 13:11 AMP)*

It should be clearly understood that not all sicknesses are demonic; some of them are as a result of natural causes. However, when your doctor is unable to "medically prove" the cause of your illness or disease, then there is a likelihood that something else, such as a demonic affliction, may be at work.

In *Luke 9:42* Jesus cast an unclean spirit out of a child and immediately the child was healed. At other times, He spoke directly to the physical sickness and the person was immediately healed. For example, Peter's mother-in-law was healed from a fever that was also rebuked.

Whenever a person is under the attack of the enemy, they may begin to experience various symptoms of disease in their body. No matter how many medical tests are performed, it may be difficult to detect the root cause of the ailment because it is not natural. I have seen people diagnosed with diabetes, various types of cancer and other diseases, only to discover that it was nothing more than a demonic attack. Whenever these people came for healing or deliverance, I had to seek God for specific direction as to how to administer deliverance to them because He is our ultimate Healer.

Once the Spirit of God reveals the root of the problem, the onus is on the afflicted person to receive his total deliverance and healing. I have encountered scores of people who have activated their faith, received their miracle and allowed God to change their negative medical report to a good one. If you feel that you are being afflicted by the enemy, aggressively take authority over every unclean spirit and command them to leave, in Jesus' name; rebuke every demonic symptom and plead the blood of Jesus over your life.

THE DAY MY HAIR FELL OUT

The glory of every woman is her hair. Whenever it starts falling out she tends to feel as though she has really lost something of great value.

I can remember the day my hair fell out during my season of affliction. I am not sure if it occurred as a side effect of the medications, a reaction to the treatments, or stress from the entire ordeal.

One morning as I was grooming myself, I looked in the mirror and suddenly noticed that my hair had started falling out in "clumps." Needless to say, I became frantic and almost hysterical as I held large amounts of hair in my hand. I shouted for my husband who quickly ran to me when he heard the desperation in my voice. He was equally surprised at what he saw. However, not wanting to further alarm me he calmly said, "Wow babes, you look nice with short hair." He continued by saying, "We'll just have the beautician even it up for you." Although, I truly appreciated my husband's sensitivity, this was another big "why" that I had for God. I could not conceive that, in addition to everything that had already happened, my hair was now falling out.

I eventually got over the hair loss and began thanking God for the fact that He had spared my life. As much as I was devastated over my hair loss, I realized that God had worked a miracle in my life. The mere fact that I had survived this diabolical attack means that I can say, "I *am* a living miracle!"

I officially renamed "The Day My Hair Fell Out!" to "Today I Am A Miracle!" *"My hair could be replaced, but my life could not ... it is priceless!"*

SURVIVING AFFLICTION
"Many are the afflictions of the righteous: but the LORD delivereth him out of them all." (Psalm 34:19)

Although you may have survived your affliction, "survival" simply means that the ordeal did not kill you. However, merely surviving is not enough, in my opinion. In other words, if you are still dancing around the same fire twenty years later, celebrating what you survived, it means that you are stuck and have not moved.

I believe that when you come out of any life-threatening ordeal or situation, that experience should catapult you to your next miracle. The previous disability should serve only as the "door of opportunity" to your next success story.

God does not place affliction and hardship on His children; however I believe that there are times He permits or allows afflictions. Further, I believe He does this because He wants to bring us into a "wealthy place":

"10For thou, O God, hast proved us: thou hast tried us, as silver is tried.
11Thou broughtest us into the net; thou laidst affliction upon our loins.
12Thou hast caused men to ride over our heads; we went through fire and through water: but thou broughtest us out into a wealthy place." (Psalm 66:10–12)

On the other hand, when the enemy brings affliction to you his intent is to defeat you *(John 10:10)*. Satan did not have the legal right to afflict Job because the Bible says he was an upright man. However, God allowed him to be afflicted; not to prove to satan that Job was faithful, but to prepare Job for a spiritual promotion.

God allowed the enemy to test Job because, first of all, he knew that he would pass his test and, secondly, God wanted to place a double portion blessing upon his life. *(Job 42:12)*

The Bible says that after Job endured his season of testing, God turned his captivity when he prayed for his friends. *(Job 42:10)* I believe he got a spiritual promotion that day because in the midst of his trial he had matured to the place where he looked beyond what he was going through and prayed for someone else.

God does not want you to just survive, He wants you to live a victorious life beyond the storm. Once the demonic spirit of affliction is cast out of your life, God wants you to:
- Overcome your disposition
- Write the story
- Tell the truth about the ordeal
- Discover why God allowed you to go through the dilemma
- Help others who are facing the same or similar dilemma

If you do not make a decision to move forward, to start to live and begin to put active measures in place to fortify the change in your life, the demon spirits which once had you bound in a previous season will seek to come back and afflict your life again.

Demons are very territorial and once they are cast out, they will seek out "dry places" or "places" which are void of the presence of God in which to take up habitation. If they do not find that "place" they will return with seven demons worse than themselves seeking to gain re-entry in your life. They, for the most part, enjoy taking the credit, sometimes even for damages for which they are not responsible.

God wants you to move and progress in every area of your life. He wants to "show you off" and display His glory through you. Therefore He may allow you to go through trials which may be challenging. These experiences are never designed to harm you; for the most part God permits them in order to spiritually elevate or promote you.

The size of your storm is a reflection of the size of your anointing!

THE "UNIVERSITY" OF ADVERSITY
"Surviving The Struggle!"

God has graced me with the privilege and honor of taking the message of the gospel around the world. As the power of God is demonstrated in my services, many times people would approach me and ask which school of theology I attended or at which university did I matriculate?

Although I studied at various institutions of higher learning and obtained several degrees, awards and recognitions, I have never allowed anyone to leave my presence without revealing to them that it was not the degrees and awards posted on my wall that prepared me for ministry. Rather, it was the school of adversity, difficulty and hardship that became my training ground for learning the strategies of spiritual warfare and deliverance. It was through the dry and lonely seasons in my life where I learned to trust God and how to travail in prayer.

It was during the times it seemed as if "the gates of hell" had waged a personal, relentless warfare against me and I had to fight for my life that I learned the strategies of spiritual warfare.

166

I cannot credit any institution or university for what the seasons of adversity have taught me. It was during the times that my back was against the wall and I was learning how to survive through a period of affliction that the anointing on my life became greatly cultivated. It was during times of overcoming struggles and learning how to use the weapons of prayer and spiritual warfare that I began to grow in the things of God.

I would be remiss if I led anyone to believe that they can go to any school other than the *"School of Adversity"* to begin walking in the power and authority of God. Believers have been known to quote this saying for years, and it is true: *"Salvation is free for everyone, but there is a price to pay for the anointing!"*

Ask any man or woman of God who has gone anywhere and done anything outside of that which is "normal". They will all tell you of their long, arduous nights, winter days of aloneness and seasons of despair. However, they will also tell you that it was truly worth it all!

CHAPTER SIX

THE PRICE OF GREATNESS

WARNING SIGNS

God only wants the best for His children. As a believer He will show you His divine will for your life but He will also warn you of the traps or snares the enemy has set for you. He always gives warning signs similar to those on a car dashboard which alert you to impending danger. Such alerts may include, but are not limited to: *check engine, change oil and low fuel.*

You must see the warnings, heed the warnings and act on the warnings.

These are a few of the warnings we see when our cars are in need of servicing. We can all agree that failure to heed these indicators and act on them can lead to expensive consequences.

Prophetic Road Signs

At times the Spirit of God may also speak to you through various spiritual dashboards, which I call *prophetic road signs*. These prophetic signs are usually symbolic and may be correlated to road signs we normally see on our streets which instruct us to yield, detour ahead or slow down. Further, they advise us when we are approaching roundabouts, curves, men at work, and construction zones. We may have other signs which indicate *no left turn, road slippery when wet, one way, wrong way, no u-turn* and more. These signs are strategically placed to protect and benefit all drivers. Failure to adhere to their warnings may prove be detrimental or even deadly.

Warning signs are given to enforce laws and boundaries but, moreover, to warn, caution and protect road users. Similarly, God sends various prophetic road signs as the vehicles to warn, caution and ultimately protect His children from impending danger. Some of these signs include dreams, visions, spiritual impressions, prophetic insights and more.

These prophetic vehicles are profound and can tell us what is about to happen. They expose the plans of the enemy and provide godly prophetic foresight and spiritual awareness. These signs should never be ignored, and every measure should be taken to accomplish the will of God.

Prophetic road signs are there to instruct you as to what action to take, and they should never be ignored!

The Spirit of God is a secret revealer and a protector. Whenever my life was in danger, He gave me numerous warning signs. Some signs were symptoms in my physical body while other signs were things he showed me through dreams. I noticed that whenever I ignored the "warning signs", I paid a price. When I acknowledged and heeded the warning signs I obtained total victory.

Warning To The Housing Station – The Body

In the physical realm, our bodies have been built and constructed by God to also warn us of impending danger to our overall health or well-being. The physical body houses the spirit and soul of man. God formed the body from the dust of the earth and ultimately it will return to the dust when man dies.

No matter how great or powerful you may be, the body must be properly maintained in order to carry the weight of the anointing. Your spiritual mandate on earth can be jeopardized if your physical body is incapable, ill-prepared or ill-equipped to carry it out. You must always remember that your physical, *finite* body hosts an *infinite* anointing and is the carrier of the eternal weight of the glory of God.

Faith, Facts or Foolishness

Your relationship with God will be qualified by your willingness to walk in either faith, facts or foolishness. In James 4:17 the Word of God tells us that *"...to him that knoweth to do good, and doeth it not, to him it is sin."*

- Your *faith* can be defined as simply taking God at His Word, and is demonstrated by your acts of obedience to do what He has called you to do.

- The *fact* is that you are a human vessel, a triune being that requires proper care and maintenance in order to fulfill your God-given mandate here on earth.

- It would be *foolish* to believe that you can fail to administer the proper due care and attention to your entire being – body, soul and spirit – and still expect to function.

THE WEAK & THE WEARY
"Resting is a must!"

The enemy preys on the weak and the weary. For this reason you must take time to rest. No matter how strong you think you are, failing to take the necessary time to regroup can prove to be detrimental. In like manner machines, after a certain amount of usage, need refueling and servicing or they will eventually malfunction and shut down.

As mentioned earlier, God uses dreams to send warnings but He has also designed your body to send warning signs, letting you know when something is wrong and that you may need to slow down or take some time to rest. Most times, however, we ignore these signs and keep going.

I had fully mastered the art of operating in "overdrive." In fact, I knew how to jump from one event to the other without finding time to take a break or even rest. Everybody needs at least six to eight (6–8) hours of sleep to effectively function. At times I worked twenty-two hour days and hardly slept. *This cost me, greatly!*

One day, my husband bought me a brand new cell phone. I was so fascinated by it and all of the modern "apps" and unique features it had, that I never turned it off. Like a kid with a new toy, I left the phone on all day and night because I was so intrigued by it until one day I tried to send a text message and, to my surprise, the phone started to malfunction. It skipped to another page, started dialing numbers on its own, the alarm went off continuously and the text refused to go. I tried to resolve what was happening. My husband took the phone from me and asked me the most embarrassing question, *"When was the last time you turned this phone to its "off" position?"*

"OFF?" I said, with my "intellectual" voice. *"What do you mean? I plug the charger in every night!"*

He smiled and said, *"Charging it is fine, but everything in this whole world needs sufficient rest if it is going to function properly."*

The moment was priceless! Within seven (7) minutes of turning my phone off and on again; my phone was back to normal and began working perfectly.

R.E.S.T.

A lack of rest is a "set up" for disaster! Just as God rested on the seventh day, I had to begin to train myself to find a moment for me. This was one of the hardest things to do because I was so accustomed to being busy all the time. In *Psalm 23:2* the Psalmist David wrote, *"... He maketh me to lie down in green pastures:.."* This simply indicates that, at times, even God has to "make" us rest.

Here are three (3) tidbits on why you should consider resting:
- Lack of rest alters your emotional state of being and will cause you to respond inappropriately
- Lack of rest results in your making irrational decisions
- Lack of rest causes you to miss divine opportunities

R – Restore ◊ E – Energy ◊ S – Strength ◊ T – Timely

R.E.S.T. restores energy and strength to you in a timely manner.

"WHEN YOU REST, YOU REGAIN STRENGTH; TIME THEN BECOMES YOUR FRIEND AND NOT YOUR ENEMY."

WISDOM IS THE PRINCIPAL THING

Wisdom is the ability to appropriately apply the knowledge you have in order to achieve a positive result. Further, wisdom speaks to knowing what to do, how to do it and also knowing when is the right time to take action based on your experiences, understanding and knowledge. In life you may have to endure various experiences. However, some adverse encounters can be avoided when wisdom is applied.

Taking time to plan and receive good or, rather, godly counsel on your journey may prove to be more beneficial and worth your while. A weakened, "unrested" body is always a good candidate for disaster. No matter how anointed you are, you can only function to the capacity that your body is able to endure.

I hardly ever rested. I kept working without ever taking any breaks. I would preach fifteen services back to back and then travel from city to city without taking a moment to rest. Even on vacation, I managed to "smuggle" work no matter where my family and I went. My unwillingness to rest eventually caught up with me

Once I gained wisdom I had a better understanding of how to utilize the knowledge I had to more effectively manage my schedule.

- *Knowledge* speaks of being in possession of the facts, information and awareness of or insight into something.

- *Understanding*, on the other hand, is having the ability to make a right decision; it is possessing the comprehension, discernment and interpretation of something.

- *Wisdom* should always be the premise and foundation upon which your life is built. Once you add wisdom to your daily life, you will begin to experience a greater level of peace and fulfillment. However, without the framework of Wisdom governing your affairs, you become vulnerable and, therefore, susceptible to the attacks of the enemy.

Types of Wisdom

I have come to learn that people tend to ascribe to various types of wisdom in life, such as divine wisdom, satanic wisdom, worldly, and man's wisdom. I further learned that I also had to discern among the various types, continuously seeking out and incorporating godly wisdom in everything I did.

It is important to note that we should only seek after the wisdom of God as the principles and standards by which we govern our lives. There is man's *(sensual)* wisdom, worldly *(natural)* wisdom, diabolical *(satanic)* wisdom and divine *(godly)* wisdom.

- **Man's (Sensual) Wisdom** is intellectual, experiential, gathered from education or based on man's experiences

- **Worldly (Natural) Wisdom** is "cognitive" knowledge or wisdom that you were born with, such as the ability to identify your mother's voice, discern her scent, etc.

- **Satanic (Diabolical) Wisdom** is demonic information, principles, ideas and ideologies which originate from the realm of darkness and are transmitted through witches, psychics, diviners, etc.

- **Divine (Godly) Wisdom** comes from God; Godly wisdom solves every problem you will ever experience and is one of the greatest gifts you can possess.

MY TURNING POINT

There are some experiences you go through solely because you did not consult or take heed to the wisdom of God. On the other hand, there are other tests and trials, like Job's experiences, which God allows us to endure in order for us to gain a greater level of spiritual attainment. There are some afflictions that we suffer because of our own ignorance and failure to seek or follow godly counsel.

God should never be blamed for our own foolish mistakes and pitfalls. I did not understand how I could be traveling around the world, preaching the gospel, administering the healing power of God and still be battling various ailments. Each time I visited the doctor I received another devastating report.

I could not comprehend what was happening to me and it seemed as if no one else had the answer. I endured many attacks in my life as a "frontline warrior." The weapons were formed; however, they did not prosper.

As my body became disfigured and my health steadily deteriorated, I slowly began to realize that the enemy wanted me dead. Many days I had to pray and cry out to God. I called on my intercessors, prayer warriors and family to pray for me, which they immediately did.

This continued for over a year. However, my condition did not improve until the day I finally made a decision that I, like Hezekiah, would turn my face to the wall, go on a fast, and petition God on behalf of my own health and my very life.

I wanted to know if He was going to supernaturally heal me or if I should follow the instructions of the doctors. At this point of desperation, whatever God said, I was prepared to obey. It was then, when I got alone in my room, just God and I, that I settled in His presence and He began to speak to me. Once you seek Him, the Spirit of God will always reveal Himself to you because His grace is endless.

176

BEYOND THE BOUNDARIES OF GRACE

It is unwise for you to focus solely on your kingdom assignment to the detriment of your physical wellbeing. God wants us to do what He has called us to do. However, He also wants us to be healthy and take care of our physical bodies. Whenever we neglect our health, we may suffer adverse consequences.

"Beloved, I pray that you may prosper in every way and [that your body] may keep well, even as [I know] your soul keeps well and prospers." (3 John 1:2 AMP)

In some cases, we suffer many things because we think God will automatically forgive us, even when we step beyond the boundaries of His grace; after all... ***God is love!*** It is true that He is a loving God. *However,* He began to share one of the greatest revelations with me that I know will radically change the lives of believers everywhere, which is this...

God is an eternal judge; but He does not judge us based on the Word that we do not know. He does hold us accountable for the Word that we do know but to which we refuse to take heed. When we do not heed His consistent warnings, we frustrate the grace of God in our lives and can step beyond the boundaries of what He has ordained. Subsequently, He is not obligated to protect that which He has not authorized, sanctioned or approved.

After I understood this revelation, I realized that I was now suffering the consequences of my own actions. At that moment I had to repent before Him. He was like a father whose daughter had gotten in trouble because she chose to break His rules and was now paying for it. He sees the bigger picture concerning me and had set these boundaries in my life, *because* He loved me and wanted to protect me.

There are penalties attached to our disobedience in not heeding godly counsel. For example, you cannot spend all of your money then, at the end of each month or year, wonder why you are in a financially challenging position. You cannot continue with poor eating habits and then question God when your health is adversely affected. Obedience is still better than sacrifice and "to hearken" or to give heed or listen, is better than the fat of rams *(1 Samuel 15:22).*

BREAKING THE HEDGE
"For rebellion is as the sin of witchcraft and stubbornness as iniquity and idolatry..." (1 Samuel 15:23a)

From the day you were born, the plan of the enemy was to destroy you, but he was not able to do so because you remained under the protective covering of the grace of God. As long as you abide in the presence of Almighty God you are covered, protected and no evil can come near you. According to *Psalm 91:1:*

"He that dwelleth in the secret place of the Most High shall abide under the shadow (that is, the Protection) of the Almighty."

However, *Ecclesiastes 10:8* says, *"...that if you break the hedge, the serpent will bite you."* This means that if you walk out from under the protective covering of the Almighty God, you become susceptible to the attacks of the enemy. It is important for you to be aware that these diabolical attacks exist just beyond the hedge of protection God has built around you.

Further, it is also important to know that you can access an eternal "God" realm through prayer, worship and intimacy with God. This access builds a spiritual hedge of protection where the enemy cannot touch you.

You may ask, *"How can the hedge be broken?"* The hedge of protection can be broken around you when you operate in spirits of rebellion and disobedience.

"GOD DID NOT LIE!"

Although the enemy continued his attacks against my life, marriage, business and finances, I was determined not to give up on the call of God. God had always been faithful concerning His promises to me and I wanted to be faithful to my commitment to Him.

"I SOON REALIZED THAT PAIN IS PART OF THE PROCESS."

I thank God for every divine encounter in my life; for it was these dreams, visions and prophetic experiences that sustained me through the hard times. However, I soon learned that the process will not always line up with the prophecy. More often than not, the pain is a "necessary" part of the process.

In other words, when you are going through a test or trial, it never resembles the powerful prophecy you may have received prior to your process. Only in the fullness of time, when you have gone through the test will you clearly see the entire plan of God unfolding.

"God is not a man, that he should lie; neither the son of man, that he should repent: hath he said, and shall he not do it? or hath he spoken, and shall he not make it good?"
(Numbers 23:19)

"So shall my word be that goeth forth out of my mouth: it shall not return unto me void, but it shall accomplish that which I please, and it shall prosper in the thing whereto I sent it."
(Isaiah 55:11)

In spite of all that the enemy began to do, the Lord began opening great doors for me. Sometimes when the call of God is on your life you will find out that the enemy will set "ambushments" and send demonic assassins after you. For the most part, these attacks are an indication that you are on the right pathway of fulfilling the will of God for your life. The closer you get to fulfilling your purpose, the greater the intensity of the warfare.

"... many are called, but few are chosen." (Matthew 22:14)

One of the things I noticed is that by the time some people see what is involved in answering the call of God, the sacrifices they have to make and the spiritual warfare they may have to endure, many choose not to accept their kingdom assignment.

Some turn and walk away from the call of God because they are unwilling to endure the process on the *"road to greatness"*. If you are going to do anything significant in the kingdom of God it is going to require something of you. There is a glory to attain but you must be prepared to endure the *"story."*

THE PRICE OF GREATNESS

There is a great price for greatness. Anyone who believes that God is going to do anything in or through their life must be willing to pay that price which is a life of sacrifice.

As previously mentioned, in the United States of America it is documented that over 1,500 pastors and lay ministers walk away from their pulpit each month. Many are unable to endure the sacrifices of ministry or the onslaught of the enemy, and they tend to "break" under the pressure. Others are drawn away and enticed by a "glamorous" world system that looks more appealing and palatable to the senses than enduring the road of sacrifice.

In *2 Timothy 4:10*, Paul laments the loss of a once faithful servant, Demas, *"For Demas hath forsaken me having loved this present world..."* who was seduced out of his kingdom assignment because the things of the world looked more enticing.

It is incumbent upon believers to acknowledge that they have been called by God to do *His* work, regardless of what our adversary may bring. God says that we will be tempted but He will also, with the temptation, make a way of escape so that we can endure it.

"There hath no temptation taken you but such as is common to man: but God is faithful, who will not suffer you to be tempted above that ye are able; but will with the temptation also make a way to escape, that ye may be able to bear it. "
(1 Corinthians 10:13)

God's desire is for you to grow more and more into the image of Christ. Your tests and trials are not designed to kill you, but they are designed to form the Spirit of Christ in you so that when God demands something of you, you will be in a position to readily and faithfully obey.

The servant is no greater than his master. If Jesus had to endure the shameful death of the Cross, then there are trials and hardships that you will also endure if you are going to follow Him. God chastens those whom He loves because He wants us to grow and mature in Him. Before God can use any one of us, He sometimes allows us to be *"bruised."*

"Now no chastening for the present seemeth to be joyous, but grievous: nevertheless afterward it yieldeth the peaceable fruit of righteousness unto them which are exercised thereby."
(Hebrews 12:11)

Once we are pressed, crushed and properly "processed in the fire" then the essence of the Spirit of Christ will flow out of our lives and we will begin to prosper and be a blessing to all.

THE VALLEY OF PREPARATION

Whenever you recognize that the hand of God is on your life, you will encounter moments of preparation. I endured many seasons where I felt like giving up on what God had called me to do. I was traveling around the world, preaching the gospel of the kingdom. Souls were being saved and lives were being transformed. I loved God and treasured His call on my life. However, I remembered moments when I had to endure what seemed to be very long days and many lonely nights.

However, I can vividly recall a particular incident which occurred after a long week of traveling and preaching. I had finally settled at home only to remember that in a few days I would be gone again. My husband and some of the men in the ministry had gathered at my house to watch the Super Bowl. I never fully understood the game, so I took this opportunity to hide away, answer emails and work on other ministry projects.

I found myself in a place where I was surrounded by people but still felt disconnected. I began to understand that God was calling me to seek Him. Maybe you were in a similar place where the music played loudly and everybody danced, but you could not catch the rhythm. Likewise, you may have been in a place where everyone was laughing as loud as they could but you saw nothing funny. This is the place where you feel lost, lonely, isolated and alone.

In your valley of despair, you may look back at the mountain of extreme circumstances you had to overcome in order to bring you to where you are now. On the other hand, as you look ahead you realize that there are other mountains of greater challenges to face in order to get to where you are truly going.

I have been to that very place on numerous occasions and have had to face all of those low places on my quest to fulfill the call of God on my life. I call them my "valley" experiences. In each instance, I had to make a resolute decision that I was not going to give up and die but that I was going to press forward and live!

"Every valley shall be exalted, and every mountain and hill shall be made low : and the crooked shall be made straight, and the rough places plain:" (Isaiah 40:4)

LEAVING THE VALLEY

In our natural mind, when we find ourselves in somewhat of a "spiritual lull" we tend to either question the plan of God for our lives or we seek to understand the "way" that He is taking us. We may even ask, "If it was truly God who gave me this assignment, then why do I feel so overwhelmed?" or "Why does it seem so hard?"

You may begin to feel that if God meant for you to own a business, then it would not be so difficult for you to succeed. Or you may think that if it was God who truly ordained your marriage, then you and your spouse would not be contending all the time. Many times we seek to judge situations based on what we see or how we feel, rather than what God says. In *Romans 8:13* the Word of God declares:

"For if ye live after the flesh, ye shall die: but if ye through the Spirit do mortify the deeds of the body, ye shall live."

This scripture is letting you know that if you continue to perceive things based on what you see, hear or feel, you will die. *"Die"* here means to lose hope, give up or "lose out" on the life that God has for you. When you begin to wrestle with spirits of hopelessness, discouragement and despair, it is then that you must understand that the spirit of death seeks to steal the very thing with which God has blessed you.

It is essential for you to understand that God has not changed His mind concerning the dreams, visions and ideas He spoke over your life before the foundation of this world was laid. However, what I have learned is that although God had spoken these things over my life, I still had to fight and even endure hardships on the way to the manifestation and preservation of the promise.

In *John 10:10*, the Bible lets us know that we have an enemy who sends the spirit of death after us because his plan is to steal, kill and destroy our lives. However, Jesus has made an eternal covenant to fight alongside us so that we could experience life and live it to the fullest. But as we go through our tests, trials and difficulties we must be willing to endure hardships and make a resolute decision that we *refuse to die.*

DEATH TO DEATH

The devil seeks to have the Church in a state of confusion, dealing with issues that are not relevant to its eternal destiny. The clock is constantly ticking but the Church is standing still. As we mentioned in *Chapter Two,* the Church has become mechanical and monument-centered. It is now time to mobilize and to fulfill our kingdom assignments.

Earlier, you saw that spiritual death represents separation from God, from the things of God or from your kingdom assignment. It means to be separated from life, the God-kind of life that He had in mind for you when He created you.

Further, the spirit of death works with other demonic confederates and cohorts in an effort to demobilize you. You cannot touch it, lay hold of it or see it, but you can experience the attacks initiated by this ruthless spirit that seeks to destroy anything that is ordained by God.

"GOD HAS SPECIFICALLY DESIGNED EVERY 'VALLEY' EXPEREINCE TO EQUIP YOU FOR THE BATTLE THAT LIES BEFORE YOU!"

I truly believe that "death" and "time" normally work together. I believe this because only time truly knows when you will be born and when you will die. *(Ecclesiastes 3:2)* There is a time and a season for everything, even death. If you know that it is not your time to die, when the spirit of death visits you, you have to refuse to die. You must discern that the enemy is trying to prematurely kill you, your vision, dream or idea. You must refuse to allow death to rob you of anything that God has given you.

The process of autumn leaves changing color and eventually falling to the ground and other symbols of death are evident all around us. However, in most instances, this process occurs to accomplish a specific purpose, and when that purpose is fulfilled, then the *"time of death"* has expired.

The Bible says that *"all things work together for good for those who love God and are the called according to His purpose" (Romans 8:28).* No matter what you go through in life, every experience is designed by God so that the end result would be a "good" outcome. You have to be in a discerning posture to know when each season of death has accomplished its purpose in your life. Once that season is over then you command the spirit of death to leave your life; *you must speak death to death and refuse to die!*

WOMEN ON THE FRONTLINE

As a result of being called into ministry and what I have experienced over the years, I would like to speak briefly to other women who also feel the call of God on their lives.

More than fifty percent of the church consists of women. There is a small number within this percentage who, I believe, fully understand their purpose and assignment in the kingdom. If you feel the call of God on your life, you should seek the face of God first then align yourself with your leadership and seek counsel from them.

Further, you should endeavor to submit your gift to your local church, as there are too many women who are out of alignment with their leadership and are contributing to *some* of the confusion that exists in the Church. If your local church does not embrace your gift then you should seek God for specific direction.

It is important for the Body of Christ to understand that every pastor, pastors' wife, servant leader and minister is uniquely called by God. In many typical "religious circles", if your "type" or "style" of ministry is not accepted, then you may suffer a degree of condemnation or rejection.

We must understand that each administration of the gospel is divinely orchestrated by God and is designed to serve a specific kingdom purpose, thereby edifying the Body of Christ.

"11And he gave some, apostles; and some, prophets; and some, evangelists; and some, pastors and teachers; ...
12For the perfecting of the saints, for the work of the ministry, for the edifying of the body of Christ:..." (Ephesians 4:11–12)

Many years ago, my husband and I were both ordained as pastors and launched into full-time ministry. He was appointed as the senior pastor and I, as the "pastor's wife", was expected to be a typical "first lady."

In that season it was understood that, as the pastor's wife, you came to church, you dressed a certain way, showed up to garden parties for tea and "crumpets" and led the women's fellowship. Well, needless to say, that "suit" did not exactly fit me and I never could remember to bring the " 'kerchiefs and scones." I realized that although I was a "pastor's wife", God had called me with a unique kingdom assignment.

One of the things that I had to learn very early was that even though I was called with an assignment, I was also called to humbly serve and submit to my husband. I gladly assisted him with his mandate for the church and our ministry, as we both understood and respected the anointing that God had placed on our lives.

I feel that some women make the mistake of trying to compete with, or usurp authority over their husband's vision. This creates much confusion. One of the most valuable lessons I have learned as a woman on the frontline of ministry is the power of servanthood and how to complement, and not compete with, my husband.

It is essential that husbands and wives who are serving together in ministry, learn how to serve each other. Many ministries have been hindered because some ministry couples have not learned how to serve God first and then each other.

I have also learned to remain true and dedicated to what I believe God has called me to do, as I have seen many gifted and anointed women who are subsequently suppressed by their husbands or pastors. I believe that this is the season and the time when God is empowering you, as a woman, to rise and function in your kingdom assignment.

Therefore, it is incumbent upon you to prayerfully consider and assess what your potential and gifts are in the Body of Christ. God expects you to function in your gift and to do so in decency and order.

GOD GETS THE GLORY!

"¹And as Jesus passed by, he saw a man which was blind from his birth.
² And his disciples asked him, saying, Master, who did sin, this man, or his parents, that he was born blind?
³Jesus answered, Neither hath this man sinned, nor his parents: but that the works of God should be made manifest in him."
(John 9: 1–3)

By now, you may be wondering what happened that caused me to go through such severe attacks. Was there sin in my life? Was I praying as I should have been? What did I do wrong to cause these attacks?

In *John 9:1–3* when Jesus saw the blind man His disciples asked, *"who sinned that this boy was born blind? Did he or did his parents?"* Jesus' answer to them was that neither the boy nor his parents sinned, but he was in this condition so that the glory of God could be revealed. I want to encourage everyone, including believers, pastors, prophets or bishops and anyone who decides to follow Jesus: if you find yourself going through a difficult time where it seems as though the enemy has greatly afflicted your life, do not be discouraged.

Do not allow spirits of guilt, condemnation and shame to cause you to blame yourself for what you are going through. Just like Job, God will vindicate you and will give you total victory. At times God will allow you to go through situations because He knows that you can handle it. He knows that you will not give up in the midst of the battle, and that you will come through it bringing glory to Him. *You may gain the victory but, ultimately, God gets the glory!*

CHAPTER SEVEN

DEATH OF A RIGHTEOUS SEED

THE SEED OF THE WOMAN

Every seed that has been released in the earth realm has been given a specific assignment! The assignment of the apple seed is to produce apples and the peach seed's assignment is to produce peaches.

Likewise, since you are the result of a "seed" from your father, "planted" into your mother's womb, you were also born into that family. God sowed Jesus into the earth and we have become His children and heirs to an eternal promise. He spoke divine purpose over your life before He released you into the earth realm. Your assignment and ultimate destiny while here on earth are designed to "shake the gates of hell" and will pose a great threat to the enemy.

The Word of God declares in **Genesis 3:15** that the *"seed of the woman"* shall crush the head of the serpent. This is the reason why the enemy has declared an "all out" war against the inhabitants of the earth – be they saved or unsaved.

> *"And I will put enmity between thee and the woman, and between thy seed and her seed; it shall bruise thy head, and thou shalt bruise his heel." (Genesis 3:15)*

In **Revelation 12:3–4** it states that the enemy, himself, came up against the woman who was ready to give birth so that he could destroy her *seed:*

> *"³And there appeared another wonder in heaven; and behold a great red dragon, having seven heads and ten horns, and seven crowns upon his heads.*
> *⁴And his tail drew the third part of the stars of heaven, and did cast them to the earth: and the dragon stood before the woman which was ready to be delivered, for to devour her child as soon as it was born."*

It is the plan of the enemy to destroy you from the day you were born because he does not want you to come to maturity, fulfill your God-given assignment or come into the full revelation of who you are in God.

Thus the enemy sends various dilemmas in an effort to destroy your life before you ever come into the divine purpose that God has for you.

Here are some dilemmas you may have experienced:
- you may have suffered rejection from the womb when your parents contemplated aborting you.
- you may have been raped or molested which scarred you physically, mentally or emotionally.

- you may have had to struggle through childhood illnesses or encountered other childhood traumas; For example you have struggled with a learning disability or some physical deformity.
- the enemy may have sent demonic spirits to torment you in your dreams which may have caused you to grow up fearful and timid.
- you may have experienced a sudden death or tragedy that you were mentally and emotionally too young to handle.
- the enemy may have sent attacks against your family where you grew up in a house that was filled with turmoil and confusion.
- you may have had to endure the divorce of your parents.

> *The intensity of the warfare you encounter is a direct indication of the threat you are to Satan's kingdom.*

Whatever the strategy, the enemy sought to do everything he could in your early stages of life to destroy you, but you are a righteous seed and it was the hand of God that preserved you until such time as He has set for you to come forth.

"The weapons of the enemy may have been formed against your life but they can not prosper." *(Isaiah 54:17)*

CHOSEN!

From an early age, I can remember fulfilling the call of God on my life. I loved God so much, that there was nothing He asked of me that I was not prepared to do wholeheartedly.

In the midst of doing what God had called me to, the enemy had launched an "all out" war against my ministry, my health and my very life. At first, I did not understand what was happening to me.

Then the Holy Ghost led me to *Job 1:8–12* and I was reminded of the exchange between God and Satan concerning Job.

I came to the realization in that season that I was probably qualified for a test. He allowed the enemy access to my life to test me, not because I had sinned, but because He was preparing me for another level in Him. God knew that after I came through it, my testimony of how He delivered me would be a blessing to many and bring ultimate glory and honor to Him.

As I look back over my life, I realize that the enemy launches a system or cycle of attacks in an effort to discourage those that are chosen and called by God. If you believe that you are chosen with a special gift, purpose or assignment then understand that the very "gates of hell" will continue to fight you. However, if you refuse to die and continue to seek the will of God for your life, in due season, you will come forth; fulfilling your divine purpose because God is with you.

THE FURNACE OF AFFLICTION

Just as you see the devil as your enemy, he also sees you as his enemy. In many cases, the purpose of the enemy's attacks against your life is so that:

- you are either unable to give birth to your dreams, visions or ideas.
- you become so overwhelmed with what is confronting you that you abort the assignment and purpose that God has given you to fulfill in this earth realm.

As you begin to seek out and inherit the things of the kingdom of God, you become a greater threat to Satan's kingdom. Satan, therefore, wages a strategic warfare against your life and sends spiritual assassins who are assigned to your life with one mission: *to destroy you.* One such assassin is the spirit of death. *(See more in Chapter Three: DEATH NEVER ACTS ALONE)*

In these instances, you must discern his plans. The Word of God says that we are not to be ignorant concerning satan's devices. Every day, we are to put on the whole armor of God so that we may stand strong when the enemy is working against us.

Even if you find yourself afflicted by the hand of the enemy, understand that God has selected you from before the foundation of the earth and He has set His seal upon you. It does not matter what it looks like now, God has not and will not change His mind concerning the assignment He has given you. We see such an example in *Zechariah 3:1– 4:*

> *"¹And he shewed me Joshua the high priest standing before the angel of the LORD, and Satan standing at his right hand to resist him.*
> *²And the LORD said unto Satan, The LORD rebuke thee, O Satan; even the LORD that hath chosen Jerusalem rebuke thee: is not this a brand plucked out of the fire?*
> *³Now Joshua was clothed with filthy garments, and stood before the angel.*
> *⁴And he answered and spake unto those that stood before him, saying, Take away the filthy garments from him. And unto him he said, Behold, I have caused thine iniquity to pass from thee, and I will clothe thee with change of raiment."*

In this passage of scripture, the Word of God reveals how the enemy came up against Joshua, who was a High Priest in Israel. The enemy's main goal was to hinder Joshua in what God had called him to do and to remind him of his shortcomings and failures.

In verse 3 of the same scripture, the Word of God reveals that whatever the enemy did to resist Joshua, it caused him to fall into iniquity and be clothed with filthy garments. The angel of the Lord declared that, although Joshua had fallen, he still belonged to and was going to be used by God. It does not matter where you find yourself in life; God has not changed His mind concerning what He wants to do in and through you.

The Rise And Fall Of The Anointed

Whenever you are "anointed", this means that God has bestowed a level of His grace upon you to accomplish His divine will. To be "anointed" means to be overtaken by and engulfed in the tangible scent, fragrance and aroma of Almighty God.

The anointing attracts His goodness and glory to your life. As powerful as this attraction and endowment may be, it does not exempt you from encountering pitfalls and other "dangers". In fact, being anointed often times attracts adversities, enemies, tests and trials *towards* you. The same applies to those who are leaders.

The Rise And Fall Of The Leader

Many people have a high respect and esteem for their pastors, spiritual leaders, employers and national or civic leaders. While this may be good, one should also remember that these men and women are also human and subject to the normal tests and trials of life.

It should be understood that leaders are not invincible and neither are they exempt from human frailty. Leaders are accepted, respected and appreciated as long as they are in a position of power. Needless to say in our society today, whenever a leader makes a mistake and falls, he is brutally criticized, condemned, disrespected or even vilified.

Although your leader may be in a season of testing and trials, it does not mean that God has not called him or is finished with him.

It does not matter what the enemy seeks to bring in your life, as a believer, God never changes His mind concerning His plans for you. I firmly believe that just as God has sealed and "branded" Joshua The High Priest, God has done the same for everyone He calls His "anointed". *(1 Chronicles 16:22; Psalm 105:15)*

SHHHH ...
INJURED AT THE HANDS OF A PREDATOR!

Growing up in a small country such as mine has its advantages and I believe a few disadvantages. One of the challenges we encounter as a people is that, because we are a small community, "news" travels quickly. Some people even say that, *"Good news travels fast but bad news travels even faster."* Based on this idea we were taught that whatever happened in the family stayed in the family, for fear that we would become the next victims of the "gossip mill." Throughout my younger years, it was the "norm" for us to *not* speak to anyone about anything negative that happened in our lives, especially if it concerned incidences of molestation.

In many communities, children are raped, molested and violated every day and, for the most part, people "turn a blind eye" and pretend as if they are unaware of what is happening. Statistics indicate that one in every four girls and one in every six boys, globally, has suffered some form of abuse as a child. Unfortunately, for me, I became a part of that statistic.

The spirit of death is no respecter of persons. He targets whosoever he wills, regardless of your nationality, gender, socio-economic status and even your status in the kingdom of God. Even if you are called to do something great for God, the enemy is coming after you, by whatever means necessary.

DEMONIC ACCESS
"The Doorway Of Abuse!"

For many years, I struggled immensely with the thought of sharing my testimony of being sexually abused as a child. When I realized years later that I was still afraid to speak of the abuse, this was an indication and confirmation to me that the enemy was using this to terrorize me. Through spirits of fear and intimidation, he sought to "muzzle" my mouth.

Eventually, I realized that this became an area of demonic access to my life through which the spirit of fear and other demonic spirits came. Although I encountered the sexual abuse as a child, I was still battling with the "spirit of abuse" as an adult. If I was going to close the door to the spirits of hurt, pain, shame, guilt, fear, and even death in my life, I knew that I would have to find the courage to expose these devastating experiences that had almost crippled me.

From about the age of seven, two distant male relatives began molesting me. I can remember the horror of being violated and was told not to tell anyone or I would be severely punished and something horrible would happen to my mother.

Every time I was touched by either of them I was threatened, warned to be silent and given a dollar bill. I was never a fearful child; however, what I did not know was that these horrible encounters were, one by one, "digging" a habitation of fear in the crevices of my soul.

This happened for several years and I found myself living as a prisoner, bound by the chains of fear, hurt, guilt and shame. It was not until my adult years, when I began seeking God for answers to certain dilemmas I faced, that the Holy Spirit began to deal with me. I found out that the enemy had sown these demonic encounters, like seeds, in my spirit in an effort to sabotage my destiny.

I had not realized the devastating effects this spirit of abuse had on my life until I understood that I had literally "shut down" a part of my mind to this childhood trauma. That is exactly what the enemy wanted. In this debilitated condition I was limited as to how far I would be able to advance in my ministry and in my life as a whole. If I was going to be all that God had called me to be, I knew I would need to go through an entire process of deliverance.

There were layers and layers of baggage that had to be unearthed and peeled away from my soul, including the fact that I wanted my father's protection from those predators. I loved my father but I felt angry because he was not there to shield me from those predators, due to his crippling addiction.

"Many are the afflictions of the righteous, but the Lord delivereth him out of them all." (Psalm 34:19)

It has not been a joy over the years to think or even speak about what happened to me, I realized, however, that forgiveness is not so much for the perpetrators as it is for the one who has been hurt or violated. Forgiveness gives that individual the freedom from his bondages and all of the hurt, pain, shame and guilt that come along with the injustice.

I made a choice to forgive both of those men who violated me and I thank God I did. My choice to forgive set me free from the years of that abuse and qualified me to administer deliverance to others who have also been hurt and abused.

SHATTERING THE GATES OF HELL
"Shatter The Silences!"

As a Prophet, I am constrained to shatter the silences of scores of thousands of people, young and old, worldwide by compelling them to acknowledge, confront and remedy what has happened to them.

Failing to shatter the silence of any vexing pattern will, inevitably, lead to other destructive cycles, not only in your life but in the lives of others close to you. I was not wholly liberated or set free until I shared my story and I believe that you can be ultimately set free as you share your story.

" IN ORDER TO SHATTER THE GATES OF HELL, YOU MUST FIRST SHATTER THE SILENCE!"

The enemy may have opened some illegal, "demonic door" to your life by way of abuse, drug or alcohol addiction, paralyzing fear, rejection, exposure to a tragic accident, the death of a loved one or even exposure to the spirit of perversion. The blood of Jesus can seal whatever demonic door to your life has been opened, so that the enemy no longer has access to you.

God wants to do more than just "break" the silence. To "break" means to split or fracture something, implying that it can be reassembled or put back together again. On the other hand to "shatter" means to totally destroy, crush or annihilate something to the extent that it can no longer be restored. God wants to shatter the very thing that has kept you in bondage so that you can be totally set free.

"whom the Son sets free is free in deed."
(John 8:36)

REJECTION FROM THE FATHER'S HOUSE

One of the greatest "burdens" that I discovered had been placed on my life was the spirit of rejection. Since my childhood, I began to realize that the spirits of fear and rejection act as demonic doorkeepers to the soul. However, I did not understand until later in my life that I suffered from the spirit of rejection.

As I mentioned before, my father was the nicest man in the whole world but he drank profusely. Throughout my years of growing up, I used to be so angry because all I ever wanted was his love and attention. Due to the fact that he was constantly drunk, we did not have the father-daughter relationship that I had expected. Even though I preached at his funeral, I never grieved this painful loss until almost seven (7) years later.

Afterwards, I spent most of my adult life searching for someone to call a "spiritual father". Many of those relationships failed and I found myself hurting again. As time went on, I began to recognize that the doorway of rejection was still open. Whenever I truly loved and built a covenant relationship with someone who greatly disappointed or betrayed me, I became disheartened.

I fully understand now what people experience when they suffer a divorce, separation or the death of a loved one, especially, if they do not have a strong support system in place. In the world, it is called "separation anxiety" but I call it the *"doorway of rejection"*. Everyone deals with rejection differently. The seed of rejection is born out of hurt. For example, while carrying her baby during pregnancy a mother may experience a traumatic hurt, but it is the baby that suffers rejection.

Whenever someone is hurt by a person they trust or believe in, this can cause a devastating wound to the soul. Rejection is an emotional feeling of being unwanted, unloved, undesired, unaccepted, unappreciated, unimportant and insignificant. Whenever these feelings manifest you may choose to react either passively or aggressively.

People who may react *passively* tend to withdraw themselves becoming isolated and unhappy. This further opens the door to self-pity, loneliness, hopelessness, depression, despair, addiction and even suicide. On the other hand, people who react *aggressively* tend to develop a nonchalant or a "don't care" attitude. They act as if they are not affected and tend to put on a harsh exterior while deeply hurting on the inside.

One of the things that I learned is that people *will* hurt you. The Word of God reveals in *Jeremiah 17:5* that, the arms of flesh *will* fail you. However, you have a choice as to how you will deal with or respond to this hurt. God does not want you to build up walls and other barriers in an effort to protect yourself or keep others "out" of your life. But He does want you to respond to any hurt you may experience in your relationships according to the Word of God.

Sadly, there are many people in the Body of Christ who have been affected by the spirit of hurt or rejection and are silently suffering, finding it difficult to live. It is very important that you deal with every type of hurt you experience because of the simple fact that *"hurting people tend to hurt other people."*

PROPHETIC PRAYER NUGGET (PPN)

Pray this powerful prayer right now and take authority over every spirit of hurt and rejection in Jesus' name!

Father God, in the name of Jesus I forgive everyone who has ever hurt or disappointed me. I release them and let them go right now in Jesus name. Father God deliver me from every spirit of hurt that opened the door to the spirit of rejection in my life.

Jesus, only You can heal a wounded soul. Heal me now and fill every void in my life and make me whole. I rebuke every spirit of hurt, rejection, disappointment, hopelessness, self-pity, despair, bitterness, anger, resentment, by the power of the Holy Spirit and the blood of Jesus. I command them to go and leave my life right now, in Jesus' name.

I activate the law of life, acceptance, peace, joy, love and prosperity over my life right now in Jesus name! ***Amen!***

WHO DROPPED YOU?

I was traveling on a ministry engagement not so long ago and, as I entered the security checkpoint at the airport, I placed my belongings, including my laptop and iPad on the conveyor belt. By the time I came through the scan machine, I noticed that my laptop had fallen off the belt because the checkpoint officer was distracted by a conversation he was having with his co-worker.

"Oh, my God!", he exclaimed. *"Ma'am, I am so sorry. Please turn it on and see if it is still working."*

To everyone's surprise, including mine, it came on. He said, *"Thank goodness! I thought I might have broken it."*

Everyone was relieved and I continued on my journey. However, little did I know that all was not as well as it seemed. Several days later, I was working on completing one of the chapters in my book, only to discover that, although my laptop was powered and able to be turned on, it was malfunctioning. It took a very long time to "boot up" and, when it finally came on, it made a loud buzzing sound.

Unfortunately, it sustained "internal injuries" and no longer performed some of the usual basic functions it did prior to being dropped. *Someone dropped it...and it was never the same again!* Later in this chapter I will share with you the account of the story of Mephibosheth, the grandson of King Saul, who was also "dropped".

Has it ever occurred to you, that you may have been dropped? If this did happen...*who dropped you?* You may have been dropped at some point in your life but as time passed you had almost forgot about it and can hardly remember who or what "dropped" you.

The "dropped" to which I am referring represents some experience that happened *to* you which has had a traumatic or devastating effect *on* you. In some cases the effects of such experiences may leave you physically, mentally or emotionally scarred or challenged. It may have happened at the hands of someone you did not know or someone who should have helped and protected you but, instead, this person "dropped" you. This crippling experience opened the door to the spirits of rejection, hurt and pain.

As it is in the natural, so it is in the spiritual. If a caregiver mistakenly drops a baby, the defects caused by this may go unnoticed as long as the child is an infant. However, as this child grows into a teenager or adult, some of the signs of being "mishandled" may begin to manifest.

If this has happened to you, eventually this "brokenness" may leave you vulnerable to the "entrapments of the enemy" who seeks every opportunity to keep you "crippled" and in a place of obscurity. Further, you may begin to struggle with all that God has for you in a new season. This new season may bring new connections and opportunities but because of the misfortunes you experienced in your past seasons, you struggle to embrace them.

It is not the will of God that you remain in a crippled, dysfunctional state. In some instances, these experiences may act as a "yoke around your neck", keeping you bound and tied to demonic burdens of suffering and hardship. Although having been mishandled has left you struggling through life's seasons of "ups and downs", this is not the will of God concerning you. He wants to remove every burden and destroy every yoke of the enemy.

DEFEATING THE ENEMY OF YOUR PAST
"Rescued From Lodebar!"

The "enemy of the past" is what has been destroying many people. What most of them do not realize is that although they have overcome devastating experiences, the enemy seeks to use the "spirit" attached to all of those encounters to keep them living in the past. For example, when you still struggle with the spirit of pain that is associated with a tragic experience such as a bitter divorce or the loss of a job, you are still in some level of bondage to your past. I call this place *"Lodebar"*. *It is a hiding place or a place of crippling where the enemy wounded you and left you for dead!*

I am calling this *Lodebar* because whenever something has happened to you and others have moved on but you are still stuck in that same place, it means that you are adversely affected by the situation or crippled by this event.

"THE ENEMY IS MORE AFRAID OF YOUR FUTURE THAN HE IS OF YOUR PAST!"

2 Samuel 4 records the story of Mephibosheth which is set against the backdrop of a bitter war between the houses of King Saul (Mephibosheth's grandfather) and King David. Mephibosheth, who was the son of Jonathan and grandson of King Saul, was dropped when his nurse fell while holding him as she ran to safety during the conflict. This tragedy in Mephibosheth's life crippled him from childhood, a dysfunction that remained with him even throughout his adulthood. Although he was the son of a king and later became a father, he spent his life in a crippled condition.

In *2 Samuel 9: 1–5, 7*, years have passed, the war is over and King Saul is now dead. We see where King David is asking if there is anyone left of the house of Saul that he may bless because of a covenant he had made with Jonathan.

¹And David said, Is there yet any that is left of the house of Saul, that I may shew him kindness for Jonathan's sake?
² And there was of the house of Saul a servant whose name was Ziba. And when they had called him unto David, the king said unto him, Art thou Ziba? And he said, Thy servant is he.
³ And the king said, Is there not yet any of the house of Saul, that I may shew the kindness of God unto him? And Ziba said unto the king, Jonathan hath yet a son, which is lame on his feet.
⁴ And the king said unto him, Where is he? And Ziba said unto the king, Behold, he is in the house of Machir, the son of Ammiel, in Lodebar.
⁵ Then king David sent, and fetched him out of the house of Machir, the son of Ammiel, from Lodebar.
⁷ And David said unto him, Fear not: for I will surely shew thee kindness for Jonathan thy father's sake, and will restore thee all the land of Saul thy father; and thou shalt eat bread at my table continually.

Could you imagine what Mephibosheth must have thought? Here is a man who was in a debilitated condition all of his life. More than likely, he had been rejected by many and tolerated by some because, although he was the son of a king, he was crippled. Now that his father was dead and a new king ascended to the throne, what was to become of him? One day, Mephibosheth received the message that the king was looking for him to bestow a blessing on him.

Some of you have been in your "Lodebar" long enough and, in this season, God is calling you out of your "hiding place" because He wants to bless you. Today, God wants to set you free because you have been there too long.

Just as King David called Mephibosheth out of Lodebar, so is God calling you out of your Lodebar, your crippling place. He does not want you bound by the chains of your past. He has so much more in store for your future and He will touch the hearts of kings if He has to, in order to get a blessing to you.

"IT'S TIME TO COME OUT OF YOUR HIDING PLACE; DEFEAT THE ENEMY OF YOUR PAST AND MAKE A DECISION TO LIVE."

THE POWER OF FORGIVENESS
"Breaking The Spirit of Limitations!"

As I shared earlier, one of the demonic gatekeepers the enemy had set up in my life was the spirit of fear, which entered through the doorway of abuse. I later discovered that this demonic nemesis had also opened the door for the spirit of limitations, which kept me suspended in various seasons in my life.

"THE ENEMY OF YOUR PAST WILL BECOME THE ENEMY OF YOUR FUTURE IF YOU DO NOT CONFRONT IT!"

I felt as though I was not attaining the level that I knew was possible for me. There were times I should have moved forward, however, the spirit of fear along with the spirit of limitations kept me intimidated and too afraid to step up and do what God was telling me to do. I believe that if I had obeyed, I could have gone farther or done more with the assignment.

Unfortunately, many people live their lives in constant torment or fear as adults, even if the abuse happened during their childhood. Once I began to seek out the answers for my deliverance, I realized that during that season of being sexually violated as a child, I was what I call "dropped".

It was difficult for me to make the connection between the abuse that happened to me as a child and what was now affecting me as an adult; mainly because the experience had happened so many years ago. What I did not know was that because I had been so inwardly traumatized I grew into adulthood with this defect in my soul, which was now challenging my destiny.

As a child I knew that I was being exploited but was powerless to do anything about it. Worst of all, in my mind, I felt like there was nobody I could turn to who would protect me, or even help me. This may have been true then, but it was no longer a reality in my adulthood. I also came to realize that I was not that helpless little girl anymore and I was now ready to move forward in life.

In order for me to break free from this restricted, limited state I knew that I would have to forgive everyone that I felt had wronged me. This meant also forgiving the two men who violated me and most importantly my father, who I felt should have been there to protect me from those two predators. The spirit of limitations made me feel as though I was trapped in a literal cage. Further, I had to remain in constant prayer and worship in order to break completely free from this restricting spirit.

Many people may find themselves stuck and imprisoned in this type of bondage to their past as well because they have never forgiven the people who have hurt them. For a long time, I too felt as if I was trapped in an invisible cage not able to progress. Finding the courage to forgive my adversaries, destroyed the power of the steel cage and iron bars; setting my soul totally free.

If you are ever going to experience total freedom, it all starts with forgiveness. Forgiveness does not mean that what the person did was right but what it does mean is that you are willing to rid yourself of the bondage of unforgiveness so that you can be set free.

What the spirit of unforgiveness will do is hold in place a strong man called the "spirit of entitlement." As a victim, the spirit of entitlement makes you feel justified in being angry, bitter and resentful. It makes you feel that if someone has wronged or hurt you then that person should be the one apologizing.

It should be clearly understood that you do have the right to your feelings as a result of what has happened to you. However, you should be aware that you will remain perpetually bound to that dilemma until you are willing to forgive and let go of that situation, person or event.

Forgiveness does not in any way mean that you have to be in fellowship with the perpetrator. It simply means that you have released them from your heart and you are no longer resentful towards them. I am much stronger now and am able to share the experience of how God delivered me; however, it was a very delicate process that led me to experience the total freedom I now have from the destructive spirit of abuse.

If you believe that you were "dropped" or "injured", meticulous time should be taken to bring total healing and deliverance in your life. Remember, there may be numerous internal fractures within your soul which, not even you are able to detect. You must be willing to unravel the hurt and pain that may be hidden within the crevices of your soul.

Be comforted that the Holy Spirit will bring you into total healing and deliverance, for it is He who is able to perform a finished work in your heart. *Once the process of healing is complete, you will no longer be a prisoner to your traumatic experience and, best of all, you will no longer be afraid.*

PROPHETIC PRAYER NUGGET (PPN)

"Pray this prayer right now and take authority over every spirit of limitations in Jesus' name!"

Father God, in the name of Jesus I take spiritual authority over and I bind every spirit of limitations along with the spirits of fear and intimidation that seek to control my life. I bind the spirits of sabotage and hindrance along with the spirits of demonic interception, interference and interruption that seek to keep me from living my life to the fullest measure in You.

I silence the false accusations of the enemy right now in the name of Jesus and choose to walk in forgiveness. Whom the Son sets free is free indeed. I decree and declare that I am free to be all that God has created me to be, in the mighty name of Jesus! AMEN!

CHAPTER EIGHT

THE "WEIGHT" OF DEATH

THE SPIRIT OF HEAVINESS
"1 The spirit of the Lord is upon me for the Lord has anointed me ...
2 To proclaim the acceptable year of the LORD, and the day of vengeance of our God; to comfort all that mourn;
3 To appoint unto them that mourn in Zion, to give unto them beauty for ashes, the oil of joy for mourning, the garment of praise for the spirit of heaviness; ...." (Isaiah 61:1–3)

The spirit of heaviness is a subliminal spirit which acts as an agent of satan assigned to attack every believer. It hides behind other spirits such as the spirit of tiredness, fatigue and weariness. It also seeks to manifest through the spirits of rejection, grief, self-pity, chronic fatigue syndrome, depression and extreme mood swings *(eg. manic-depressive disorders)*, hopelessness, despair and excessive-compulsive eating disorders *(eg. anorexia, starvation, bulimia, binging, gluttony)*.

This foul spirit of heaviness seeks to keep you bound and totally "weighed under". It will emotionally bind you, keeping you discouraged, depressed and in a constant state of worry.

The diabolical tactics of the spirit of heaviness are evidenced by its ability to do the following:

- weigh you down (gross depression, despair, hopelessness, etc.)
- block, hinder and stifle your growth and movement
- burden, anchor or bolt you down, increasing immobility
- bring with it the "cares of life"
- bring worry or anxiety (mental fatigue)
- bring guilt (shame, condemnation, regret, self-pity)
- attack your emotions (sorrow, grief, pain, heartache, etc.)
- bring anger (frustration, rage)
- draw you into isolation

The spirit of heaviness penetrates the very core of your soul, thereby giving place to the spirit of suicide, death, self-destruction, self-mutilation and may sometimes drive you to bring destruction to others.

During these times we must learn how to earnestly pray and trust God *with* everything and *in* everything. It is when we are pressed and bruised beyond what we believe we are able to bear that we become positioned to see the anointing and power of God manifested in ways we could never imagine.

THE NATURE OF GRIEF

Grief is mental anguish or the emotional response to loss. This may occur as a result of the death of a loved one or the loss of something that is endearing or valuable. It is an automatic reaction to an unexpected traumatic experience, an affliction or tragedy. When a person is grieving, this generally means that their soul is in distress.

Anything your soul is tied to and loses can spark intense feelings of grief. However, how you choose to deal with the grief will determine the outcome. I have discovered over the years that many people also grieve as a result of major losses such as:

- financial loss
- loss of health
- loss of job
- retirement
- loss of a pet
- loss of a marriage as a result of separation or divorce
- loss of a home
- loss of a good friendship
- loss of a cherished dream
- emotional instability after experiencing *a trauma*

In *Isaiah 53:3* the Word of God says, **"He (Jesus) is despised and rejected of men; a man of sorrows, and acquainted with grief:"** Although, He was "acquainted" with grief, Jesus was not overcome or overtaken by the spirit of grief. *(See more in this Chapter)*

People deal with or express their grief through the process called "mourning". If you have never lost someone near and dear to you there is a possibility that you may not understand what it feels like to truly grieve. Jesus always felt the hurt and pain of those around Him. In *Luke 7:11–15*, when the widow of Nain lost her son, the Bible says that Jesus was so *moved with compassion* that he restored her son to her; He even felt the pain of this grieving mother.

Jesus also understands the grief that comes to a husband or a wife who experiences the sudden loss of his or her spouse, especially after decades of being together. He knows the pain that parents go through as a result of the tragic loss of a child to some unexplainable dilemma. In any relationship, whether short or long, it is important to note that grieving the loss of a loved one is never easy.

WHY MARRIAGES DIE

When any marriage "dies", fails or ends in divorce, I believe that spouses grieve due to this loss. Marriage, as defined by the Word of God in *Genesis 2:21–22* is a covenant union between a man and a woman. This was God's original design with Adam and Eve in the Garden Of Eden. God's plan for this intimate covenant was that a man and a woman would live together in perfect harmony; loving and caring for each other. He designed a healthy marriage as part of His master plan.

Satan, on the other hand, seeks to corrupt and pervert everything that God ordained. Therefore, he craftily manipulates the mindset of each individual as it relates to the key components of marriage. Some areas he attempts to target include money, sex, communication and spiritual views, in order to bring division, separation and ultimate destruction to this God-ordained institution.

I also believe that marriages are challenged due to internal issues which originate between spouses. Unfortunately, one of the primary reasons I feel why many marriages fail is because people simply fall out of love with God and each other. Even though this may be attributed to many different external factors, I strongly believe that the absence of constant and relevant communication between spouses gives way to demonic interferences in a marriage.

Further, one person's mindset, goals, aspirations, expectations and outlook may begin to mature beyond that of their spouse. This discrepancy may cause both spouses to become indifferent, prone to disagreements, and uncertain of their perception and love for each other.

In *Amos 3:3* the Bible asks, *"How can two walk together except they agree?"* To "agree" means to be on one accord or to have perfect harmony with something or someone. When couples can no longer agree or see "eye-to-eye" on any matter with no clear resolve in place, then emotional, mental, sexual or physical separation is inevitable. In other words, they begin to "war" with each other, generating anger, tension, disagreement, jealousy, selfishness, hatred, rejection, abuse and various destructive behaviors. These and other issues sometimes open the door to irreconcilable differences and infidelity.

In these instances, negative attitudes of unforgiveness, unwillingness to forbear and share responsibility make reconciliation difficult, opening the door to satanic interferences and eventually termination of the marriage covenant.

LIFE AFTER DIVORCE

Statistically, it has been proven that over fifty percent (50%) of marriages end in divorce. I also believe that more people are filing for divorce in this decade than any other time in history. Unfortunately today, many lovers and soul mates are finding it difficult to stay in love with each other, persevere together or remain faithful.

I believe one of the biggest mistakes that couples make is spending more time planning for their wedding than planning for their marriage. If any God-ordained marriage is going to survive, couples must be prepared to put forth great effort to make their marriage work.

God does not want His children heartbroken, and He certainly does not want His ideal covenant of marriage severed by the devastating practice of divorce. If a couple believes that their marriage is ordained by God, I believe that they should do everything within their power to avoid divorce and fight for their marriage.

Everyone that has ever gone through a divorce should consider some level of deliverance for healing purposes. Moving on into another relationship or marriage without being healed and delivered will only lead to more pain and disillusionment. There is an adage which says that, "Hurting people hurt other people" and, worst of all, hurting people will hurt again if their soul scars are not healed.

If you are going to live after the "death" of your marriage, you must consider the following:

- Pray and ask God to give you the courage and strength to overcome any devastation your soul may have experienced
- Seek out a pastor or prophet for deliverance from any soul wounds or soul scars uncured as a result of the divorce or unsuccessful marriage
- Undergo a *"spiritual detox"* and forgive your spouse for any wrong that you feel may have been committed against you
- Be mature enough to acknowledge where you may be at fault and also forgive yourself, if necessary; only take ownership for what you are responsible for, do not blame yourself for anything that you did not have the power to change
- You must let go of any bitterness, anger, pain and resentment in your heart towards your spouse in order to be set free and move forward with your life
- If necessary, break every covenant agreement with any demonic spirit husband or spirit wife *(See more in Chapter Four: DEFEATING THE REALM OF DARKNESS)*
- Allow yourself to be healed of any hurts, disappointments, rejection or abuse experienced in your marriage
- Take time to pamper yourself
- Put measures in place to let go of the past and move forward with your life after the divorce (i.e. move to another home, remove photos of you and your spouse, remove objects that may keep your soul tied to your spouse,...)

- If you and your spouse have children together, be careful not to defame your spouse in their eyes
- Be mindful as you go through a divorce, that this separation will also affect your children, seek to cover and protect them; reassuring them of your love for them, regularly
- Be proactive and put measures in place to safeguard your mental, emotional and spiritual health as well as that of your children *(See more in this Chapter)*

GONE TOO SOON!

I could not help but notice over the past several years that whenever someone died, people wore a t-shirt with the face of the deceased and the words **"Gone Too Soon"** inscribed on it. At first, I was not sure why they wore these t-shirts. Then I noticed that these insignias were worn at funerals, regardless of the gender or age of the deceased.

In my opinion, it all "looked like an oxymoron" or a businessman's idea to make a few dollars at the expense of the bereaved. Nevertheless, I later came to understand their rationale. Regardless of the person's age at death, those who were left to mourn felt as if their loved one had died sooner than they would have wanted.

The words *"gone too soon"* convey the common idea that someone has died, prematurely, and imply that they may have been unable to completely fulfill their life's purpose.

CONSOLING THE BEREAVED

Whenever a person dies someone mourns their death. Every individual processes grief differently. People grieve based on their faith, personality, life experience, mental or emotional stability, history of witnessing death and finally, based on the nature of the loss.

In some cultures, people may adorn themselves with sackcloth and ashes or even rip their garments.   While in other cultures, family and friends attend what is called a "wake" in memorial and silent celebration of the life of the deceased. I believe that it is good, even healthy, for you to mourn and shed tears; this may help to alleviate some of the pain.

I believe that we, as the Body of Christ, must know how to deal with someone who is grieving and be able to minister to them until they are back on their feet.   Remember, everyone grieves differently. Some persons may cry while others prefer to sleep. Some may even find themselves consuming alcohol or seeking some other means to suppress their pain.

Although, a person may be grieving, and I sympathize with his or her pain, I do not believe that anyone should engage in self-destructive or violent activities such as drinking, smoking, lashing out in anger or any other counter-productive behaviors. I believe that these negative behaviors will, on the contrary, only serve to perpetuate the pain, especially if you are not prepared to confront your tragedy.

"Blessed are they that mourn for they shall be comforted."
(Matthew 5:4)

GRIEVING THE LOSS OF A LOVED ONE

Your emotions, along with your will and intellect, are housed in the realm of your soul. Your emotions are the elements of your soul through which you express how you feel about your life experiences. Whenever you experience loss, it is one of the most deadly assaults against your soul and, more than anything, it is your emotions that become affected.

If you ever face the loss of a loved one, the grief you experience can sometimes become overwhelming. It is imperative that whomever you surround yourself with be able to help you survive this difficult time. This is extremely important because many times the enemy uses your weak moments to seek to gain an advantage over you. With grief, he typically deploys demonic spirits of pain, sadness, regret, depression, anger, bitterness, resentment and more to keep individuals forever bound to the tragedy that caused their loss.

It takes a heart filled with much compassion and graced with wisdom to know how to help others walk through their period of grief and eventually get their lives back.

GRIEVING THE LOSS OF A SPOUSE

One of the greatest tragedies that anyone can face is the death of a loved one, especially the loss of a spouse. It is one of the most painful and difficult things to experience, especially if the couple had been together for a long time. However, whether long or short term, it is an extremely painful loss.

The grieving spouse is left to contend with the fact that the person they once shared their life with is no longer there. Now all they have left to hold onto are the memories created with their deceased loved one. This thought alone is painful enough.

The surviving spouse is also confronted with the harsh reality that they will never be able to create any new memories because the life they had with their loved one is over. This type of grief can be almost unbearable.

I can distinctly remember when one of my faithful members experienced the sudden, tragic loss of her husband. One morning they were at home preparing for the day, and the next moment, due to an "unexplainable" accident that happened while he was fixing an automobile, he was gone.

He was one of the most dedicated and loving spiritual sons that my husband and I had the privilege of nurturing and "growing" in the faith. The news of his death swiftly traveled throughout the church, piercing the hearts of everyone in the ministry, even the children. His wife, at the time, was pregnant with their first child.

Many reminisced about how he would talk nonstop about the arrival of the baby and the excitement of becoming a first-time father. He would share all of the plans he had for his baby. He was so excited about bringing a child into the world … little did we know that he would never live to see that day. At the age of twenty-eight, with his whole life yet to live…he was dead.

As we all tried to "make sense" of this tragedy, our initial response was not prayer, nor was it to sing shouts of praise. At first we grieved. Some people screamed, some cried and others embraced. Even the children were crying. Some were too young to understand what was happening and wanted to know why everyone was so sad. Some persons never spoke a word as they tried to come to terms with the fact that he was gone forever and, definitely, *"gone too soon!"*

Having been married for less than two years, his wife bore the brunt of the sorrow. We immediately established a support system around her. We laid out specific rules in an effort to guard her soul. No one was allowed to visit her looking sad or depressed. We told everyone to allow her to talk or cry if and when she wanted or needed to.

We had a few women from the ministry stay and pray with her twenty-four hours a day. We never left her alone, especially considering the fact that she was also pregnant. Two of her friends agreed to move in and kept speaking to her about the happy times she shared with her husband but also reminded her to be strong for their unborn baby.

It was not an easy process but, by the grace of God, she buried her husband and a few months later gave birth to a beautiful baby girl. The support network stayed in place until we felt she was emotionally, mentally and spiritually sound. We all still assist her with the beautiful little girl who is now attending pre-school.

THE GRIEVING PARENT

One of the other major forms of grief occurs when a parent unexpectedly loses a child. In many instances, parents do not expect to outlive their children. The pain of losing a child is unbearable for any parent.

Many parents live in regret and guilt laboring under the prevalent belief that they could have done something to prevent the child's death. Ultimately, in the mind of parents the child's safety and protection is their responsibility. Many parents also carry the burden of dwelling on *"what could have been."* Their minds are tormented by the thought that their child will never live to be all that they envisioned.

Parents must be surrounded by the "right people" who are able to coach them through their season of grief, offer words of encouragement, and "lend" a sympathetic ear. These factors will help them to rebound from such a loss.

THE GRIEF OF A CHILD
"Surviving Divorce!"

There is no pre-requisite regarding the age at which someone may experience grief. Even children grieve as they face various tragedies. Whether because of death or divorce, the stages of a child's emotional recuperation from the grieving process must be fully addressed in order for healing to take place.

Depending on the age and maturity level of the child, one of the most common struggles they experience is the emotion of guilt. They automatically begin to believe that their parents' separation is their fault.

Oftentimes people can genuinely sympathize with a child who is experiencing the death or loss of a loved one or pet. However, many people may not realize that one of the most devastating experiences for any child occurs when his parents decide to separate or get a divorce.

As a result of their own personal pain, sometimes it is difficult for parents to fully comprehend the extent of the hurt, guilt, confusion, disappointment and sadness that the child also feels. It is very important for parents to understand that this rift in the family dynamics can cause extreme emotional trauma in a child's life.

THE PROCESS OF RECOVERY
"What About The Children?"

The road to the child's recovery will vary depending on the child's age and the level of emotional impact his parents' separation or divorce had on him. The response of the adult to that child may require a combination of spiritual sensitivity and use of proactive emotional healing strategies. For example:

- **Ages 5-11** Children in this age group need to feel confident that they will be cared for and their physical needs will be met. They need constant assurance that they are loved and protected from both parents.

- **Ages 12-17** This age and stage is a crucial one as teens are going through the adolescent period. Therefore, the separation or divorce of their parents, the death of a loved one or even the death of a pet can be a traumatic experience for them. We must deal with them prayerfully, with the appropriate care and attention, because they are at that stage of transitioning from childhood into adulthood.

At this age, they can become susceptible to destructive behaviors such as alcohol or drug abuse, isolation from the family and more. They may also experience a gamut of emotional reactions during this time; from becoming introverted to exhibiting "out of control" behaviors.

It is very important for the child to be reassured that:

- their parents' separation or divorce is not their fault and they have done nothing wrong
- both parents still love them and care about how they feel
- it is okay to feel angry, sad or unhappy
- they will not always feel the hurt and pain they are currently feeling; everything is going to be alright!

THE GRIEVING "FIRST LADY"
Losing a Husband and Pastor

The "first lady" is whom we commonly refer to as the pastor's wife. When a pastor dies, it is an experience that grips an entire church and places the congregation in the mode of grief and suffering.

Generally, because the pastor had a more intimate relationship with the members, in some instances, his wife and children may be neglected by the local church. These women are sometimes forced to endure an entire lifestyle change due to the sudden shift in dynamics. Some are even forced to now find a suitable means for survival for them and their children.

However, in *James 1:27*, the Word of God says: ***"Pure religion and undefiled before God and the Father is this, to visit the fatherless and widows in their affliction..."***

In *Acts 6* there was a major dispute which arose in the early church regarding the fact that the widows were being neglected and not cared for properly. Seven deacons of good reputation and full of the Holy Ghost and wisdom were appointed to deal with matters pertaining to them.

In some instances, due to extreme adverse circumstances some widows and orphans have been forced onto the streets or in shelters, having to find other means of survival. As the Body of Christ, we should make every effort to support our widows, especially the pastor's wife.

THE GRIEVING CHURCH
"Losing A Pastor"

Losing a pastor, may be of great discomfort and distress to any church. Nobody even wants to entertain the possibility of the thought of losing their spiritual leader. Therefore, prayer should be constantly, consistently and fervently offered on their behalf.

In some regards, the loss of a pastor or spiritual leader can greatly impact not only the local church, but, depending on the extent of the church's outreach can devastate an entire community, country and nation at large. Great care and attention should be given to comfort and console each member of the congregation.

On the other hand, the loss of this "one" life can affect the lives of "thousands" and even "millions" of others. Careful care and attention should be taken to bring consolation and comfort to those who are grieving and resolve to those who are asking the question,

"Why" or "Where is God in the midst of this tragedy?"

As a member, although you may have lost a pastor, spiritual father or renowned leader, it is important to understand that you are not hopeless nor are you without hope. Further, *1 Thessalonians 4:17*, assures us that we will see him again, one day.

While it is important that we hold onto the legacy of our pastors and great leaders, we should also be careful that we do not erect monuments or shrines to them which we worship after their death. Many people make the mistake of stopping and giving up on God, after their leader has died. You should endeavor to continue to advance your leader's vision even if he is no longer alive. I believe that your ability to continue your pastor's vision will be a greater testament to the strength and validity of his legacy.

When Moses died the children of Israel had come to a place of total despair, grief and uncertainty. They had become comfortable in their wilderness place and were afraid to go forward. God emphatically spoke to Joshua and said, *"Moses my servant is dead, take these people and cross over to the other side." (Joshua 1:2)*

Joshua loved Moses but, if he did not move forward, he risked the same fate of dying where Moses died; in the wilderness, never entering the Promised Land. If your leader passes away, it is understandable that you will experience some level of sadness and grief. Despite this tragedy, you must forge ahead in the things of God.

CAUGHT IN A SCANDAL
"The Fall Of A Leader"

In the previous section, we addressed how grief can affect a member, due to the death of his leader. Alternately, people can suffer or come under grief, as a result of the fall of anybody they view as a role model or public figure. Over the years, many men and women of great renown have fallen. This, no doubt, has devastated persons who held them in great esteem and high regard.

These scandals have not only led them to reputational demise and public humiliation but have also caused distress to the people who once admired and respected them. Some people may even become angry and feel a sense of betrayal, extreme disappointment and abandonment. However, great care should be taken that we do not stereotype every leader in that arena because of the few who have fallen from grace.

Again, you should never seek to deify anyone and exalt them to a place above God. We should not ignore the human element of our leaders, who are mere mortals, and susceptible to making mistakes. However, I do believe that every leader should seek to live a life that is spiritually and morally sound.

EXPOSING THE SPIRIT OF GRIEF

I truly believe that grief is a natural response to loss and people should be allowed to mourn for as long as they deem necessary. However, it is important to note that excessive periods of mourning may inadvertently open the door to a *spirit of grief.*

When you experience prolonged periods of grief this, along with the spirit of heaviness, can open the door to oppression, suppression, depression and, eventually, demonic possession. *(See more in Chapter Ten: "CARRY ME OUT, I'M WOUNDED!)*

I believe that there is a time and a season to everything, even the grieving process. However, when that time is over you must find the courage and strength to move beyond that tragedy or disappointment.

The *spirit of grief* is not just limited to natural or physical death. This deadly spirit seeks to emotionally, mentally and spiritually demobilize you. Therefore, it must not be tolerated or "entertained" at any age. The spirit of grief has as its demonic counterparts the spirits of despair, hopelessness, self-pity, gloom, rejection, depression, oppression and anguish.

Again, this is an unclean spirit that must not be tolerated. If you are struggling with a spirit of grief, according to *Isaiah 61:3* God wants to give you, *the "...the oil of joy for mourning, the garment of praise for the spirit of heaviness..."*

GRIEF VS GUILT

Whenever you have lost a loved one, and years later still find yourself crying over a photo, an article of clothing or when your loved one's name is mentioned, this may be a sign that the *spirit of grief* is present.

In some cases, when the enemy seeks to keep you in prolonged seasons of grieving he may employ the spirits of heaviness and grief to "fabricate" or "manufacture" an emotion or feeling of sadness that becomes more of a "habit" than an authentic emotion. This false disposition keeps you in a destitute mindset long after the loss and even after the grieving period has passed. The Word of God states, *"The spirit of a man will sustain (him in) his infirmity; but a wounded spirit (soul) who can bear?" (Proverbs 18:14)*

You may also suffer feelings of guilt and condemnation:
- if you were unable to bring closure to unresolved issues
- if you were not able to say "goodbye" to your loved one,
- if you were not present at the time of their death or
- if the death occurred suddenly by some tragic event

Do not allow the enemy to condemn you over your loved one's death. The reality is that they are gone now and, no matter how guilty you feel, this will never bring them back.

Guilt and condemnation are diabolical strategies the enemy uses to keep you in a mental or emotional prison. Forgive yourself if you must, and grieve freely without the added burden of taking responsibility for something you have no power to change.

VISIBLE SIGNS OF THE
SPIRIT OF HEAVINESS AND GRIEF

There are a number of visible signs to indicate whether or not a person is naturally grieving or whether he is being oppressed by a *spirit of heaviness* and *grief.*

Again, I believe it warrants repeating that it is very important to understand that grief is the *natural emotion* you experience after some tragedy or devastating loss. The expression of that grief is typically followed by "mourning." A period of mourning is necessary if you are going to move forward with any level of resolve.

Deliverance from the spirit of grief and heaviness may be necessary if you experience extreme or prolonged occurrences of any of the following:

- frequently expressing extreme guilt for your loss or adverse situation years after the experience occurs
- when thoughts of the loss or adverse experiences cause prolonged bouts of acute depression or mood swings
- extended periods of uncontrollable weeping
- repetitive feelings and thoughts of suicide, or expressing a desire to die as well
- becoming dysfunctional or losing the ability to perform basic duties at home, work etc.

- intense feelings of worthlessness and a lack of desire to go on or move forward many years after the tragedy
- complaints of hearing voices or seeing things that are not real, especially the voice or image of your loved one
- erratic thoughts and unexplainable behaviors
- chronic fatigue, weariness or anxiety

DEALING WITH SPIRITS OF HEAVINESS AND GRIEF
"My Daddy"

Growing up, my father was one of the nicest men you could ever meet. However, all of his life he struggled with an insatiable addiction to alcohol. There were rare moments when my father was sober. It was during those moments he would play his guitar as we sang country music and laughed with him. I loved my father and wished I had more time with him.

After years and years of battling with a number of health issues, including liver and stomach ailments, he eventually succumbed to the deteriorating health condition with which he struggled. I also believe he became tired of being tormented and controlled by his nagging habit and ultimately gave up.

The day my father died, was one of the saddest days of my life. I was at the church office dealing with several matters when the hospital called for me to come because his health had taken a turn for the worse. By the time I got there, however, it was too late as he had already died and his body had been taken to the morgue. I was so angry and devastated that I never even went to see his body.

For a long time I was mentally and emotionally numb because my dad, the love of my mother's life, her "Kermy", was gone and he was not coming back. Worst of all, I felt cheated and robbed of the opportunity to say "goodbye".

My father's Pastor came to visit the family a few days later and asked if I would be able to deliver the eulogy at his funeral. I accepted the request; however, I must admit that right then I was still angry and bitter because I felt that he had died way before his time.

At the funeral I preached a sermon about Dives and Lazarus from *Luke 16:19–31* and wanted everyone to know that they needed to "get right." In other words, they needed to get their lives in order. For the most part, many of them were too drunk to even "pay attention", but I preached as the Spirit of God empowered me to do so.

It was not until several years later that I grieved my father's death. I had been so busy trying to be strong for my mother and siblings that I took no time to feel anything for myself. I can clearly remember that while sitting in my living room with no one else around me, I eventually released all of my pent up anger, bitterness and frustration. I broke down and began weeping uncontrollably. It seemed as if I wept for hours.

I cried because I missed my father and I only had a few memories of a little girl's "daddy" moments. I cried because of the bedtime stories he never read. I cried over every car that was "totaled" by my father who crashed them because he was driving drunk; I cried over every slumber party I did not have because I was too embarrassed to have my friends over; I cried because I was only allowed to enjoy a fraction of the man that my father truly was; I cried because my father was gone and he was not coming back. I cried and, this time, I did not have to hold back my tears and be strong for anyone.

I grieved openly and freely until finally I felt a spirit of relief come over me. Now, whenever I think about my father, I can look back without anger, resentment or bitterness. To be honest, there is a twinge of sadness that comes over me whenever I think about him and what he could have become.

Do I wish he was still here? Yes, many times! Do I wish God had delivered him from the spirit of addiction so he could be all that God had intended for him to be? Of course! Instead, soon after my dad gave his life to the Lord, he passed. Do I love my father? Yes, I love him very much; I miss him ... *and I always will.*

OVERCOMING GRIEF

It is very important to remember that just as everyone deals with pain differently, everyone also grieves differently.

There are, however, a few basic nuggets that I will share with you as you continue to gain the victory over the spirit of heaviness and grief, which include:

- Acknowledge that you have lost something or someone of great value or importance to you
- Allow yourself some time to mourn. It is alright to cry, as this is an excellent way to relieve some of the pressure.
- Surround yourself with the right people who will encourage you but not push you further into a state of depression
- In the midst of your pain you must find time to worship
- When the enemy attacks you with depressing thoughts begin to renew your mind with the promises and the Word of God; encourage yourself with scriptures that give hope.
- Do not harbor the bitterness or anger you may feel as a result of your loss

- Forgive, quickly! Forgive the situation or circumstance that cheated you of your loved one or even forgive yourself if you must
- Remind yourself that you will not always hurt

God is able to turn your "mourning into dancing" *(Psalm 30:11).* He promised in His Word that, weeping truly may endure for a night but the joy of the Lord will come in the morning *(Psalm 30:5).* These precious promises give hope that you will not mourn forever.

PROPHETIC PRAYER NUGGET (PPN)

"Pray this prayer, taking authority over every sprit of grief, in Jesus' name!"

Father God, in the name of Jesus, I give you all glory, honor and praise. Lord, Your Word declares that You came to set the captives free. Your Word also declares that whom the Son sets free is free indeed. I therefore declare my liberty, breakthrough and deliverance from every spirit of grief and heaviness this day in the name of Jesus.

I now agree with your Word that the law of life that is in Christ Jesus sets me free from the law of sin and death. I take control of the spiritual, emotional and mental climates of my life and I bind the spirits of grief, mental torment, emotional anguish, deep pain, suffering and loneliness from off of my life in the name of Jesus. I render them powerless under the blood of Jesus Christ.

Your Word declares that all things are working together for my good. Thank you for turning my mourning into laughter and for giving me the garment of praise for the spirit of heaviness, in the name of Jesus. I declare total victory in my life, right now in Jesus name! AMEN!

CHAPTER NINE

'TIL CHRIST BE FORMED IN YOU!

I DIED A "MILLION" DEATHS!

There are times when "death" or "dying" are necessary. These times are pivotal to your overall spiritual development and maturity. Rejection, hurt and pain all have a way of making you feel numb or "dead". If you do not deal with them spiritually, eventually you will succumb, or become indifferent and callous to the environment around you.

Whenever God calls you with a unique anointing, do not expect to fit into every "circle" or clique; it will not work. I spent many years in frustration and anger because I was trying to fit into what I call "elite circles": the "women that preach" group, then I tried the "women that prophesied" group and let's not forget the "women who go shopping" group. What I had to realize at the time was that God did not want me to be a part of any of these groups because of what He was calling me to do. However, I believe that something was "peculiar" about me.

I soon came to understand that the Spirit of God was drawing me to Himself. I did not sound like everyone else; I preached loud, sweated, ran and in their opinion I was overly demonstrative. Whenever the hand of God is on your life, you should be very careful not to entertain the voices of your enemy.

I can vividly recall the numerous times I slipped into bouts of depression, not knowing or understanding why I was going through my trials. There were times that I desired to sleep and could not; I wanted to eat and could not find the appetite. I became weakened to the state of listlessness, devoid of all strength to function.

I felt as though I had died a million deaths before I began to live my one life!

On many occasions I had to use the spiritual weapons of prayer and worship to pull me out from under these attacks. There were specific inspirational songs which motivated and "carried" me through these seasons. At the time, these encounters were very intense and almost unbearable. However, they all eventually pushed me to a place of yearning and desiring more of God, which propelled me further into His presence.

Now, all I wanted was to hear His voice. All I desired was to feel His touch, His warm embrace and His tender love assuring me that I was His own and that we belonged together.

I continued to pursue the call of God on my life. It seemed as though *I had died a million deaths* in my quest to "fit in", only to discover that I *"paid"* my own price for what God had already freely given me. In other words, I had endured many needless pangs of anxiety, worry and fear in order to attain another level in God.

Sadly, many people go through their whole life, struggling to fit into circles or what they perceive as "elite groups" not realizing that the greatness they are searching for is already on the inside of them. Many face the same travesty of fighting to receive validation or acceptance from people who have, no doubt, already excluded them.

What you fail to understand is that God may have promoted you far beyond the level that you are trying to attain because you paid the price when you overcame your last trial. There were even times when I felt as though I was exposed to what I call the *"church mob"* society. For the most part, these people do a good job of making you feel inferior or as if you are of a "lesser brand".

They make it very clear that you do not belong in their group, however they will ruthlessly exploit your gifts and talents for their own selfish gain. For all of you who may be new to and coming up in ministry, *BEWARE OF SUCH SOCIETAL ORDERS. (See more in book by author, "IT'S MY TIME TO LIVE!")*

Nevertheless, I count it all joy and appreciate every level of warfare, pain and shame I overcame at each "season" of my spiritual journey, as they led me deeper and deeper into the "secret places" of God. Over the years I discovered that learning how to "find God" in the midst of my "death-like trials" increased my desire to seek His presence more and more. Now I willingly climb into the "secret place", the place where He dwells, where He lives; *"....a path which no fowl knoweth, and which the vultures eye hath not seen; The lion's whelp have not trodden, nor the fierce lion passed." (Job 28:7-8)*

My *"million death encounters"* drove me to a new realm of faith and have pushed me into a deeper place of prayer and consecration. I am sure you feel the same way I do, perhaps having also survived similar "death experiences". You survived and can now feel totally safe and protected from any attack, onslaught or diabolical plan of the enemy.   Your life is secured in this "secret place" where you are totally overshadowed, and surrounded by the presence of God.

The depth of suffering that you or I may have endured will never be compared with the glory that shall be revealed in our lives once we continue to overcome the enemy.

After many incidences of "falling down and getting back up" in my mind, I then realized that I *had* "died a million deaths". Looking back, it would seem as though they were par for the course because during these "death experiences", although I felt as if I had died, I gained so much more.

I died to …

- the opinions of others so that I would no longer be hindered by what they thought or said about me

- low self-esteem so that I could fulfill my assignment with boldness and confidence

- being tolerated by friends and learnt how to celebrate myself

- vulnerability to rejection and learnt to activate the "law of acceptance" over my life

- being lonely and came to understand that God had divinely orchestrated my "solitary places" so that He could endow me with a unique anointing

- wanting to "fit in" and understood that no matter how hard I tried, I would never fit into a "circle" when God had divinely created me to be a multi-faceted "diamond"

God reserves a commanded blessing for warriors who have, at times in their lives, *"DIED A MILLION DEATHS"*.   As a valiant warrior I refused to conform to a worldly system or measure up to the status quo, choosing instead to cultivate an anointing that could only be found in a "secret" or solitary place. I admonish you to continue soaring far above the eagles, defeating challenges, overcoming pitfalls and surviving the irony of *"dying a million deaths"*.

> *"YOUR VALLEY EXPERIENCES CAN CULTIVATE IN YOU AN ANOINTING THAT COULD NEVER BE CULTIVATED ON THE MOUNTAINTOP!"*

IS THIS GOD OR THE DEVIL?

"And we know that all things work together for good to them that love God, to them who are the called according to his purpose." (Romans 8:28)

When things begin to go wrong in a person's life, the questions asked are, "Why Is This Happening To Me?" and "Is this God or is this the devil?" Whenever God is seeking to develop the character of Christ in you, He allows various tests and trials to hit your life.

On the other hand, the enemy seeks to co-opt God's strategies in order to fulfill his diabolical plan. Unlike God, the enemy is not seeking "to process or bring anything good" out of you; his ultimate intention is to *kill* you!!

Again the question one would have is, "How will I know if my test was instituted by God to bless me or by the devil to destroy me?" or "How do I know if it is God pushing me forward or the devil tempting me to stop and turn around?"

One of the first points to understand is that the enemy is never going to push you towards anything that is going to bring honor and glory to God.

Once you discern the source of your "storm", you must begin to deal with it as Jesus did. You can do this by:

- Rebuking the confusion (storm) and causing it to become calm
- After silencing the commotion around you, find a quiet place to seek the presence of God; by spending time in prayer.
- Further, allowing the Spirit of God to impart the instructions, direction and wisdom you need

Once you identify where your "warfare" is coming from, if it is God you can make a resolute decision that you are going to pass the test. However, if you discern that it is from the devil, then you can emphatically resolve that you will outlast the attack and defeat your enemy.

In some respects we must also be willing to admit that there are some issues existing in our lives and even some needless pains we have borne because we did not seek and obey the wisdom of God prior to making decisions. For example, there are some things that God spoke to us and told us to do, however, in our own disobedience and rebellion we chose to do something else which may have caused our lives to come into hardship. *Delayed obedience is disobedience.*

God may have also given you a ten-step process to your victory or breakthrough but if you only fulfilled a portion of the instructions then you must assume responsibility for whatever difficulty you encounter. In *1 Peter 5:10*, the Word of God declares:

"But the God of all grace, who hath called us unto his eternal glory by Christ Jesus, after that ye have suffered a while, make you perfect, stablish, strengthen, settle you."

When tests and trials come, they fulfill a specific purpose in your life, be it positive or negative, depending on their source. For example, as explained earlier, God allows various challenges in your life in order to forge the character of Christ in you. The enemy, on the other hand, sends attacks to your life in order to sabotage, derail, demobilize or debilitate you.

You can also create various issues in your life, knowingly or ignorantly, by "opening demonic doors" through your own disobedience or rebellion. Some ways diabolical attacks may also come to your life are due to:

- *something that has happened to you* via abuse, neglect, abandonment, etc.
- *generational curses* which work through you
- *what has happened because of you* by negative words you have spoken against yourself, the doors you have opened through willful sin, involvement in occult practices, , and the like.

By whichever means the trial or test comes to your life, it is important to know that God is able to make all things "work together for your good" *(Romans 8:28).* As you continue to seek God for answers in your life, He will begin to show you the way through and out of your dilemma. It is not His will that you be consumed by the "heat" of your trial or the "will" of your enemy. He will never allow you to be confronted with more than you are able to bear. *(1 Corinthians 10:13)*

IDENTIFYING THE ORIGIN, ROOT, SOURCE AND FRUIT

In spite of what transpires, as a best practice or principle you must always earnestly seek God to gain the answers as to what is happening in your life or in the life of your family. You cannot truly solve a problem until you are able to identify the origin, root and source of that problem.

❖ **The Origin** – exposes the place where something has started, the seed from which something initially grew or the event that triggered it. The origin speaks to the "seat" of your situation. For example it could be some form of childhood abuse, trauma or tragedy; a rape, a bitter divorce, the death of a spouse, loss of a job, etc. *The origin represents the seed of a tree.*

❖ **The Root** – reveals what is hindering you from moving forward. The "root" is the thing that has legal rights to keep this demonic situation "tied" and "bolted" in your life. It could be in the form of bitterness, unforgiveness or some deviant mindset. *Just as tree roots go deep into the earth to find water and food to nourish the plants, in this context the root of your issue lodges deep in your soul in order to cripple you.*

❖ **The Source** – is the pre-existing unresolved issue that gives strength to or accommodates the mindset of what is happening or has happened to you. It is the "thing" that is supplying or giving nourishment to the persistent problem you are facing. It can be considered the "enabler" or the "energizer". The source can be encapsulated in both internal factors or pre-existing issues such as guilt, self-pity, low self-esteem, pride, etc. and external factors such as the negative input of others. Therefore, the source should not be confused with the "root"; in that the root represents the conduit through which the source flows as it "gives strength to the issue." *The source, in the natural, can be similar to the soil and all of its nutrients.*

❖ **The Fruit** – is the physical manifestation of what you are experiencing as a result of the original event. It is the resulting illness, divorce, rebellious child, bankruptcy or broken relationship that you are now struggling to manage. It is the negative thing that you are now confronting because of a demonic seed the enemy planted, that either you were not aware of or you never dealt with in its infancy. *The fruit is the result of what was planted; apple seeds produce apples; orange seeds produce oranges; etc.*

In the case of someone who was raped, the rape is the *origin*, the bitterness, hurt, anger or shame they feel represent the *root.* The *source* may be insecurities, low self-esteem and self-condemnation. Finally, the *fruit* is manifested through a life of promiscuity.

It is not God's plan to bless or curse you. Regardless of what has happened, Jesus has given you authority over the works of the enemy in your life.

ANOINTED IN A SOLITARY PLACE

Sometimes you can become so wounded in your soul that it brings you to a place of destitution; this is what I call a "solitary place." The enemy may seek to use these moments as opportunities to convince you that because you are now in a solitary place, you are no longer anointed, God is no longer with you and can no longer use you. *This is a lie from the enemy!*

A primary example of this is the story of David in *1 Samuel 22* where he finds himself on the run from King Saul who had become jealous of his anointing and was now his enemy. Saul and his army of men were trying to kill David, who was forced to leave his home, his family and his throne. Hiding in a cave to save his life, David finds himself in a solitary place, seeking the face of God. It was in this "solitary place" that David penned *Psalm 57*, which begins:

"Be merciful unto me, O God, be merciful unto me: for my soul trusteth in thee: yea, in the shadow of thy wings will I make my refuge, until these calamities be overpast." (Psalm 57:1)

In his solitary place, the kingly anointing on David's life never left him; neither did the anointing of the Psalmist. It was in the cave that men, who were destitute, disadvantaged and *"dispositioned"*, found David and followed his leadership.

Sometimes God, Himself will bring you to these "low" places just so that He could bless you. *"How can I get a blessing out of a destitute situation?"* you may ask. If you would be truthful, it is in the solitary places of your life where God has demonstrated Himself to you the most. In these places you learned to hear the heartbeat of God as He drew you closer and closer to Himself.

Your "solitary place" could have been a "broken heart", the betrayal of a close friend, the death of a loved one or acute bouts of depression and fear. Whatever it was, it was during these times that you learned to trust God with all of your heart.

In *Psalm 23:4*, King David said, *"Yea though I walk through the valley of the shadow of death, I will fear no evil for Thou art with me; thy rod and thy staff they comfort me."*

This was the very David who was a man after God's own heart, king of Israel and an intimate Worshipper of God who found himself walking through the "valley of the shadow of death". David took comfort in this because he knew that God had promised to never leave him nor forsake him, and He was with David. I want to encourage you today that God will also be with you, even as you go through your "solitary place".

THE BELIEVER'S DEATH WALK
"The Irony of Death!"

In order to become more like Christ, we must "die" to our flesh so that the spirit of Christ can come alive. Whenever you hear about death, it usually brings about a very morbid and dreary feeling.

242

People immediately begin to think about grief, pain, sadness or despair. Some people even feel fearful talking about graveyards, funerals and the like. As much as we may not like to talk about it, "death" is an element of our humanity that is inevitable.

In *Ecclesiastes 3:1–3*, the Bible declares that to everything there is a season and a time to every purpose under the heaven. It clearly mentions in verse 2 that there is a time to be born and a time to die.

This scripture clearly points out that death in every form has its time and purpose, including the time of dying to your flesh. I believe that in order to fulfill the will of God for our lives, it requires a mandatory "death walk." The Apostle Paul declares in *1 Corinthians 15:31, "I die daily!"*

In *Hebrews 5:8* the Word of God further reveals that even Jesus, as the Son of God, learned obedience through the things He suffered. Even He had to go through a process in order to learn how to be obedient to God, but He was willing because He wanted to fulfill His divine purpose *in* God. This process is what I call *"The Believer's Death Walk."*

As difficult and as painful as they can be at times, there is a purpose for your "death" experiences. For the most part, they can *purge us from* the works of the flesh and *sanctify us to* the call of God on our lives.

"For I reckon that the sufferings of this present time are not worthy to be compared with the glory which shall be revealed in us." (Romans 8:18)

The process of "death" can be seen in the transition from the Autumn Season to the Winter Season, during which time everything dies. It is one of the most colorful times of the year. Trees which had only green leaves now begin to shed brown, orange and yellow leaves.

These leaves eventually fall off and die. This process takes place every year in due season.

When things, situations or people are being "shed" from your life you must understand that the season for that person or that thing has come to an end.   The "shedding" process is only a sign of better things to come. God says, I know the plans I have for you, plans to prosper you; to give you hope and an expected end *(Jeremiah 29:11)*. However, before these things can manifest you must go through a process of shedding; shedding old ideas, old habits, old practices and any remnant or sign of the previous season that you have just left.

This "shedding" may be a very uncomfortable, difficult or painful process but it is necessary to shed the old, before you can embrace the new.

"I HAD A SPIRITUAL MAKEOVER!"

It was during these seasons, as everything was being shaken and "shed" around me, that I came to understand there was only one thing I could do, which was to fall into the bosom of God.

Further, if you are going to find your way out of any situation, you must assess where you are and what you are going through then implement a plan of action to come out with the victory. Far too often, during the time of major testing and hardship, people make the mistake of running away from God rather than running to God. It is of grave importance that you find the pathway to God.

In one such season, I willingly placed myself in "solitary confinement" pulling away from everyone and everything, posturing myself to seek the face of God. I locked away in my room with the bare essentials and did not entertain any phone calls. I was desperate; I needed to hear from God and stayed in the Word of God morning, noon and night. During this time I also immersed myself in worship to keep the atmosphere set for the Spirit of God and to repel demonic thoughts and influences.

At first, I did not want to hear them, but at the time that I could not pray, I played the very prayers that I had prayed on CD for others for myself. I fasted and prayed. I told God everything that was going on around me, *as if He did not already know.* I asked Him to give me direction, to speak His counsel to me and show me the way that I was to take during this season. I asked Him to speak to those around me; to open their eyes so that they could perceive what was going on in my life and know how to pray for me.

There are times when you may find yourself in a struggle and left to bear alone because others around you may not be sensitive to what you are facing. In these instances, you may also find yourself constantly in a quandary, seeking to be fully understood.

As I laid on my threshing floor in much prayer and travail, I heard the Spirit of God begin to speak to me. I sat up and postured myself to receive whatever counsel, instruction or direction He was about to release to me because I believed that He had heard my prayer.

I will never forget that day. For hours the Spirit of the Lord gave me one of the greatest revelations of my ministry – He showed me myself. In those precious moments, He began to perform an intensive reconstruction on me, I knew that He was giving me a *"spiritual makeover."* He revealed to me my strengths and weaknesses. I became so broken in His presence that I wept for countless hours. I felt such a profound love emanating from the presence of Almighty God that I did not want to leave.

I was so desperate to get to the next level in God that I was willing to do whatever it took, even if it meant staying all day in His presence.   Although it was extremely uncomfortable at times, I stayed in His presence until the entire process was over.

That day I learned that no matter how much you may accomplish as a believer, what level you may have attained in ministry or how much you truly loved God, every now and then you need to ask the Holy Spirit to give you a *"spiritual makeover"*.

I believe that if God is going to use you in any capacity, you must become broken and yielded before Him.   Once you have gone through your process of spiritual reconstruction, God then prepares you to help birth someone else to their next level in God.   In other words, He takes you through the process so *Christ be formed in you* first so that you can be a spiritual midwife to someone else *'til Christ be formed in them! (Galatians 4:19)*

'TIL CHRIST BE FORMED IN YOU

"For our light affliction, which is but for a moment, worketh for us a far more exceeding and eternal weight of glory;"
(2 Corinthians 4:17)

It is important for you to know and believe that God is in control of everything.   He knows every heartache and disappointment that you will ever experience.   His master plan is designed to bring you into a place where He gets all the glory out of your life.   God's aim is to provoke you to a place in Him where you discover levels of prosperity, peace, love and joy that you would never experience outside of His perfect will for you.

The Apostle Paul discovered something that is true about every human being, himself included.   In *Romans 7* he discovered that there was no good thing that dwells in man's flesh.   He further realized that there was only one thing left to do with the flesh, and that was to kill it.

246

Once he had made a decision to do what God had called him to do, Paul understood that this would only be possible if he made a commitment to "dying daily". What did he mean by this? *He was crucifying his flesh and bringing it under subjection to the will of God, every day.*

God is never surprised; neither is He left in "shock and awe" when difficulties, hardships or challenges come your way.

He was not allowing how he felt to dictate how he served God. He refused to do what he wanted to do, but every day he submitted his will to the purpose and plan of God.

There is no good thing in your flesh. The flesh must die so that the life that is in Christ Jesus may come alive in you. The Word of God says in *1 Peter 4:12, "Beloved, think it not strange concerning the fiery trial which is to try you, as though some strange thing happened unto you:"*

Further, according to *James 1:3-4, "Knowing this, that the trying of your faith worketh patience. But let patience have her perfect work, that ye may be perfect and entire, wanting nothing."*

I believe that you are purged spiritually when you are able to overcome the trials of life which are designed to "test", "stretch" and "try" you. In other words, trials come to press you into another dimension in God. Your response in the midst of the test will determine whether you are prepared for spiritual advancement. Although there were times I felt within myself as if I would not survive my season of testing, it was the Word of God, among other things, that sustained me.

In *Isaiah 54:16* God reveals that it was He who created the "smith" that bloweth on the coals. In other words, He created the maker of any weapon that is "made" and is, therefore, able to control whatever "fiery trial" you must endure. God is at the master controls and He will not *ever* give you over to the will or desire of the enemy.

It may be challenging for some people to accept the notion of another trial, especially after experiencing numerous difficulties in life. The idea of having to endure another adversity may be one thing, but accepting that God actually allowed it is another, especially when they feel as though they do not deserve to undergo another challenge.

The enemy may be sending the "heat" but, ultimately, God is in control. He will not allow the "smith" to put more on you than you are able to bear; His desire is to purge you until you become pliable in His hands and Christ is formed in you.

God is in complete control!!

"There hath no temptation taken you but such as is common to man: but God is faithful, who will not suffer you to be tempted above that ye are able; but will with the temptation also make a way to escape, that ye may be able to bear it."
(1 Corinthians 10:13)

"HE WHO HAS BEGUN A GOOD WORK ..."

"Being confident of this very thing, that he which hath begun a good work in you will perform it until the day of Jesus Christ." (Philippians 1:6)

God allows you to go through the "fire" so that He can purify you from the imperfections in your flesh. He knows just how hot to make it so that every unclean spirit seeking to attach itself to your life is purged away. He does not want His children wrestling with spirits of fear, doubt, pride, anger, bitterness, envy, strife or the like. God knows the exact nature of the test or trial needed in order to purge you of every spiritual imperfection.

God carefully orchestrates every test and trial so that it accomplishes the "cleansing" in your life that He desires. He also knows exactly the right situation to place you in so that you would experience His power of deliverance.

Always remember that God is in the midst of every situation in your life. He is not trying to hurt you; He wants to help you. God's ultimate will, purpose and plan for you is that you be conformed to the image of His Son. Again, His desire is that the Spirit of Christ be formed in you. This means He is committed, focused, meticulous, diligent and faithful when it comes to the work that He is doing in your life. He does not haphazardly send tests and trials to your life. However, if He allows them, they are there to accomplish a specific purpose.

God sits as a skilled silversmith with eager anticipation, for He knows that upon completion of the purging process there will emerge a vessel so refined, so magnificent, that its price will soar beyond earthly value.

In *Hebrews 11*, the Word of God talks about the apostles and how they walked this earth as *"ones of whom the world was not worthy."* The anointing on your life is so precious that God will bruise you, press you, crush you, and allow you to go into the fire in order to purge you from the realm of your carnal flesh and un-rejuvenated soul. He does this so that the pureness of what He breathed into your spirit at inception can come forth.

THE PAIN IS NECESSARY FOR YOUR PROGRESS

"Thou has caused men to ride over our heads; we went through fire and through water; but thou broughtest us out into a wealthy place." (Psalm 66:12)

I am sure you will agree that, from the time God gave you a promise to the point where it manifested the process was, at times, unusually difficult. This "process" is the place between "here and there," or what I call the place of *divine* preparation. It is divine because God ordains and designs it with you in mind. It is tailor-made and uniquely engineered by God to produce a specific outcome in your life.

God also sets in place processes and procedures to achieve *His* desired results. God is divine and all-powerful. His desire is that we become more and more like Him. No two individuals are alike; neither are their processes "equally identical".

If you are going through a difficult time in your life, you may have come to a place in the process where your transition seems to be unbearable, and even overwhelming. For the most part, it is filled with tests, trials and much uncertainty. You must begin to embrace the fact that where you are is exactly where God wants you to be – even if only for this season. Moreover, the things that you are going through are designed to usher you into a blessed place.

"For which cause we faint not; but though our outward man perish, yet the inward man is renewed day by day."
(2 Corinthians 4:16)

I want to encourage you to go through your process however difficult it may seem. If you would be completely honest, you know that you learned to pray more fervently when you were faced with adversity. You also know that after surviving your last trial your priorities have changed and you have learned to value the "gift of life."

Once you pass your test, you will begin to embrace life in a different manner. You have now emerged with a greater level of compassion, love, peace, patience and now find yourself refined, walking in a higher dimension of the anointing and more mature *"fruit of the spirit."*

In other words, as you walk in a more refined fruit of the spirit, you become a better or more authentic representation of the spirit of Christ. If you do not abort the process, but endure to the end, you will see that there was purpose behind every pain!

"YOU HAVE BEEN DISPOSITIONED IN ORDER TO BE REPOSITIONED FOR A SPIRITUAL TRANSITION!"

CHAPTER TEN

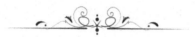

"CARRY ME OUT, I AM WOUNDED!"

HEALING FOR THE WOUNDED

Have you ever been wounded in your life? Can you remember the pain and trauma you felt as you tried to "process" what had just happened to you? Being wounded is one thing; knowing how to deal with someone else who has been wounded is another.

To *"be wounded"* means to be damaged, impaired or injured; mishandled, hurt or afflicted. It is a tragedy or, rather, a modern day "conundrum" that most people in today's society do not know how to accommodate or properly care for people who have been hurt. In fact, those who are "wounded" are often viewed as weak, degenerate and deserving of mistreatment. In *Luke 10:30–35,* Jesus clearly teaches us how to minister to wounded people in the parable of the "Good Samaritan."

The man who was beaten and robbed on his way from Jerusalem to Jericho was placed on the Samaritan's donkey and taken to a nearby inn or hospital for excellent medical care. This Samaritan by the way, was a total stranger of a different race and class than the man who had been wounded. However, the Samaritan was moved with such compassion that he paid the wounded man's bills and did what was necessary to care for the man's wounds.

God, no doubt, wants you to develop a practice or skill for helping to heal the wounds of others. Once we learn how to care for the wounded and love them beyond measure, we will begin to see them rise above their adversities.

"CARRY ME OUT, I'M WOUNDED!"

"...So Ahab said to his chariot driver, Turn, carry me out of the battle, for I am wounded." (2 Chronicles 18:33 AMP)

Have you ever been to a place in your life where you were busy in the kingdom and became wounded? There are numerous people that I know of who truly loved God but were critically injured in the midst of battle. This percentage is high, especially for those at the forefront of ministry, namely apostles, prophets, evangelists, pastors and teachers, who may find themselves needing to say, *"Carry me out, I am wounded!"*

Although this is true for the leaders and those at the forefront of ministry, this does not negate the number of casualties which also exist in the lives of ordinary people. I have seen many people *not* on the frontline of ministry, such as an usher at the door, who were also wounded in battle while serving in various aspects of the Church. Many such casualties have ensued, while others remain oblivious.

As the Body of Christ, we need to be in a spiritually discerning posture to perceive that someone is suffering in silence. It is important that we "pull these people to the sideline" or a place where they can be medically and spiritually restored. As a believer, it is important that your armour is securely fastened around you so that you do not become a casualty of war.

Sometimes when struck by the arrows of the enemy it appears difficult for frontline warriors to simply "turn aside" from the battle. Instead, most of them feel the need to "stay on board" fighting and leading while severely hemorrhaging. What they do not realize is that failure to tend to their wounds may result in them becoming "spiritually anemic", and they run the risk of bleeding to death.

In *2 Chronicles 18:33* King Ahab was struck by an arrow while fighting the Syrian army. Once he realized that he was hit, he begged his servant to take him out of the battle because he was wounded.

Similarly, in *2 Samuel 21:17* David found himself having to do the same thing when his men noticed that he was sick, weak and unable to continue in battle. Understanding the value and the importance of King David's survival, even for the whole house of Israel, his men went to battle and fought for him while he was left in a safe place. This gave David sufficient time to heal and regain his strength.

It is very important to note that exiting the battlefield does not mean that you have turned back, given up or surrendered to the will of your enemies. During your time of "retreat", your recovery may entail "re-strategizing" and regrouping through times of concentrated prayer, worship, reading, studying, declaring the Word of God and the like.

Whenever you find yourself wounded in battle, regardless of your rank or position, you must seek God for refuge in order to be restored, revived and totally healed.

BATTLEWORN

Many times people become overwhelmed when faced with the day-to-day challenges of life. In some instances, the struggle for survival can prove to be difficult and can foster a sense of hopelessness. Nevertheless, true warriors never give up and are not easily defeated. Even if they become critically wounded and weary on the "battlefield" they will continue fighting to gain the victory. I have had numerous experiences of this nature as I, too, have had to deal with satanic missiles which came to overwhelm me.

"RETREAT IS NOT ALWAYS A SIGN OF WEAKNESS; IN SOME INSTANCES IT IS AN ACT OF WISDOM!"

I have learned that you have the power to choose whether or not to allow life's tests and trials to consume you. It is God who gives you power to overcome every demonic oppression, suppression, depression and ultimate possession of the enemy.

- **Oppression** is the feeling of being heavily burdened, mentally or physically, by troubles, adverse conditions, anxiety and the like, which seek to bring you into bondage. Oppression can come about as a result of something that happens to you by way of exterior forces which bring you under heavy, harsh or cruel captivity. As a result of your being "weighed down" the enemy then seizes the opportunity to further afflict you with spirits of doubt, fear, torment or discouragement. Oppression makes you feel helpless or powerless and can create a "slave-like" mentality. Prolonged oppression may eventually lead to suppression.

   The Word of God encourages you in Luke 21:34 that we are not to become overburdened or consumed by the cares of life.

- **Suppression** occurs as a result of external forces which adversely affect the mind to such a degree that they subdue you and make you feel trapped and restricted. Further, suppression represents a failure to develop to your fullest potential and can put you in a state of mental slavery to the point where you may not be able to function; instead of progressing, you may find yourself stagnant or in a state of regression. Prolonged suppression takes you to the next level of demonic bondage, which is depression.

  The Word of God encourages you in Galatians 5:1 that we are to stand fast in the liberty wherewith Christ has made us free and not be entangled again in a yoke of bondage.

- **Depression** is a condition of extreme sadness which can occur as a result of prolonged periods of suppression. Due to a lack of development and prolonged suppression you can become depressed. In this depressed state your mind and body may begin to "shut down". Further you may become dysfunctional and daily tasks may become overwhelming and challenging. Chronic depression may eventually open the door for demonic entrance into your life, ultimately leading to demonic possession.

  The Word of God admonishes you in Psalm 42:11 that you do not have to be cast down in your soul, you can hope in God.

- **Demonic Possession** is a condition or state where you may have become vulnerable, thus opening the door to demon spirits who enter your life; taking complete control.

  The Word of God encourages you in Colossians 1:13 (AMP) that the Father "has delivered *and* drawn us to Himself out of the control *and* the dominion of darkness and has transferred us into the kingdom of the Son of His love."

STRESS: A "SATANIC" KILLER
"A false balance is abomination to the Lord: ..." (Proverbs 11:1)

Believe me when I tell you *stress can kill you.* Stress is your body's way of responding to some type of excessive demand or requirement that has been placed upon it, whether stimulated by a good or bad event. It is a feeling that is created when you react to something that has happened to you such as being violated or mugged. It can also arise due to something that you have experienced such as witnessing the tragic death of a loved one.

The enemy will create challenging situations then sit back and watch your responses to them. Can you imagine the strain placed on the body when you allow stress and frustration to linger? This increase in the mind's activity sends a message to your body that it is being invaded. It therefore goes into attack mode, increasing the production of adrenalin in the body. Unfortunately, when the body cannot find anything to attack in response to the stress, it attacks itself and, eventually, breaks down.

Self-afflicted stress is a "satanic" killer.

In the midst of all that is required of you, you must be in a position to operate and function in a balanced manner. In *Proverbs 11:1* the Word reveals that a "false balance" is an abomination to God. You must do everything in your power to keep the doors of your life closed to demonic oppression in any form.

Jesus gave *you* the key to stop every satanic infiltration in your life and to release the power of God so that His favor, blessings and increase will cause *you* to prosper. *Do Not Stress!*

It is the plan of the enemy to bombard your life with so much activity that you do not find the time to go into the presence of God to get the refreshing that you need. In the midst of your daily routine, you must find time to spend with God, for in His presence there is fullness of joy and at His right hand there are pleasures forevermore. *(Psalm 16:11)*

I HAD A "NERVOUS BREAKDOWN ...!"

I somewhat "skirted" around this topic in an effort to avoid speaking about it. In my opinion, out of everything that I have spoken about, this is by far the most difficult to share. Why? Because no leader, pastor or anybody wants to ever admit that they have had a "nervous breakdown" or that they have gone through a season where they became "burnt out." I mentioned in *Chapter Five: "This Is My Story!"* how I had gone through a season of relentless warfare. I was under a severe attack and became so ill that I lost my desire to fight.

During that season of my life when I was greatly afflicted, I lost my memory and, with it, I felt as if I had lost my mind. This was particularly devastating because I always prided myself on my ability to remember everything and quote entire chapters of the Bible. However, after this horrific ordeal, I could barely remember anything. I found myself at such a low place in my life and discovered that in order to rebound I had to follow a daily routine of quoting the scriptures and earnestly praying my way into a "sound mind." God literally rebuilt and restored my mind.

A STRONG WORD OF ADVICE:
"LOSE EVERYTHING, BUT KEEP YOUR MIND!"

It is a commonly held perception that if you have a nervous breakdown, you are weak. That is not necessarily so. The truth is there are scores of people around the world including doctors, lawyers, bankers, corporate executives and pastors who have all experienced some level of mental distress.

In some churches there are many people, including pastors' wives, who are stretched and stressed beyond measure and are on the verge of having a "nervous breakdown", or who may have already had one. If you find yourself in such a dilemma there is no need to be ashamed. Moreover, God still loves you and has designed a healing plan for you.

Whenever someone experiences a nervous breakdown there is a commonly held belief that this is a sign they may have been completely "stressed out", stretched beyond their limit or have experienced some trauma to their soul. This is evidenced in the life of some people who may go through a divorce, the loss of a loved one, a rash of traumatic incidences, exploitation by authority abusers, and the like.

Moreover, we are seeing this happening every day in the lives of believers. One may ask the following questions: "Are they *weak*?; Is this an attack from the enemy?; or Are they simply experiencing a test, like Job?" Whatever the conclusion, you should render prayer for them, get in the fight on their behalf and administer healing and deliverance.

"SPIRITUAL NERVOUS BREAKDOWN"

There is a form of "Church Hurt" that demobilizes some people who sincerely love God but have been severely hurt and abused in the Church. These are people who may have come to the Ministry loving God, with a pure heart and willing to serve, but the enemy released an onslaught of attacks, working on their "spiritual nerve" and afflicting their soul, using others in the ministry to bring offense and disappointment, in order to frustrate their progress or purpose.

Over time, many of these people experience what I call a *spiritual nervous breakdown*. They become numb, disillusioned and begin to disconnect from the Church and the things of God. Similarly, even if they regularly attend Church they exist as "spiritual zombies" in the pew and become totally disheartened with God and anything related to God.

It is vitally important to understand that the hurt people of whom I speak are not those operating in a spirit of Jezebel, rebellion, or disobedience. Neither are they fault-finders, easily offended, thin-skinned or unwilling to change; those groups are who I call the *"she-bellions, militia-ites, terror-ites", and other "ites"* in the Church.

A person suffering from a *spiritual nervous breakdown* also exhibits other spiritual maladies and may become non-responsive, apathetic, bitter, angry, offended, outrightly antagonistic, critical, and more. Eventually, many of them leave the church. Some of them, however, remain and suffer in silence, slipping into a backslidden *"comotosed"* state, while others become a menace, engaging in all-out warfare against the church and turning into ungodly insurrectionists, redirecting their efforts now to discrediting the church, and undermining its leadership.

These people remain in the church having a personal vendetta bred out of hatred, spewing bitter venom upon every activity, operation and function as they tear down the Church. If you are not careful their poisonous disgruntlement will spread like a cancer, infecting the lives of others.

The Pitfall, Downfall and Mistake of A Believer

Whenever someone falls or makes a mistake, how we choose to deal with them is extremely important. Many people are trapped in the snare of shame, gilt and condemnation because of a mistake they have made or some sin they have committed. The enemy uses the guilt of their mistake to discourage them and further push them away from God. It is not the will of God that His people be bound by any oppression of the enemy. Therefore, we should seek to restore or re-instate them, in brotherly love. *If we find our brother taken in a fault, we should restore that one in the spirit of meekness. (Galatians 6:1)*

Unfortunately, some people choose to place themselves in a position where they become unreachable. As a result of the spirit of pride, many such people hide themselves behind the sham of the spirit of guilt and shame; not realizing that this deceiving spirit of pride is the strong man that is keeping them bound.

Likewise, there are some people who retreat into a shell because they feel that "no one cares" and no one will probably understand what they are going through. These are all demonic entrapments used by the enemy to further perpetuate his ultimate plan to kill, steal and destroy. *(John 10:10)*

If you have made a mistake or committed some sin, I believe that your first position should be to pray and seek God for forgiveness and divine direction. Then you should find a spiritual authority that you can confide in and with whom you can be transparent.

If you do not address your issue with your spiritual leader or some other person in a position of spiritual authority, then you are going to succumb to your affliction. If you feel as though you are unable to address your issue with your pastor, then you should find another person in spiritual authority in whom to confide. The truth is, if your spiritual leader leaves you alone, you will die. If you die, there is a possibility that you will die hopeless, thinking there was no help available.

REMEMBER: *"ISOLATION IS A SATANIC DEATH TRAP!"*

You must realize that there is help available to you; there is something that God can divinely inspire your spiritual leader to speak into your spirit that can improve your situation. You do not have to stay in isolation or bound by the lies and deception of the enemy. God can restore you, regardless of whatever mistake you have made *(Psalm 23:3)*.

THE BREAKING POINT

It should be understood that everyone has what I call a "breaking point" or limit on how far they can go and the level of stress they are able to endure.

Once this breaking point is reached, you may begin to experience various emotional, mental and physical signs, such as lethargy, exhaustion, depression, isolation and mental fatigue; not wanting to be bothered by anyone. You may also appear to have lost some resilience as a result of the pressure felt.

"Thou wilt keep him in perfect peace, whose mind is stayed on thee: because he trusteth in thee." (Isaiah 26:3)

If you feel as though you are under any level of attack, it is incumbent upon you to wage war against the enemy and gain immediate control of your mind. Many times people who are on the brink of a breakdown are left alone to suffer, in some cases because the people around them are unaware of their struggle. The enemy stands a greater chance of gaining an advantage over you whenever you are left to fight a battle alone.

When the spirit of death seeks to destroy your mind, it bombards you with a series of failures, heartaches, pain and negative thoughts in an effort to *push you over the brink.*

The mind *is* the greatest battlefield. The enemy already knows that if you lose your mind; you will lose in every area of your life. Being no respecter of persons, the enemy targets everyone: the old and the young, the affluent and the poor, male and female, black or white, it does not matter.

The enemy typically uses subtle tactics of depressive thoughts and mind battles in an effort to overwhelm you. He will then inundate you with the "cares of life" until you implode. If you are ever in this position, it is very important that those around you take measures to help you through the experience and facilitate a healthy recovery.

A nervous breakdown can occur gradually but I believe that it negatively affects every aspect of a person's life immediately. This is evidenced by the malfunction of their mind, will, intellect, emotions and physical demeanor. This is a subtle, strategic attack that the enemy wages against your mind in an attempt to cause you to have a debilitating mental breakdown. However, just as Jesus can heal you physically, He can also heal you mentally. *(Isaiah 53:5)*

Many people who have suffered a nervous breakdown tend to hide it for fear of how they may be viewed by others. In fact, in most families it is kept hidden and "swept under the rug" in order to avoid shame or embarrassment.

It is vitally important that you fight to avoid ever experiencing a "breakdown". However, if you have a nervous breakdown, know that it is not the end of the world and your life is not over. God is faithful and as He has promised, He will deliver you.

Recovery and Preventative Measures

The following are steps you can take to recover from or prevent a nervous breakdown:
- Put on the whole armor of God
- Rely on the grace of God to help you overcome

- Pray for peace of mind
- Do not allow yourself to be overwhelmed by the cares of life
- Protect your mind, body, soul and spirit
- Know when to rest
- Know when to say "no"
- Know your limitations and regulate what comes into your life

If you or someone you know is at a breaking point, it is important that you pray a prayer of peace and take authority over every spirit of heaviness in Jesus' name. *Psalm 91* is an excellent scripture that speaks of God's divine protection over your life and against the relentless onslaught of the enemy.

WARFARE AT THE GATES
"Mind Battles!"

God has already devised a master plan to keep and protect you. The enemy seeks to launch an all-out diabolical attack against the people of God that is designed to destroy the life of the believer.

"Di-abolical" *speaks to the fact that it is a* two-fold attack occurring in more than one realm or dimension. The attack has been launched in the realm of the spirit but has targeted the soul.

In this warfare, you will find that a person's mind, will, intellect and emotions are under siege. The enemy bombards the realm of the soul with demonic thoughts, feelings and emotions of doubt, fear, unbelief, hopelessness, defeat, discouragement and more. It is his ultimate plan to bring so much confusion and distractions to your mind that you become frustrated and eventually give up. If you are going to win this attack against the enemy, you must first wage strategic warfare and position yourself to win this battle in the realm of the spirit.

During many of the deliverance sessions that I conducted I realized that many of the ailments people were complaining about in their physical body were, subsequently, due to what was going on in their souls.

In such cases, people had literally maladapted and begun to take on the very nature of the unclean spirits that were taunting them. As a result, these demon spirits sometimes hid in the cavities of the soul of the person, eventually attaching themselves to various organs in the body. These demonic invasions in the soul actually caused organs or systems in the afflicted person's body to malfunction. *Such malfunctions manifest in the form of numerous ailments, diseases and in some cases traumatic disorders.*

For example negative emotions such as:

- Self-hatred, bitterness, resentment and unforgiveness can cause multiple sclerosis, rheumatoid arthritis, lupus, chronic joint pain, ulcers, cysts, fibroids a list of autoimmune disorders and more
- Hatred, anger and hostility towards others can cause heart disease, hypertension and strokes.
- Holding or repressing anger can cause back and joint pains, fibromyalgia, migraines and much more.
- Fear and anxiety can cause breathing disorders, irritable bowels, and palpitations.

It is true that *stress* is known as the "silent killer." It is said to be the body's response to adversity, triggering the release of various hormones, toxins and other harmful agents which can cause the body to deteriorate.

For many people their first resolve is to "medicate" their symptoms without seriously considering that there may be a deeper-seated root to the problem they currently face. Please understand, I do believe that medication may serve a purpose in helping to treat a symptom. However, I also believe that in some cases, in order to receive ultimate healing, some people must be prepared to deal with underlying issues such as hurt, pain, rejection, bitterness and negative mindsets. This would bring the total healing in mind, body and soul.

THE BATTERING RAM

The spirit of death sometimes works like a battering ram. This relentless spirit "beats" and "hits" at your soul just like a battering ram on the iron gates of a city until it breaks through. The pressures of life seek to "knock" at your mind, day after day until you become weakened, frail and ready to give in.

Whether it is a "battering ram" or a "straw lightly stroking a camel's back", do not allow anyone or anything, great or small, to "overpower you to death." This means, do not allow anything to push you to the point where you want to give up or die!

Just as the enemy has used the concept of the battering ram to bombard your mind to defeat you, you should seek to use the concept of a battering ram through prayer to break through the onslaught of the enemy.

THE EMBATTLED MIND

As mentioned earlier, it is very important to understand that whenever satan wants to attack your life, he usually targets your mind. The battle in the mind is a "one on one" combat with an archenemy whose only motive is to destroy and totally wipe you out. It begins as a silent, non-verbal warfare in the emotional and mental arena of the soul.

Satan suggests and launches thoughts of incompetency, inadequacy, failure and the like. He sends a barrage of "mental missiles" to torment and frustrate you into believing that you are "no good", useless and serve absolutely no purpose.

In **Proverbs 4:23**, the Word of God admonishes you to keep your heart with all diligence, for out it flows the issues of life. In this context, the "heart" refers to the soul and mind. God wants you to protect your mind and keep it guarded because this is the arena that satan attacks in an effort to destroy you completely. Eventually you become what you think.

According to **Proverbs 23:7 (AMP)** *"... As a man thinks in his heart, so is he."* When you entertain negative thoughts in your mind, you will eventually begin to speak them out of your mouth. Your words are powerful and they immediately begin to form pictures that take on motion. They become what I call, *"motion pictures"*.

It is your words that both justify and condemn you. Whenever I found myself in the midst of gruesome mind battles, I had to take authority over the *"raging warfare."* No matter how many scriptures I read, I realized that if I was going to live I had to fully engage my mind in order to counteract the attacks that were coming against me. Inundating my mind with the scriptures, ultimately gave me the victory.

It has always been said that the eye is the gateway to the soul. Therefore, the renewal of the mind positions you to embrace a new perception of the kingdom whereby you begin to see yourself as God sees you. Once I changed the way I thought, my spiritual vision became clearer. I began seeing things differently. I saw myself as a child of the king seated with Christ in heavenly places. I began to speak differently. This changed the way I responded to every situation. The moment I began thinking, seeing, speaking and applying God's Word to my life, I saw dramatic changes in my health.

You have the power in Jesus' name, to win the warfare at the gates of your soul. Trust the Spirit of God and begin leaving every battlefield with total victory as you boldly declare the Word of God.

WHEN THE PROPHET BECOMES THE PROPHECY

It is certain that you will pay a price to function in any level of the anointing. Any great man or woman of God can attest to the fact that they did not just become powerful overnight but that there was a process.

There was a season in my life I realized that the prophecies I had spoken over the lives of others to bring them through their seasons of afflictions, were the very same prophecies, I had to declare the same words over my life if I was going to survive.

I had to "pull on the same grace" to overcome. I then realized that when I could not find anyone to prophesy me to my breakthrough I had to prophesy myself to the place where I needed to be. In this I, as the prophet, became the prophecy.

THE MOUNT CARMEL EXPERIENCE
"Calling Fire Down From Heaven"

Just like Elijah, you may have an experience where God uses you mightily but you are later confronted with challenges. In *1 Kings 18:30–33* the Word of God gives an account of how God uses Elijah to call fire down from heaven, but he is later attacked.

"30And Elijah said unto all the people, Come near unto me. And all the people came near unto him. And he repaired the altar of the LORD that was broken down.

---

³¹And Elijah took twelve stones, according to the number of the tribes of the sons of Jacob, unto whom the word of the LORD came, saying, Israel shall be thy name:
³²And with the stones he built an altar in the name of the LORD: and he made a trench about the altar, as great as would contain two measures of seed.
³³And he put the wood in order, and cut the bullock in pieces, and laid him on the wood, and said, Fill four barrels with water, and pour it on the burnt sacrifice, and on the wood."

It is important to note that during Elijah's confrontation, he had expended a lot of energy. Not only did he have to resist the wickedness of eight hundred and fifty false prophets, according to the Word of God, he also:

- *Repaired the altar of the Lord that was broken down*
- *Found and brought twelve stones*
- *Built an altar with the twelve stones*
- *Dug a trench around the altar*
- *Gathered wood and laid them, in order, on the altar*
- *Cut the sacrifice in pieces and placed them on the altar*
- *Had the men that were there to pour water on the altar*

We know the end of the encounter and the great victory that was won that day and that is the part we all get excited about. We love to celebrate how God sent fire down from heaven, humiliated and eventually killed eight hundred and fifty false prophets, how the hearts of the people returned to God and how they experienced one of the greatest Revivals of that day.

In our Bibles, this passage of scripture is highlighted, underlined and filled with asterisks and exclamation points because we desire to be used of God in the same way. *There is nothing wrong with that!*

However, we must also consider what happens when the encounter is over, the lights are out, the people all go home to talk about "what a move of God that was" but, in some cases, the man or woman of God goes home ... *alone.*

UNDER THE "JUNIPER TREE"

There comes a time in your life where you may have an "Elijah" experience. Many people can identify with the "Elijah" on the mountaintop calling fire down from heaven but cannot relate to the "Elijah" under the juniper tree suffering from discouragement. This is why I encourage resting or a time of spiritual refueling in the presence of God.

As we can see, Elijah had just called down fire from heaven, slain the false prophets but yet found himself under a Juniper tree wrestling with the thought of dying. I believe that he was suffering from spiritual exhaustion, and the need to be spiritually revived and rejuvenated.

Many times, you may experience varying degrees of discouragement and disappointment because you are:
- Overworked
- Under much stress
- "Burnt out" and vulnerable
- Under an extreme demonic attack
- Overtaken by what is going on around you

These extreme attacks leave some people battling for their lives, their ministry and even their relationship with God. Elijah ran away, sat under a Juniper tree and wished to die, not because he was *not* courageous or did not believe in God, but I believe that he ended up in a state of depression because he was *overly tired.*

Just like Elijah, you may find yourself battling with spirits of discouragement after God uses you in a mighty way. I have found myself in this same position on numerous occasions. Many times after I have ministered under the anointing of God and there is a major move of God

After hearing a powerful sermon, people may go home and watch television however, the "prophet" goes home, enters the shower ... and weeps!

through my ministry, I would find myself needing to be refreshed.

You should take some time to be refreshed after the spirit of God has used you. Although I am sometimes tired after ministering, I have to find time to get in prayer and allow the presence of God to refresh me. We saw this throughout the life and ministry of Jesus, whenever He was finished with His revival services, He always found time to retreat to the other side where He prayed, ate and rested until the next Crusade.

BINDING UP THE BROKEN-HEARTED

" 1...he hath sent me to bind up the brokenhearted, to proclaim liberty to the captives, and the opening of the prison to them that are bound;

2 To proclaim the acceptable year of the LORD, and the day of vengeance of our God; to comfort all that mourn;..."

(Isaiah 61:1-2)

I believe that there are too many people suffering from a broken heart in today's society. Many of them have been hurt and devastated by some adversity that caused severe pain and anguish. In most instances, this pain emanated from rejection, neglect, abandonment, separation, divorce, the death of a loved one and more. These people tend to find themselves in a place of emotional and mental distress, exhibiting grief, uncontrollable sorrow, depression and generalized isolation.

I believe that a broken heart can open the door to various demonic attacks, which provides easier access to spirits of infirmity and may even lead to suicide or death.

"A merry heart doeth good like a medicine: but a broken spirit drieth the bones." (Proverbs 17:22)

Over the years, I have had to administer deliverance to so many people who were on prescription drugs while their condition was only getting worse. The Spirit of God began to reveal to me that the root cause of their problems was a broken or "shattered" heart. Whenever I conducted these mass deliverance and healing services for the broken hearted there would be scores of people *(men, women and children)* weeping.

In fact, once the presence of God entered the building, I saw chains breaking off of people's lives like a thread popping off of the feet of an elephant. I watched grown men who were imprisoned in their mind cry out for deliverance from the bondage of their past wounds. Children who were gravely ill, and even some who displayed erratic behaviors, were changed once healed from their broken hearts.

God wants you and I to "bind up the broken-hearted". His will is that none should perish but, rather, that every wounded soul should receive total healing and deliverance. Being healed from a broken heart takes courage and the process can only begin with the willingness to forgive those who have hurt you.

"The Lord is nigh unto them that are of a broken heart; and saveth such as be of a contrite spirit." (Psalm 34:18)

"YOU HAVE TOO MUCH TO LIVE FOR!"

I believe that many people give up on life because they feel as though they do not have anything to live for. In my season of affliction, I can remember being so overwhelmed by what was going on around me that I felt as though I wanted to give up. The encouragement of my husband, beautiful children and grandchildren inspired me to keep going.

I know that some of you can share the same testimony of going through some of the most difficult times in your life and coming to the realization that God was not finished with you yet. Wherever you may find yourself in life, just hold on because you have too much to live for.

Although Elijah's Juniper tree experience was a place of depression and discouragement, God used that place to prepare him with an anointing for the next generation. Later in *1 Kings 19*, God used Elijah to anoint Elisha, Jehu and Hazael into their kingdom assignments. If you can endure whatever you are going through right now, God will give you the anointing to mantle the next generation of world-changers.

CHAPTER ELEVEN

THE STING OF BETRAYAL

THE STING OF BETRAYAL

Have you ever been betrayed by a trusted friend, relative or anyone else for that matter? I know firsthand what betrayal feels like. It is one of the most painful and heart–wrenching experiences that anyone could imagine. Betrayal can penetrate the very core of your being and pierce the soul. I have known people who were betrayed and it took them years to rebound.

"Paradidomi", the Greek word for "betray" which is also the root word of "betrayal" appears one hundred and twenty-one (121) times in the Greek New Testament.

Further, it can be translated into several English words meaning:
- to be false or disloyal to
- a breach in the confidence of
- to give information or aid to any enemy of

- to commit treason against
- the violation of a trust or allegiance
- to deliver into the hands of the enemy

THE SEAT OF BETRAYAL

The seat of betrayal is envy, jealousy and strife *(James 3:16)*. By definition "jealousy" is an envious resentment of someone or their achievement, possession and *perceived advantages*. On the other hand, "envy" is defined as *a feeling of discontented or resentful longing aroused by someone else's possessions, qualities,* or good fortune.

A spirit of covetousness motivates the seat of envy and causes you to desire what another person has. The seat of jealousy is motivated by an adverse anger, hatred or deep dislike for someone. It is fueled by one person's animosity towards another based on what the other person has or the perception of what the other person has. The spirit of jealousy can provoke you to literally destroy or even kill.

The seat of strife is motivated by a spirit of dissatisfaction with or a strong disapproval of someone or something. When a person is operating in strife they will spitefully inflict distress, promote contention or cause discouragement.

According to *James 3:16, where envying and strife is, there is confusion and every evil work."* In other words, these forces will drive somebody to betray you and are breeding grounds where spiritual contaminants fester and grow. Therefore, betrayal is a heinous, evil crime carried out by people possessed with spirits of jealousy, envy and strife. This is what I call the seat of betrayal.

"THE ENEMY WITHIN THE CAMP"

The Roman Empire ruled supreme by economic, political and military might and was known to be a formidable empire. After numerous failed attempts, no one from the outside could conquer the city or overthrow its ruler, Julius Caesar (100 – 44 BC). Therefore, Rome became known as the impregnable city.

History also records, that the enemy convinced Brutus, Caesar's trusted friend and servant, to betray him by stabbing him in the back. This betrayal was the catalyst the enemy used to topple the entire Roman Empire.

The spirit of death will come after you at one of the weakest moments in your life. It is amazing how people expect you to be strong and can set "unfair" expectations on you as a Christian. Many times the enemy will use your times of weakness and despair to launch his greatest attacks against your life.

Many years ago I was betrayed by someone I trusted. The betrayal was so painful that it took me some time to get over it. It takes some people time to get over the pain of the betrayal because in that moment they are so hurt and devastated by what has happened that they feel as though they will never get over it. This is due in part to the fact that they have shared intimate details of their lives with this person who can no longer be trusted. This now leaves them feeling uncovered, vulnerable and even violated. *The hurt is what happens but the pain is what lingers.*

The question may arise, "How could they and why would they do this to me?" Eventually I rebounded gaining a few valuable lessons in the process. No matter what you go through in life, there is always a lesson that you can learn and, no doubt, teach someone else.

THE SPIRIT OF BRUTUS STILL LIVES
"Et Tu Brute'?"

It was Judas who betrayed Jesus, his spiritual leader, and Brutus who assassinated his friend, Julius Caesar. For both of these great men, their saboteurs were not strangers but people who walked closely and intimately with them.

While you do not want to build walls of mistrust and suspicion, there is a need to use much wisdom in every season of your life. Therefore, it is of paramount importance that you continually discern the hearts of those around you. The spirit of sabotage and death can move in your life if you allow people to become overly familiar with you, especially when you have not established boundaries or limitations.

In *Psalm 55:12–13* even the Psalmist David speaks of the devastation felt after being betrayed by a close friend:

"12For it was not an enemy that reproached me; then I could have borne it: neither was it he that hated me that did magnify himself against me; then I would have hid myself from him: 13But it was thou,...mine acquaintance."

It was Brutus' betrayal that brought the demise of Julius Caesar, one of the greatest rulers of Rome and ultimately destroyed an entire empire. Brutus, the man may be dead, but the spirit of Brutus still lives on today. Hence, my word of advice is you should not hastily trust someone to the extent that you *totally* let your guard down around them. People sometimes may mistake your meekness for weakness. Hence, you must continue to guard your heart and mind from the possible "sting of betrayal."

THE CURSE OF GEHAZI

I believe that one of the reasons why so many leaders in the Body of Christ have been "compromised" is because they have innocently opened their lives to the "wrong" people, or allowed people to walk with them who may not have been prepared for this level of assignment.

Some of these people were not able to appreciate walking in such close proximity to a man or woman of God. Some leaders have opened up and embraced these individuals simply because they expressed their willingness to follow or serve that leader. Ultimately, they were not spiritually equipped for that level of responsibility! They either abused their position, took their leaders for granted or simply refused to change, eventually causing more harm than good.

In *2 Kings 5* the Word of God reveals how Gehazi, Elisha's servant, pursued wealth and possessions from Namaan, a Syrian Leader who was healed of leprosy by the Prophet Elisha. Following his healing, Namaan sought to bless the Prophet with various gifts in order to demonstrate his appreciation but Elisha did not wish to accept his gift.

However, later in the chapter, Gehazi betrays the wishes of his leader by operating in deception and greed. Gehazi secretly persuaded Namaan to give him the gifts which Elisha had previously refused. Eventually, God revealed to Elisha what Gehazi had done. This betrayal resulted in a curse of leprosy being released on Gehazi's life and his entire family.

It is very important that servant leaders understand that God requires faithfulness and loyalty from them as they serve in any level of ministry. Many people are attracted to the "lime light" and power which is sometimes associated with ministry. However, these same people are not prepared to endure the sacrifice necessary to serve effectively.

As a servant leader, called to walk with a man or woman of God, you are required to live a consecrated life, first before God and then before your leaders. If you are not careful, instead of being a blessing, you may become a curse, hindrance or even an enemy.

"ANYTHING THAT YOU PERCEIVE OR PURSUE AS A BLESSING, CAN BECOME A CURSE IF IT IS NOT THE WILL OF GOD FOR YOUR LIFE."

THE MAKING OF YOUR ENEMY

Leaders do not extend the right hand of fellowship to someone with the mindset that one day this same person will become their enemy. A leader never believes that a member of his church will take all of the biblical teaching and training received and use it against the leadership.

It is amazing how people will join a church as babes in Christ, receive a revelation about the kingdom of God and esteem themselves as "experts", "qualified" and "certified" to function in various areas of ministry. However, when these same people who think they are "strong" in the things of God begin to gain the respect of others, they may either betray or even "turn their backs on" their leaders.

In some cases, where they were once *praying for* their leader, they may now find themselves *praying against* their leader. These things should not exist in the Body of Christ, yet these types of betrayal are happening every day. Further, it is this type of betrayal that generates the confusion that causes many churches to split.

The enemy knows that in order to destroy you as a leader, he has to raise up or "possess" someone who has already infiltrated your system – these are the people you taught who inadvertently become a tool in the hands of the enemy.

As a leader, you may never be aware of the identity of your enemy. Some people come into your ministry very sincere and willing to serve but may become contaminated over a period of time. It is very important that you remain in a discerning position, encouraging those who walk with you to continue to pray that they do not "weaken their guard" and allow the enemy to use them.

MY SERVANT IS SICK
"The Spirit of Death In The Church & Workplace!"

A *"servant"* is a person who humbly submits himself to perform duties for others, without hidden agendas, underlying motives or impure intentions. A true servant is necessary in almost every arena in life and is vitally important to the overall success of organizations. Some of these "servant" positions include, but are not limited to: secretaries, receptionists, bodyguards, chauffeurs, housekeepers, nannies, maids, ushers, protocol officers, security officers, ministers, deacons and, especially armorbearers.

In the truest sense we are all servants regardless of what title or position we hold in the kingdom. Therefore, we should all posture ourselves to surrender our gifts in serving the King. In *Matthew 23:11, Jesus said that he who will be greatest among you, let him first serve.*

Some of the following are qualities of a good servant:
- a trusted servant is willing to bear the armor of his leader; (assists his leader with fulfilling his assignment, call or duties)
- a faithful servant goes beyond the call of duty
- someone who is willing to sacrifice himself for the benefit of others
- someone who is willing to give of himself freely and unselfishly to someone else

- someone who is loyal and dedicated to the call of God, the ministry and to the one they are called to serve;
- someone who is willing to protect his leader
- *someone who is a true warrior and serves with a pure heart.*

Every great leader knows that the strength of his organization depends on the strength of those serving with him. Just like every President needs servants, kings and queens need courtiers, and every warrior needs a shield-bearer; every leader "on the frontline of battle" needs armorbearers.

I believe that the first and truest estate of any servant is to have a heart to serve. When you, as a leader, have someone serving you who becomes contaminated by spirits of resentment, jealousy, bitterness or unforgiveness, this provides an opening for the enemy to launch a deadly attack against the life of the leader.

You must be prepared to "guard your heart" from spiritual contaminants if you are going to be effective as a servant. This positions you so that you can effectively guard and protect the one you were called to serve.

A spiritual death can take place in any arena of society, even in the workplace. However, in this section I would like to address how spiritual death takes place in the church.

For the most part the church has been known as a spiritual hospital. It is a place where sick people go for healing from whatever ailments or diseases are plaguing them, whether spiritual, physical, mental or emotional. Unfortunately however, some people have "died" because the Church was ill-equipped to handle their dilemmas.

It would be a tragedy if you went to the emergency room of the hospital to be treated for a minor condition, only to discover that you have contracted a life-threatening disease. The greater atrocity is that you contracted this disease while receiving medical care from the "nurse" on duty.

Clearly, this would cause you to become angry and disillusioned because you expected your health to improve when you went to the hospital. Instead, you became contaminated and were left battling a more vexing condition. This is a typical example of what happens when people serving in ministry have not come into their full deliverance from past issues.

"Nurses" can represent anybody who is serving in any capacity of the helps ministry in the local church, be it ushering, protocol, armorbearing, administration, etc.

These servant leaders or "nurses" of the ministry are responsible for lending assistance to their leaders in caring for the members or anyone who may come through the doors of the church.

Can you imagine having a bad case of the flu, cold or cough and being asked to pour a glass of water for your leader without washing or sanitizing your hands? Your leader may trustingly drink the water only to show up the next day sick and in pain, with the same or worse ailment that you had. As it is in the natural, so it is in the realm of the spirit.

At some point in life, servant leaders may have experienced some level of hurt or pain from which they has not been healed. They may find themselves struggling with bitterness, resentment, anger, low self-esteem and other issues. As a result of this, these hurting, wounded servants who are "leaking issues", in turn tend to hurt other people. Unfortunately, this may sometimes include wounding or hurting their spiritual leaders.

I have realized that if the issues which are plaguing a servant leader or anyone called to serve in ministry are not resolved, they can be transferred to the leader. No Christian or servant should be left to die. We should do whatever it takes to save that person's life.

In *Luke 7:2–10* as Jesus was passing through the city, a Centurion captain diligently sought for Him. He approached Jesus with urgency because his servant was lying ill at home, ready to die. He insisted that Jesus only needed to speak one word and he knew that his servant would have been healed. Jesus spoke the Word and, as he had believed, his servant was healed immediately.

As a trusted servant, you should make every effort to constantly examine yourself for any lingering issue that can cause insult or injury to the Kingdom of God. When necessary, confess your faults and watch the power of God deliver you. Whatever you do, conduct regular evaluations to determine the state or condition of your heart.

"Don't Let A Wounded Soldier Die!"

Throughout my time of ministry, I have discovered that some "servants" may come to you sick while others become sick while working with you. I have seen genuine, loving, humble people working with their leaders only to discover after years of serving, they become bitter, rebellious and disrespectful to the same leader. *How does this happen?*

Far too often, people know that they are spiritually ill but fail to take radical measures to bring healing to themselves. If you find yourself wounded and vulnerable you must earnestly seek to prostrate yourself on the altar and cry out to God.

Sometimes you may have to drive yourself to the "spiritual hospital", especially when there is no one around or if there are people present but who are unwilling to assist you. *The "hospital" to which I now refer is the presence of God.*

You must position yourself to be totally healed. You will never resolve an old wound by "sticking a band-aid on it." More often than not, you stand the risk of infecting other people if your "spiritual ailment" becomes contagious. Most wounds tend to heal quickly when they are exposed, treated and left uncovered.

> *"REGARDLESS OF YOUR TITLE OR STATUS, ALWAYS BE WILLING TO HUMBLE YOURSELF AND UNDERGO A HEALNG PROCESS BEFORE ENDEAVORING TO HELP OR ADMINSTER HEALING TO OTHERS."*

The enemy will seek to exploit your vulnerability at this time by whispering in your ear to gain an advantage over you. He seeks to use your own pride to prevent you from finding a place of brokenness and repentance. You should never just allow yourself to die spiritually. You must become desperate for your own soul's survival. Whenever you become sick or contaminated, much prayer is needed in order to restore your mind and spirit to the right position.

MAINTAINING YOUR SPIRITUAL POSITION

Although you may have been blessed with the privilege of connecting with your spiritual leaders, you must be careful of satan's devices which seek to pervert or contaminate this relationship. It is important for you to "maintain your spiritual position."

You can only preserve this relationship if you maintain a pure heart. The enemy also knows this. Therefore, he sends traps and snares your way in an effort to pollute your spirit, weaken you and ultimately compromise your position with your spiritual leaders and in the kingdom of God.

He may also seek to use whoever he can to sow seeds of discord and stir up confusion, all in an effort to frustrate you out of your kingdom assignment.

If you are going to be effective in the kingdom, it is important that you do the following:

- You *must* cultivate and maintain the presence of God in your life through prayer, fasting and reading the Word of God
- You must guard your heart with all diligence; the Word of God says that the issues of life flow out of your heart *(Proverbs 4:23)*
- You must be strong and courageous enough to defend and protect the anointing on the life of your leader as well as guarding your own heart from spiritual contaminants
- You must maintain your confidence in the call and assignment that God has placed on your life
- You must be confidential and trustworthy in the eyes of your spiritual leader
- You must have the ability to encourage the one you are serving and also "encourage yourself in the Lord".

OVERCOMING BETRAYAL

The closest thing that I can liken a betrayal to is a "rape experience" someone may have had. Although I am not downplaying the magnitude of such an experience, it is my opinion that the effects of betrayal are similar to being violated.

Betrayal can happen on any level. I have seen people betrayed by trusted servants, colleagues, spouses, business partners and even family members. Regardless of who you were betrayed by it can carry the same sting of pain.

Betrayal can be so devastating that if you are not careful the spirit of discouragement can take control of you. If you allow it, this demonic spirit can shatter and ultimately wound your soul.

Many years ago, I was preparing to host a major conference and prior to the event I was betrayed by somebody that I trusted. I can remember being so disappointed that I almost cancelled the entire event because of what I had just endured. As painful as it was, I found myself bearing down in a time of prayer to receive the necessary strength and power to overcome what had just happened. God supernaturally gave me the wherewithal to continue the assignment; the power of God fell mightily and the people were tremendously blessed. This was, in my opinion, one of the most powerful moves of God I had ever experienced.

If you are ever faced with such a painful ordeal, where you feel as if somebody has betrayed you, my advice to you is to pray. Most people come out of betrayal pledging never to trust again.

Many people in leadership positions sometimes make the unfortunate mistake of "moving on" without ever dealing with the wound of betrayal. In addition to bearing down in prayer, however, you now have to ask yourself the relevant questions, "Are you too trusting?" or "Are you divulging too much of your personal information without using wisdom?" and the like.

In other words, *"the less information people know about you, the less they have to "betray" you!"* When people have little to no personal information about you, the less opportunity they will have to betray you. You should never trust anyone to the extent that if they betray you, it alters your entire state of being and you can no longer function.

The most important thing to remember is to maintain your confidence in God. The Word of God assures in *Psalm 125:1,* that they which trust in the Lord shall be as mount Zion. Further, *Psalm 118:8* says it is better to trust in the Lord than to put confidence in man.

"DO NOT IGNORE THE WARNING SIGNS!"

The spirit of betrayal and disloyalty has caused many ministries to fall apart and split. Joshua served Moses faithfully; Elisha served Elijah faithfully.

Some of the signs or signals of disloyalty and possible betrayal are people who:

- Operate in an independent spirit; seeking to do their own thing; not following the directions of their leader
- Think they know more and are wiser than their leader
- Have difficulty sowing into the life of their leader and into the ministry
- Have not been delivered from past hurts and previous affiliations (for example, "church hurt")
- Do not support and defend their leaders if they are being accused by others
- Are inconsistent with their attendance at church services and other ministry-sponsored events
- Are easily offended, cannot receive rebuke and make repetitive excuses
- Are not willing to be corrected by their leader
- Are unwilling to take responsibility for their actions and are unreliable
- Are unwilling to serve after services and special events

It is evident that spiritual death can occur at every level and strata of our society, even in the Church. In *Matthew 10:16* the Word of God warns us that we are to *be wise as serpents yet harmless as doves.* We must remain in a strong and spiritually discerning place so that we can identify the enemy as he seeks to destroy the Body of

Christ with spiritual death. Although the Body of Christ has not come into the fullest measure of the demonstration and power of God, I believe that neither the spirit of death nor the gates of hell will be able to prevail against the church *(Matthew 16:18).*

DEATH OF A LIFE-GIVER
"....smite the shepherd, and the sheep shall be scattered."
(Mark 14:27)

The death of a leader may be considered one of the most tragic events that can occur in a person's life. It can leave an impression so indelible that it is lodged in the deepest recesses of a person's mind long after the event has taken place.

Over the years we have seen how many great leaders have fallen or have been slain. The enemy knows that in order to debilitate or sabotage any movement, cause or interest group, all he has to do is destroy the Leader.

According to *Mark 14:27*, once you "smite" the shepherd (the Leader), the sheep (the followers) will scatter. Once you destroy the Leader, you automatically afflict the followers and, in some cases, totally destroy their cause.

INJURED LEADER...The Breakaway Sheep

I can recall, during my season of affliction, how the warfare also became intense amongst some of our members. For some reason several people suddenly did not know what to do or how to function. In many instances, people became more easily offended by others no matter how nicely information was communicated. It seemed as if the spirit of Babel took over and no one understood each other. There were unexplainable arguments, disagreements and the "I'm doing my own thing" syndrome dominated.

"Then saith Jesus unto them, All ye shall be offended because of me this night: for it is written, I will smite the shepherd, and the sheep of the flock shall be scattered abroad." (Matthew 26:31)

Many people cannot handle the idea of their spiritual leader being under any level of warfare. In fact, there is an almost subtle belief that the Leader is exempted from the attacks of the enemy. This, however, is not scriptural as every great man or woman of God, from Genesis to Revelations, has had to confront some level of spiritual warfare. However, the actions taken by their followers during these times, generally help to determine the lifespan or longevity of the vision and the visionary.

The people who scatter when their Leader is under attack are in my opinion, spiritual weak cowards and frail sheep. These are usually people who have spent very little time in prayer and are unfamiliar with God's plans and satan's tactics. Further, these are the people who probably never captured the spirit, spiritual fragrance or teaching of their Leader and were only following His ministry for the *"loaves and fish"*.

Intervention 101

During this time, I realized that I had been so accustomed to micro-managing that I was not aware that some people were not carrying their share of the weight. As a result, my husband and I immediately developed a multi-level mobilization plan in order to recapture the minds of the people back towards their kingdom assignment and responsibility to God. This plan involved strategic prayer, planning and a better execution of their daily routine. Further, we also empowered our auxiliary leaders to function in various capacities so that the work of the ministry would continue.

Everyone who dares to stand for God in this hour will endure some level of testing which may involve public probing, examination, persecution or an affliction of some sort. Holding fast to your faith in God will be the catalyst to your breakthrough and ultimate victory. As you continue to overcome these afflictions, spiritual promotion and increase will be inevitable.

Everyone who is a part of a ministry or organization must learn how to wage war against the attacks which may come to the life of their leaders. As a believer, you must also learn how to engage in prayer and spiritual warfare you fight the good fight of faith. If you love your spiritual leaders or pastor, then you should commit to pray for them, especially if they may be under an attack of the enemy. Failure to do so may also make them susceptible to the attack of spiritual vultures and demonic piranhas.

Spiritual Vultures and Demonic Piranhas

Vultures are huge birds of prey which are scavengers which seek to devour the carcass of any dead animal. They seek out weak, wounded or dead prey to feed on their flesh. Piranhas on the other hand are small aggressive fish which devour living flesh "faster than you can imagine". Unfortunately, these represent some of the spirits that many leaders, including pastors, sometimes, tend to operate in when another Leader is afflicted or falls. They attack, seeking to further assassinate the disadvantaged Leader in hopes that they will gain more members, followers or some other benefit. This is unscriptural and, certainly, ungodly.

Jesus said that we should restore our brother in the spirit of meekness and not celebrate or take advantage of their weakness. This is what I call "illegal poaching" in the Church.

Illegal Poaching

In other words, illegal poaching is the act of preying on another innocent, weak or afflicted individual for personal gain. Illegal poaching is always done to benefit the deliberate poacher while killing or robbing someone else.

Spiritual poachers are typically motivated by spirits of envy or jealousy as they seek to illegally gain the favor, esteem or respect of another, by any means necessary. In the world, we see such behaviors condemned regarding the hunting of tigers for their fur, bones or whiskers; sharks for their fins and the elephants for their tusks. It is unfortunate that Christians are fighting other Christians and Leaders are relentlessly fighting other Leaders...*just for a "tusk"*.

I declare an end to all illegal pirating activities in the Church and instead, I decree that fervent prayer be rendered for all the afflicted. (See more in book by author, IT'S MY TIME TO LIVE!)

The World's Eye View

It is amazing how the people in the world respond to each other when they are under an attack. They unite in a time of solidarity, supporting whatever cause or crises is at hand. They organize street marches, rallies, protests, boycotts and the like, in order to show their unity in fighting a cause. In some instances, they may even coin slogans, chants, decrees, declarations or songs to show their support of those who are hurting.

On the other hand, it seems that when individuals, particularly Leaders in the Church are "under siege", people become divided and even segregated. A similar travesty occurred right before Jesus' crucifixion. He spent hours trying to get His disciples to tarry in prayer, but to no avail. They failed to pray and, in the hour of testing, as Jesus was arrested, they became scattered, confused and hopeless.

True servants pray, cover, uphold, support, hold fast and remain committed during the time of their Leader's trials. True servants do

"Greatness is born out of adversity!"

292

not buckle or bend in the face of adversity but, rather, they diligently seek to bind themselves together in unwavering faith and love. This is why prayer should be offered on behalf of all Leaders, whether they are social, political, spiritual or otherwise.

They are the "life-givers" of every organization or movement. Once the Leader is killed, the Visionary or the "Vision Carrier" is killed and without a vision, the people will perish. *(Proverbs 29:18)*

DEATH BY ASSASSINATION

To *"assassinate"* means to murder someone of prominent status by way of a surprise attack. There are certain individuals who are destined to make a global impact for the kingdom of God. For the most part, these are the people at whom the enemy seeks to launch his most diabolical attacks. God begins to prepare them for the call and the assignment on their lives, from an early age. Satan is also aware of this and assigns demonic assassins to their lives in an effort to hinder them from becoming all that God has created them to be.

If you sense the call of God on your life, beware of demonic assassins. The enemy will seek to use all forms of tactics to destroy or sabotage your destiny.

It is not the enemy's plan to simply injure or demobilize you; it is his plan to totally destroy the mission, ministry or mandate that God has placed on the inside of you. Therefore, you must be sober, vigilant and wise not to succumb to the devices of the enemy. If you are carrying something great, it is important that the enemy does not gain access to your life and that neither you, nor the assignment, dies.

JESUS, THE ULTIMATE LIFE-GIVER!

For His disciples, the Crucifixion of Jesus in that day must have been extremely painful.. He had spoken of His death. He had even prophesied the way in which He would die but, when the actual day came, it was still a very tragic experience for those who followed, loved and believed in Him.

As painful as the experience was to those who loved Him, Jesus' death was a great detriment to satan's kingdom. If the enemy knew the impact that Jesus' death would have on his kingdom, the Bible says in *1 Corinthians 2:7–8* he never would have crucified the Lord of Glory:

"7But we speak the wisdom of God in a mystery, even the hidden wisdom, which God ordained before the world unto our glory: 8Which none of the princes of this world knew: for had they known it, they would not have crucified the Lord of glory."

Please understand that Jesus paid the price which brought you salvation. In so doing, His life liberated you from the "sting of death" and gave you the "victory over the grave." He is the ultimate life-giver and because of His sacrifice, *you can live!*

A WORD TO THE WISE IS SUFFICIENT

As distressing as the "sting of betrayal" was, there were a number of valuable lessons I gleaned from my experience that I want to share with every leader:

- As a leader, it is important that you remember to "put a space" between you and the people, even those you may call trusted armorbearers, servants, helpers and the like.
- It is easy to become comfortable around the people who are called to serve you, however, you must define their boundaries.
- Your friends or associates should never be "their friends" *(Joshua 3:3–4).* For example, it is a conflict of interest to have your friends also be friends of your servant leader or

armorbearer because he is placed in a position where his loyalty may now be challenged

- Keep your private affairs private, no matter how much your helpers or armorbearers seek to convince you that they can be trusted.

- *Pray!* Seek out seasoned and proven spiritual leaders to cover you. Having no covering means you are an open target for "spiritual vultures or sharks."

- Do not allow anyone to serve you who does not have a consistent prayer life or attend prayer sessions.

- Watch people's attitude toward your times of victory. Pay attention to whether they are able to celebrate your successes. If they cannot celebrate you, then they are only tolerating you.

- A good servant will take advantage of every opportunity to be a blessing to his leader. People, armorbearers, servant leaders and helpers who honor you will sow into your life and ministry. Be careful of people who call you their leader but struggle to bless you.

- If your armor bearer, servant or helper steals from you once, chances are they will steal from you again. *They obviously cannot be trusted.*

- If someone is bringing a blessing to you; that *does not* mean that they have to bring a blessing for your armorbearer as well.

- Pray over your food and be careful of what you allow yourself to ingest.

- Pray over everything, including the information that your servants bring you.

- Never make anyone think that they are so powerful that you cannot make it without them.

- Look out for signs and signals of betrayal. Never ignore them. Remember a lie is a lie, no matter what color it is.

PROPHETIC PRAYER NUGGET (PPN)

"Pray this prayer right now as a covering for spiritual leaders, in Jesus' name."

*Father God, in the name of Jesus I cover spiritual leaders everywhere. I praise You because You have given us pastors and leaders after Your heart. I pray that they will be steadfast and immovable, always abounding in Your work so that their labor will not be in vain. Your Word declares, "**how beautiful are the feet of those that preach the gospel**", so God anoint their feet afresh. Let them run through troops and leap over walls in the mighty name of Jesus.*

No weapon formed against our leaders shall be able to prosper. Lord, bless them super abundantly above all that they can ask, think or imagine, in the mighty name of Jesus! AMEN!

CHAPTER TWELVE

ON YOUR WAY TO VICTORY!

THE BREAKING OF DAY

I know that it was the grace of God that transitioned me through what I considered to be the darkest season of my life. I can remember many times I would lie in bed, terrified at what the night would bring. During the night watches, I was unable to sleep. I would spend most of the night in prayer. I kept worship music and scriptures playing as I prayed for morning to come.

I knew that with the breaking of day the night torments would be over and I would have lived to see another day. If you are experiencing a difficult season in your life, just know that "trouble does not last forever." I want to encourage you that there is a time appointed for the "day to break" over your situation and, if you do not lose hope or give up on God, He will cause the sun to shine again.

THE ROAD TO RECOVERY

"Behold, I give unto you power to tread on serpents and scorpions, and over all the power of the enemy: and nothing shall by any means hurt you." (Luke 10:19)

The road to recovery from my season of affliction was painstakingly slow and almost as agonizing as the attacks I suffered. During this time, I required the utmost due care and attention. I had a supportive husband and a wonderful family who prayed earnestly and helped to take great care of me. I intensified my time of prayer and worship before the Most High God and committed to taking communion and declaring the Word of God back to Him several times a day.

At times, I questioned whether I would be able to walk or minister again. However, every time I doubted, the Spirit of God assured me that I would preach the gospel. I started having prophetic dreams again as God began showing me how He would use me in time to come.

I was determined that I was not going to prolong the time of my total healing and recovery. On the other hand, I did not want to rush this process and risk injuring myself.

Right now you may be experiencing one of the darkest times in your life and wondering if you will ever see the "light of day". I want to encourage you that every season, good or bad, eventually comes to an end and when the time is up for your season of affliction, you will begin to see the "breaking of day!"

GOD MIRACULOUSLY HEALS!

During that season I truly learned the value of life and what it meant to have a family. I experienced a dimension of God's grace and favor that taught me how much He really loved me. Not only had He preserved my life, but He had provided everything I needed to survive in that season.

At times, He may pull you back for a short season in order to prepare you for another. I was no longer able to travel as I used to and had to come off of local television. The medical bills were escalating not to mention all of the other bills that were now extremely "past due". I had learned how to solely trust in the Lord as my Provider. God took me through those very difficult and dry seasons and I will forever be grateful to Him.

The years of being sick and afflicted forced me to assess my relationships, especially during the weeks and months when I could not preach or accept an engagement.

When I faced these challenging times, I believe that God used them as opportunities to expose exactly who my friends and enemies were. It is in such times as these that you must steadfastly hold on to your faith, knowing that God is your Healer and Deliverer. He has never failed. *(Exodus 15:26)*

Woman Thou Art Loosed

In *Luke 13:11* the Bible gives an account of a woman who was bound by a spirit of infirmity for eighteen (18) long years. It is amazing that in her debilitating condition, Jesus had compassion on her and healed her.

There are several implications in this account:
- Her sickness was caused by a demonic spirit
- She was bent over and could not lift herself
- She did not see Jesus but Jesus saw her
- Jesus healed her on the Sabbath, a day of rest for all. Although everyone rested she could not because her condition kept her in torment.

299

- She was bound for eighteen years which represents three seasons of six; where 6 represents the number of man or her reliance on man and 666 represents the mark of the beast.

- Although she had remained in this affliction for eighteen years, one touch from Jesus, immediately set her free.

- When Jesus loosed her, the curse of her affliction was shattered and destroyed from off her life; this "loose" (*Greek* word *Luo* means to loose, demolish, abolish, set a prisoner free). This means that all penalties, obligations, debts, condemnation were removed from her life and, now she was totally vindicated; never to be bound again. In that one declaration everything in her life totally changed and all her constraints and restraints were gone. After that day, she owed no one anything. She was loosed from everything that had once held her bound and now she could no longer be hindered.

During my season of affliction, I felt just like this woman, bound by circumstance, bent over, and destitute; left alone to die. I had tried to get the comfort and consolation I needed from other people; not realizing that God had already devised a plan to set me totally free. Whenever you feel as though you have lost everything, be encouraged because every problem has an expiration date. God sees, hears and knows what you are going through and in time He will also come to set you free.

"YOUR FAITH IN GOD WILL AUTOMATICALLY PRODUCE MIRACLES REGARDLESS OF HOW GREAT OR SMALL THEY MAY BE."

PERSISTENT FAITH
"...for he that cometh to God must first believe that He (God) is and that He is a rewarder of them that diligently seek Him."
(Hebrews 11:6)

Faith speaks to the simplicity of taking God at His Word. It is the act of believing God regardless of what situation or circumstance confronts you. I believe that one of the greatest mistakes you can make in life is to lose your belief in God. God will reward you with healing, prosperity, favor and a blessed family as long as you have faith and believe in Him.

The greatest sin in life is not fornication or adultery; it is unbelief!

During my seasons of intense spiritual warfare I had to activate the Word of God in me in order to maintain my faith in Him. Too often people lose hope and begin trusting in their own strength.

"18 Who against hope believed in hope, that he might become the father of many nations, according to that which was spoken, So shall thy seed be.

19 And being not weak in faith, he considered not his own body now dead, when he was about an hundred years old, neither yet the deadness of Sarah's womb:

20 He staggered not at the promise of God through unbelief; but was strong in faith, giving glory to God;

21 And being fully persuaded that, what he had promised, he was able also to perform." (Romans 4:18-21)

"WHATEVER YOU PUT IN YOUR SPIRIT IN YOUR DAYS OF STRENGTH WILL SUSTAIN YOU IN YOUR TIMES OF WEAKNESS."

It was in this season that I had to lean on every Word and promise God had ever spoken to me. My faith in God as my Healer and Deliverer propelled me to my breaking of day.

In my earlier years when I was growing in God I spent countless hours studying and praying the scriptures. I spent seasons investing in good books and teachings on how to live victoriously as a believer. I had no idea that somewhere in my spirit these were the scriptures that would come back to revive and strengthen me. During my process I even had to rely on some of my own prophetic prayer CD's and messages.

"I BELIEVE IN MIRACLES!"

I watched as God began to turn everything around and miracles began happening in my life. I began to experience the healing power of God in my body and every day I felt a new level of strength returning to me. I started walking on my own and eventually discontinued most of the medications. I had to eat the right foods and my kids made sure I laughed every day. I also began to celebrate God for every miracle and every milestone.

On one day in particular, as I prepared for my doctor's appointment, I experienced an unexpected move of God. As I began to exit the vehicle my shoe fell off my foot. My daughter and I were totally amazed because just a few short minutes earlier, due to swelling in my feet, it was difficult for me to put my shoes on. I cannot explain what happened but my feet had miraculously shrunk from a size ten (10) back to a size seven (7), which was my original shoe size. I soon realized that I was looking at a miracle. That day, the shoe falling off was a sign to me that my healing process had begun. My entire staff, my children and I celebrated this major milestone and continued to celebrate every other miracle in my life.

It is almost unbelievable to see what God has done. For a season I was afflicted in a valley of despair and hopelessness, but God raised me up again. He took me out of the grave with resurrection power and gave me my life back! In that season of affliction it felt as though I had died. Because of Jesus' victory on the Cross I am now experiencing the favor and blessings of God I had only dreamt about. I view life from a different vantage point and am now totally free!

I also experience new realms of glory every day as God manifests miracles, signs and wonders through the ministry of healing and deliverance every time I mount the pulpit.

"...A TIME TO LIVE!"
"Living vs Merely Surviving!"

"To every thing there is a season, and a time to every purpose under the heaven:" (Ecclesiastes 3:1)

After my experiences I realized that there was yet another spiritual level of attainment that involved so much more than just surviving. I had made a conscious decision to do more ... I decided that it was my time to live!

Most people spend their entire lives merely surviving or "just getting by" after experiencing some extreme hardship. God does not want you to just survive or barely make it out of your situation; He wants you to thrive to your next level and live, but He wants you to *truly* live!

> *You can choose to remain a slave to sin and the spirit of death, just barely surviving in life, or you can decide to break free and live!*

The expression *"to live"* means "to have a peaceful, God kind of life", not merely existing but enjoying and living each day to the fullest. This is the essence of seizing each moment and maximizing on the value of it, fully embracing every experience, every encounter and every divine connection.

To *"live"* means to have the ability to maintain all vital functions in life. It is the pleasure of greeting each day with profound love in your heart for God, His people and yourself. It is to possess the means necessary to sustain and support your daily needs while helping to fulfill the needs of others. Having this kind of life means that you will have vigor, vitality and vivacity.

The Greek word for *"live" or "life"* is *"Zoe". (Job 10:12)* It speaks to the absolute fullness of life where the word spoken by God actually takes on a vibrant, active nature with the ability to function and give life as God intended. Through the shed blood of Jesus, God gives this kind of life that causes you to prosper, enjoy and abound in all good things.

Moreover, "living" is choosing life beyond that which is dead, mundane and purposeless. It is a dimension and state of total confidence in God as the One who sustains and upholds you regardless of what "shakes" and "breaks down" around you. It is the ability to find joy, peace or contentment in the midst of a chaotic situation. *A good dose of laughter a day will keep the stress away.*

"LAUGHTER – MEDICINE FOR THE SOUL!"
"A merry heart doeth good like a medicine: but a broken spirit drieth the bones." (Proverbs 17:22)

I can remember traveling, preaching, counseling after preaching, working all through the night, conducting programs, performing hospital visits, cooking, cleaning, "worrying" about the bills, going to work, directing the praise team, youth ministry, women's ministry, hosting radio programs, leading the prayer ministry, conducting follow up calls and more, I was going nonstop. I never took a day off to rest. My husband and kids would be in the pool having fun while I, on the other hand, would be locked up inside the house having some type of meeting or finishing off projects.

In earlier years I seldom laughed and every time my kids would joke around, I told them that they were too "carnal". Well, I now understand why they were always laughing and having fun. My husband told me that laughter was a stress reliever. He said he was not going to worry about anything in this life because God had it all covered. Whenever he said that, I would get even angrier because I wanted everybody to be as serious as I was.

It is a fact that the more you laugh, the less stress stays in your body. Laughter and relaxation calm you, give you peace of mind and lower your blood pressure.

Needless to say, I laugh a lot nowadays. I am so humbled by the fact that God extended His grace towards me. He chose me for that test and better yet, kept me alive in the midst of it all. I had to make many lifestyle adjustments, including resting and laughing more. I began to enjoy the people around me with whom God had blessed me, and I literally began to enjoy life again.

You never really graduate from the trials and tests of the "University of Life." God has so designed it that you simply advance from one level to another, and from one encounter with His glory to another. In fact, when you think you have attained all that God has for you, there will be other challenges to cause you to "study", pray and build your faith again.

"SOMETIMES YOU MAY HAVE TO ASK THE TEACHER TO GIVE YOU MORE GRACE IN ORDER TO PASS THE NEXT LEVEL OF YOUR TEST!"

SEVEN PRACTICAL SECRETS TO DEFEATING THE SPIRIT OF DEATH
"Learning How To Live!"

I can truly testify that, if it had not been for the Lord who was on my side, I might not have been here today. That is not a cleverly scripted cliché it is a fact that is very real to me. I thank God that He trusted me enough to allow me to go through this.

It does not matter what lie the enemy is telling you. As long as there is breath in your body, God is not finished with you yet. You, too, can have victory over the spirit of death…just as long as you refuse to die during your season of testing.

Surprisingly, one of the major lessons this experience taught me, was how to live. After coming face-to-face with death, I made a deal with myself that I was going to keep the spirit of death "under my feet" and enjoy my life to the fullest.

I made a commitment that while maintaining my relationships with God and others I would also adopt seven practical secrets to defeating the spirit of death, and I would learn how to live and enjoy life.

As a word of advice to you, I will share my seven secrets:
1. Spend quality time in prayer and the presence of God every day
2. Take life one day at a time
3. Appreciate and celebrate yourself
4. Get pampered; have your day of relaxation and comfort
5. Treat yourself to something nice and regularly surround yourself with things you enjoy
6. Learn to laugh out loud and laugh long
7. Spend as much time as possible with people who truly love you

HERE BY THE GRACE OF GOD!

As I look back over my life, I realize that it was truly the grace of God that kept me. Even when I could not perceive His presence, He was always there with me. *(Job 23:8–10)* He was there teaching me how to build my faith; how to trust Him in the midst of adversity; how to hear His voice and how to navigate through life's various obstacle courses.

I am grateful to my God that He was always there with me to help me make it through my seasons of testing. I have always believed in the power of God but I now have a greater understanding and appreciation of grace. *Grace is Jesus paying the price for your salvation, deliverance or healing with no strings attached! It is free of charge!*

PRESCRIPTION FOR HEALING & DELIVERANCE
"Overcoming the Spirit of Death"

If you are going to defeat the spirit of death, you must recognize the power and authority you have over it and make a decision to reach towards the life that God has for you. According to *Revelation 12:11 we overcome by the blood of the lamb and by the word of our testimony.*

In other words, *you shall have whatsoever you say.* If you declare out of your mouth that you are going to live and that you will have victory in the midst of your test, trial or tribulation, then you will live.

It was also during my season of recovery that I soon realized I was not just going to wake up and walk away from the demonic attack of the spirit of death. I also realized that my entire life had changed because the enemy's onslaught had affected me physically, mentally, emotionally and even spiritually.

The Word of God is the weapon of mass destruction against the plots, plans and diabolical strategies of the enemy!

Not only did I make a decision that I was not going to die but, as I sought the Lord, the Spirit of God gave me a threefold *"prescription"* that revived me in *body, soul and spirit.*

In the natural *(body)*, I obeyed the doctors' orders, took my medications as prescribed, changed my diet, took small steps when I could and scheduled times of rest.

To revive my soul *(soul/mind)*, I surrounded myself with people who celebrated me; no one was allowed to have a sad countenance when they came into my presence. I laughed more, spent more time with my family and told more jokes.

In the realm of the spirit *(spirit)*, I launched an aggressive counter-attack against the spirit of death.

The following are some of the spiritual warfare strategies I employed against the attack of the enemy in my life:

- **Identifying and exposing which element of the spirit of death is after you** *You must identify and expose all of the cohorts of death; this weakens their activity in your life.*

- **Put on the whole armour of God** *Every day I verbally decreed and declared that I received the whole armour of God. (Ephesians 6:11)*

- **Applying the blood of Jesus** *You must appropriate, apply and plead the blood of Jesus specifically to your situation. When you do, this will remind you that the enemy, the devil, has already been defeated in your life.*

- **Releasing/Declaring the Name of Jesus** *You have to call on the name of Jesus because He has all power, even over death. Just the mention of His name releases that same power in the atmosphere and every demonic spirit of death will have to go.* **(Matthew 28:18)**

- **Praying with Power** *You must rebuke the spirit of death through prayer because life and death are in the power of your tongue. Also, I used the prayer cloth that I took into the hospitals with me as my daily reminder that God heard even my simplest prayer. As I mentioned earlier, when I could not pray, I resorted to listening to the prayers that I had previously recorded on CD and had been distributing to others.*

- **Speaking the Word of God** *In addition to prayer, you can also release the Word of God and scriptures in the atmosphere. During my "death experience" I literally "wallpapered" my room with the Word of God (scriptures). When I woke up and went to sleep, I saw the Word; I kept the Word of God before me. I would also play the audio Bible throughout my room on a continual basis.*

- **Holding on to the prophecy** *In this season you must recall every prophecy that God has ever spoken to you. Some days I replayed audio CD's reminding myself of who God said I was. This inspired me greatly.*

- **Calling on angelic assistance** *You can call for angelic assistance because the Word of God says that there are angels which excel in strength, harkening to the voice of your commands. I dispatched angels to warfare on my behalf.* **(Joshua 5:13–15)**

- **Administering Communion** *I took communion every day for three (3) months. God does not restrict you to a certain number of days or to a certain amount of times you can partake of communion. He simply said in as much as we do it to remember Him and it would commemorate His death, burial and resurrection; it reminded me every* *day that Jesus took thirty-nine stripes, three nails and a spear in his side to bring redemption and healing to my life.*

- **Enduring until the end** *You must make a decision within your spirit that you are not going to die. I believed that at the end of my test I would be victorious. I just did not know when that would be. The only thing I knew is that I was prepared to survive the attack that the spirit of death had launched against me; the Word of God declares in **Matthew 24:13**, **"But he that shall endure unto the end, the same shall be saved."** The glory is always in the finish!*

These powerful strategies helped me to overcome the onslaught of the spirit of death and live a new life of victory. You can employ the same strategies in order to defeat the attacks of the enemy in your life.

MY PERSONAL AWAKENING
"Embracing The Call!"

"Before I formed thee in the belly I knew thee; and before thou camest forth out of the womb I sanctified thee, and I ordained thee a prophet unto the nations." (Jeremiah 1:5)

I can truly say that if it had not been for the Lord who was on my side, I do not know where I would be. I know that the victories I experienced through my seasons of affliction can only be attributed to the miraculous, sustaining power of God in my life. Although this was undoubtedly one of the darkest seasons I had ever experienced, there were many times that I had what I call "awakening" moments.

Whenever you are called with a divine assignment from God you will encounter some level of spiritual warfare. It is important to remain focused, regardless of what comes against you. There was a season when I did not like my voice and the Spirit of God had to show me that I had a very unique voice which He had anointed.

The Office of a Prophet of Deliverance is what I believe God has called me to and there was nothing that I, the enemy or anyone else for that matter, could do about it. The calling of God is "without repentance". *(Romans 11:29)* God will never change His mind concerning you. He wants you to fulfill the purpose for which He has created you.

Through all that I had endured, I sincerely believe that God was speaking to me about my character and remaining true to Him. Character defines the quality and the essence of who you really are. It represents or demonstrates the "color of your soul".

"Your true personality lies within the characteristics or DNA that God has deposited on the inside of you. However, the person that you have become is a combination of what God originally placed in you and the sum total of your past experiences. In order to find the truest you, you must go back to your original "maker's design" and rediscover who you are; therein you will find your true identity."

The world is filled with so many imitators that it is difficult to find authentic or genuine people who are true to their God and to themselves. Just like the Apostle Paul, I, too had "an awakening" regarding the call of God on my life. Further, I had to recognize that *"I am who I am by the grace of God."* I had to come to the place where I would not allow people's opinions to change me into something else. I learnt one of the most profound laws of the Kingdom: The Law of Acceptance which clearly states, *"You must first accept yourself before others can accept you."*

Careful attention should be spent fine tuning and developing your character. At the end of every day, before going to bed, I conduct my personal character analysis. I check to ensure that everything I did that day was in alignment with the Word of God.

I would like to encourage you to seek God for your own awakening to your kingdom assignment. I cannot help but recall that some of the "greats" in history such as **Rosa Parks, Harriet Tubman, Leonardo Da Vinci, Albert Einstein and many others** may not have always been understood, celebrated or even liked in their day. Yet, they all somehow left an indelible mark upon the tablets of history.

A PROPHET OF DELIVERANCE
"The Cost Of The Oil!"

Answering the call of God to do something that seems beyond your own capabilities will require winning the warfare, even in your own mind. I call it *"Gaining Victory Over The Embattled Mind!"*

I must admit that there was a time in my life when I had a tendency to avoid the ministry of deliverance. However, like the Prophet Jonah, I realized that I could no longer run from the call of God.

I want to encourage you to find out who you are in God. He has given you a unique "divine purpose." You are a righteous seed destined to do great things for God. Confront your internal struggles and external challenges. Make a decision that you are going to be all that God has created you to be:

"7 But we have this treasure in earthen vessels, that the excellency of the power may be of God, and not of us.

8 We are troubled on every side, yet not distressed; we are perplexed, but not in despair;

⁹ Persecuted, but not forsaken; cast down, but not destroyed;

¹⁰ Always bearing about in the body the dying of the Lord Jesus, that the life also of Jesus might be made manifest in our body."
(2 Corinthians 4:7–10)

PROPHECY:
"THE IMPENDING MOVE OF GOD"

I can remember when a world renowned evangelist was asked on a Christian television what he felt was going to be the most profound ministry in coming times. He prophetically and emphatically stated, the "Healing & Deliverance Ministry!"

The Spirit of God spoke to me and I firmly believe that we are about to see one of the greatest moves of God to ever "hit the earth." Miracles will become commonplace and the glory of God shall be revealed like never before. The blind will see, the deaf will hear, revelation knowledge will increase profoundly and we will see God's creative genius rise to the forefront.

However, there must be a radical change in the minds of the people in the Body of Christ in order to embrace what God is about to do. Every office in the "Body" must be accepted and respected as a vital and necessary component to the overall strength of the kingdom of God.

The apostles, prophets, evangelists, pastors and teachers must be united as one. The season of "holy warfare" must end and we should see how we can sharpen each other's gifts for the perfecting of the saints and the work of the ministry.

"¹¹ And he gave some, apostles; and some, prophets; and some, evangelists; and some, pastors and teachers;

¹² For the perfecting of the saints, for the work of the ministry: for the edifying of the body of Christ:" (Ephesians 4:11–12)

"FAR TOO OFTEN PEOPLE ARE FASCINATED BY THE GIFT GOD HAS GIVEN THEM. HOWEVER WHAT IS SOMETIMES FORGOTTEN IS THAT THE GIFT MAY GET THEM THROUGH A DOOR, BUT IT WILL TAKE CHARACTER TO KEEP THEM THERE."

THE GOSPEL REVOLUTION

"For this purpose the Son of God was manifested, that he might destroy the works of the devil." (1 John 3:8)

What is a revolution? A ***revolution*** is a sudden, radical, or complete change in political, religious or economic systems. It is an activity or movement designed to effect fundamental change.

I further believe that God is releasing a radical prophetic anointing in the earth realm through the ministry of healing and deliverance. More and more we will see chains being broken off the lives of individuals and the Church will captivate the world again.

"The glory of this latter house shall be greater than of the former, saith the lord of hosts: and in this place will I give peace, saith the lord of hosts." (Haggai 2:9)

The Revolutionary Gospel of Deliverance & The Five-Fold Ministry Gifts are going to shift the demonstration of supernatural power from the realm of darkness to the Kingdom of God. People will once again see the power of God demonstrated, superseding the powers of darkness as in the days of Elijah.

POWER BELONGS TO GOD

In short, the demonstration of the power of God's kingdom is going to overshadow the powers of darkness. Instead of looking for answers from psychics, soothsayers and witches, people are going to start running back to the Prophets of God for the answers they seek.

I believe God allows you to go through a season of affliction in order to prepare you for what He is getting ready to do in your life. I further believe that God took me through to birth a new season in my ministry and life. Furthermore, I believe that many other persons are also going through their tests and trials in order to be prepared for what God is doing and what He is about to do in the Body of Christ.

I believe that people want to break free from the stagnant "religious" norms and negative stereotypes which have characterized the Body of Christ as being bound, poor, destitute, defeated and weak.

I further believe that it is time for the *Five-fold Ministry Offices* to emerge from complacency or irrelevance and rise to its position of kingdom authority, order and power. ***This is the hour of the Absolute and Resolute.***

Believers everywhere must now make a firm decision as to who they are in Christ and begin aggressively fulfilling their kingdom assignment. This is the time for all believers to begin tapping into the divine power of the Kingdom of God and revealing *this* power to the world.

People everywhere need to know that they can tap into the divine realm of God if they wish to receive spiritual enlightenment and power; they do not have to consult those operating in the powers of darkness. I believe that it is time for people to recognize that Jesus truly is the answer for the world, and that ***ultimate power*** belongs to God.

"God hath spoken once; twice have I heard this; that power belongeth unto God." (Psalm 62:11)

"Dunamis" vs "Exousia"

The word *"power"* speaks to the right, might, capacity, strength or delegated authority to operate and function. There are two words in the Greek which can describe power as we know it. The first is the Greek word, *"exousia"* which represents delegated authoritative power by God to perform and do things in the earth. It carries weight, authority and influence. It is the deciding or final authority given to believers to demonstrate their faith.

- *Behold I give you power over all the powers of the enemy. (Luke 10:19)*
- *For we have this treasure in earthen vessels that the excellency of the power may be of God and not of us. (2 Corinthians 4:7)*
- *(See more in book by author "THE POWER OF PROPHETIC REVERSAL")*

The other Greek word is *"dunamis"* which represents God's raw power. It speaks to strong, explosive or miraculous power and is the root for our English word dynamite or dynamo. It is a part of the very nature of Christ. *(Psalm 46)* It speaks to the inherent power which you possess and comes from God. It is explosive and represents the force at which something can happen or come forth. It is the ability to move in miracles, signs and wonders; demonstrating the kingdom of God and to do exploits. *(Daniel 11:32; Acts 1:8; Luke 4:36)*

Additional Scripture References:
- *"And he said unto them, Verily I say unto you, That there be some of them that stand here, which shall not taste of death, till they have seen the kingdom of God come with power." (Mark 9:1)*

- *"To the intent that now unto the principalities and powers in heavenly PLACES might be known by the church the manifold wisdom of God,..." (Ephesians 3:10)*

THE MINISTRY OF DELIVERANCE

"The Spirit of the Lord is upon me, because he hath anointed me to preach the gospel to the poor; he hath sent me to heal the brokenhearted, to preach deliverance to the captives, and recovering of sight to the blind, to set at liberty them that are bruised (bound)." (Luke 4:18)

I believe that once people get the revelation of who Jesus is, they will be set free. In *Luke 4:18*, He identifies Himself as the One whom the Prophet Isaiah spoke of in *Isaiah 61:1–3*; the Messiah, the Deliverer of the Nations, the One who would come to bring salvation to a lost and dying world.

The Word of God declares that the Spirit of God would come upon Him to do the following:

- Preach good tidings (news) to the meek
- Bind up the broken-hearted
- Proclaim liberty to the captives
- Open oppressive, demonic prisons that had people bound
- Proclaim deliverance wherever He went
- Proclaim that every demonic spirit in your life would leave
- Give beauty for ashes
- Release the oil of joy for those who were mourning
- Give a garment of praise for a spirit of heaviness

The power of deliverance comes through the grace and love of God to bring healing, restoration and reconciliation to the nations. This will break the power that the enemy has over your life so that you can be restored to a place of kingdom power and authority.

Deliverance is the *children's bread. The Ministry of Deliverance* is one of the most profound ministries that will usher in Revivals that will shake the nations of the earth, turning the hearts of the people back to the Most High God.

PROPHECY: REVIVAL OF THE NATIONS
"Of the increase of his government and peace there shall be no end,..." (Isaiah 9:7)

As chains of bondage are broken off of your life, these same bondages will be broken off families, communities, regions and nations. We will see entire atmospheres change. Regions that were once dominated by demonic spirits of drunkenness, lewdness, perversion, death, war, pestilence, suffering, poverty and lack, will now be saturated with the power of God.

I can see a Revival coming to topple demonic thrones and infiltrate demonic systems which have been erected and have kept people bound for years.

I see the *"ruach" (Hebrew – breath, wind, spirit)* of God coming with such force and power that the very gates of hell will be shaken and the backs of our enemies will be destroyed.

I can hear a prophetic sound coming through the young people in this hour; young prophets who God will raise up to impact this generation with righteousness and the demonstrated power of God. I believe that we will begin to see the prophecy in *Joel 2* fulfilled, where the Spirit of God will be poured out upon all flesh.

I see a divine infiltration of the presence of God in our homes, schools, governments, churches, economy and other social systems. However, I believe that this will only take place as the people of God begin to break free from the distractions and vices of worldly systems and begin tapping into the miraculous power of the kingdom of God.

"If my people, which are called by my name, shall humble themselves, and pray, and seek my face, and turn from their wicked ways; then will I hear from heaven, and will forgive their sin, and will heal their land." (2 Chronicles 7:14)

THE ETERNAL PLAN OF LIFE

"For God so loved the world, that he gave his only begotten Son, that whosoever believeth in him should not perish, but have everlasting life." (John 3:16)

Eternal death is an everlasting, unending separation from God. However, Jesus' plan for redemption is eternal life and is an unending unity in the presence of God; this is what is promised to the believer.

In life we all have choices. In **Deuteronomy 30:19** the Bible instructs us to choose life over death. Eternal death or separation from God is a result of man's choice to remain separated from God in sin. **Matthew 25:46** states, *"And these shall go away into everlasting punishment: but the righteous into life eternal."* Further, eternal death is also known as the second death:

"He that hath an ear, let him hear what the Spirit saith unto the churches; He that overcometh shall not be hurt of the second death." (Revelation 2:11)

"But the fearful, and unbelieving, and the abominable, and murderers, and whoremongers, and sorcerers, and idolaters, and all liars, shall have their part in the lake which burneth with fire and brimstone: which is the second death." (Revelation 21:8)

When Jesus died He went to hell because He was carrying the sins of the world on His shoulders. The enemy never knew that while Jesus was in hell, He would continue in the same ministerial functions He operated in while on earth. He became the sacrificial lamb and through the shedding of His blood we have the remission of our sins. *(Hebrews 9:22)* When He died He entered the portals of hell, where He re-established His rulership and divine sovereignty. He took ultimate authority and control over the destiny of the souls that were in hell which were fated to be bound there throughout eternity. He preached deliverance to them and, when He got up out of hell, those who received the message were delivered and set free with Him. When Jesus arose He proved that death did not have the final say in the eternal destination of mankind...***He would now hold the keys!***

In ***Revelation 1:18***, it states, *"I am he that liveth, and was dead; and, behold, I am alive for evermore, Amen; and have the keys of hell and of death."*

When Jesus took the keys of death and hell, He took the power away from death and canceled its final judgment over your soul. If the enemy had known that Jesus' death, burial and resurrection would have exposed just how powerless his kingdom was, he would have never crucified Him – but it was too late. The plan of redemption for mankind had already been sealed by Jesus' blood and now salvation is available to all:

"14Blotting out the handwriting of ordinances that was against us, which was contrary to us, and took it out of the way, nailing it to his cross;
15And having spoiled principalities and powers, he made a shew of them openly, triumphing over them in it."
(Colossians 2:14–15)

While Jesus was in hell, He fulfilled a four-fold mission so that the plan of redemption would forever be established. He was able to:
- take the keys of death, hell and the grave *(Revelation 1:18)*
- lead captivity captive *(Ephesians 4:8)*
- preach deliverance to those that were captive *(Isaiah 61:1)*
- take the authoritative power of the five-fold ministry so that when He arose He could give it to men *(Ephesians 4:8)*

Jesus confronted death, hell and the grave and won. He fought for you and defeated every enemy that could possibly keep you separated from the life that God intended for you.

His victory gives you complete access into the divine presence of God so that you can receive the grace, mercy and favor you need to live an abundant life in Him. Once you accept Jesus Christ as Lord and Savior of your life, what you are saying throughout the annals of time is that you refuse to die and you choose to live...*today, tomorrow and forever...throughout eternity! AMEN!!*

PRAYER FOR SALVATION

*The Word of God declares in **Romans 10:9,10** that if you would confess with your mouth and believe in your heart that God has raised Jesus from the dead that you will be saved. If you want to accept Jesus and Lord and Savior of your life, pray this prayer of salvation and believe that God will set you free.*

Father God, in the name of Jesus, I confess that I am a sinner. I repent of every wrong that I have done. I believe that Jesus died for me and arose from the dead so that I could have a right to eternal life. I further believe that this life can begin today as I confess that Jesus is Lord of my life and that God raised Him from the dead. I renounce satan and declare that I no longer belong to him. I choose to live my life for You and right now I believe that I am saved! In Jesus' name! Amen!

I, _____ (printed name) gave my life

to the Lord on _____ (date). ***Today I am a Christian and I am saved!***

INDEX

Only One Life

By Lanny Wolfe

Days pass so quickly. The nights come and go.
The years melt away like new fallen snow.
Spring turns to Summer and Summer turns to Fall.
Autumn brings Winter then death comes to call.

Only one life, so soon it will pass.
Only what's done for Christ will last.
Only one chance to do His will, so give to Jesus all your days.
It's the only life that pays.

If you recall you have but one life.

It matters so little how much you may own
The places you've been and the people you've known.
It all turns to nothing when placed at His feet.
It's nothing to Jesus, just memories to keep.

You may take all the treasures from far away lands
Take all the riches you can hold in your hands
Take all the pleasures your riches can buy
But what will it mean when it's your time to die?

Only one life, so soon it will pass.
Only what's done for Christ will last.
Only one chance to do His will
So give to Jesus all your days.
It's the only life that pays.

If you recall you have but one life.

DR. MATTIE NOTTAGE BA, MA, DD

MINISTRY PROFILE

Widely endorsed as a prophet to the nations, God has used Dr. Mattie Nottage to captivate audiences around the world through her insightful, life-changing messages.

Dr. Nottage is married to Apostle Edison Nottage. She co-pastors, along with her husband, Believers Faith Outreach Ministries, International in Nassau, Bahamas.

Mantled with an uncanny spirit of discernment and an undeniable prophetic anointing, Dr. Nottage is a well-respected international preacher, prolific teacher, motivational speaker, life coach, playwright, author, gospel recording artist and revivalist. She is the President and Founder of *Mattie Nottage Ministries, International, The Global Dominion Network Empowering Group of Companies, The Youth In Action Group and The Faith Village For Girls Transformation Program. She is also The Chancellor of The Mattie Nottage School of Ministry. She is the Founder of the prestigious Mattie Nottage Outstanding Kingdom Woman's Award.*

Dr. Nottage has ministered the gospel, in places such as: Ireland, Brazil, Africa, The Netherlands, throughout the United States of America and The Caribbean. Gifted with an authentic anointing, God uses her to "set the captive free" and to fan the flames of revival throughout the nations. Dr. Mattie Nottage, has an endearing passion to train and equip individuals to advance the Kingdom of God and walk in total victory.

She is the author of her bestselling books, *"Breaking The Chains, From Worship to Warfare", "I Refuse To Die" and "Secrets Every Mother Should Tell Her Daughter About Life" Book & Journal.*

Dr. Nottage is also a regular columnist in The Tribune, the national newspaper of the Bahamas. She has also written numerous publications, stage plays and songs, including the #1 smash hit CD Singles, *"I Refuse To Die In This Place!"*, *"The Verdict Is In…Not Guilty!"* and *"I Still Want You!"*

She has regularly appeared as a guest on various television networks including The Trinity Broadcasting Network (TBN), The Word Network, The Atlanta Live TV and The Babbie Mason Talk Show "Babbie's House" amongst others. Additionally, Dr. Mattie Nottage has been featured in several magazine publications such as the Preaching Woman Magazine and the "Gospel Today" Magazine as one of America's most influential pastors. She, along with her husband, Apostle Edison are the hosts of their very own television show, "Transforming Lives" which airs weekly on The Impact Network.

Dr. Nottage is the former Chairman of the National Youth Advisory Council to the government of the Bahamas and was also recognized and awarded a *"Proclamation of State" by the Mayor and Commissioner of Miami-Dade County, Florida* for her exemplary community initiatives that bring transformation and empowerment to the lives of youth and families globally.

Further, Dr. Nottage has earned her, Bachelor of Arts degree in Christian Counseling, a Masters of Arts degree in Christian Education, and a Doctor of Divinity degree from the renown St. Thomas University, in Jacksonville, Florida and is also a graduate of Kingdom University. Additionally, she has earned her Certified Life Coaching Degree from the F. W. I. Life Coach Training Institute.

Dr. Mattie Nottage is known as a Trailblazer and a *"Doctor of Deliverance"* who is committed and dedicated to *Breaking Chains and Transforming Lives*!

Music CD Single "I Refuse To Die"

This prophetic song of hope and healing is an anthem to encourage you to live a life of victory overcoming every challenge or adversity of the enemy. Get your copy today and make a prophetic declaration through song that you "Refuse To Die!"

Prayer of Deliverance for the Wounded Soul

Breaking the Spirit of Limitation

To request Dr. Mattie Nottage for a speaking engagement, upcoming event, life coaching seminar, mentorship session or to place an order for products, please contact:

Mattie Nottage Ministries, International (Bahamas Address)

P.O. Box SB-52524

Nassau, N. P. Bahamas

Tel/Fax: (242) 698-1383 or

(954) 237-8196

OR

Mattie Nottage Ministries, International (U.S. Address)

6511 Nova Dr., Suite #193

Davie, Florida 33317

Tel/Fax: **(888) 825-7568**

UK Tel: 44 (0) 203371 9922

OR

www.mattienottage.org

Follow us on:

Facebook @ DrMattie Nottage

and Twitter  **@ DrMattieNottage**